TRADE MARKS IN THEORY AND PRACTICE

Trade Marks in Theory and Practice

C.D.G. PICKERING LL.B., LL.M.
Denton Hall, London

HART PUBLISHING
OXFORD
1998

Hart Publishing
Oxford
UK

Distributed in the United States by
Northwestern University Press
625 Colfax, Evanston
Illinois 60208–4210 USA

Distributed in Australia and New Zealand by
Federation Press Pty Ltd
PO Box 45, Annandale
NSW 203, Australia

Distributed in the Netherlands, Belgium and Luxembourg by
Intersentia, Churchillaan 108
B2900 Schoten, Antwerpen
Belgium

Hart Publishing is a specialist legal publisher based in Oxford, England.
To order further copies of this book or to request a list of other publications
please write to:

Hart Publishing, 19 Whitehouse Road, Oxford, OX1 4PA
Telephone: +44 (0)1865 434459 or Fax: +44 (0)1865 794882
e-mail: hartpub@janep.demon.co.uk

British Library Cataloguing in Publication Data
Data Available
ISBN 1–901362–64–7

Typeset in 10pt Sabon
by Hope Services (Abingdon) Ltd.
Printed in Great Britain on acid-free paper
by Biddles Ltd., Guildford and King's Lynn

To the memory of my late mother

Preface and Acknowledgements

Frank Schechter opened his seminal work on the historical development of trade marking with the following quotation, suggesting that it was apposite in the context of trade mark law:

> "There is, upon some subjects, a touching absence of curiosity among English lawyers. Institutions which are the very heart of modern business life, the fountain-heads of not ungrateful streams of litigation, are accepted as though, like the image of Ephesus, they fell direct from heaven for the benefit of a deserving profession. The legal questions to which they give rise are studied with minute care, the legal relationships which they create are made the subject of microscopic analysis. But the subject itself, the really interesting and important matter, is left untouched."[1]

This was a very perceptive observation. In some areas of law, it is possible to discern intuitively and with relative ease the purpose and normative basis of a particular legal rule. For example, murder is prohibited by the criminal law because of the immorality of intentionally killing another human being; interference with another's possession may be a crime and a tort because respect for an individual's belongings is a fundament of a liberal democracy. Equally, the laws governing matters such as assisted human reproduction or the integrity of one's private life are subject to intense ethical debate by many quarters of society. What, though, of dry, unemotive trade mark law?

Certainly, as will be outlined in Chapter 1, there exists a quite technical body of rules which regulate when people may use particular symbols in a particular way. These are in fact the same symbols which permeate everyday life:

> "The British are a trade mark conscious people. After a refreshing sleep on a SLUMBERLAND mattress the average Briton is awakened by the alarm of a BHS clock. He arises, puts on his CLARKS slippers and walks on the ALLIED carpet to the bathroom. He brushes his teeth with AQUAFRESH toothpaste on a WISDOM toothbrush and applies PALMOLIVE to his beard to be removed by a GILLETTE razor. After a stimulating shower with RADOX soap, and while listening to the news from a SONY radio, he hurries into his ST. MICHAEL underwear, NEXT shirt freshly laundered with PERSIL . . . puts on his ROLEX wrist watch and rushes downstairs to breakfast."[2]

and which can indeed rise to the status of cultural icon: consider the meaning conjured by COCA-COLA, ROLLS-ROYCE, SONY or ROLEX. They are also symbols to which great value is attributed:

[1] *The Historical Foundations of the Law Relating to Trade Marks* (New York, 1925), 1 quoting E. Jenks, *Select Essays in Anglo-American Legal History*, iii, 51, who was writing in the context of the early history of negotiable instruments.

[2] Adapted from J. R. Lunsford, "Consumers and Trade Marks: The Function of Trade Marks in the Market Place" (1974) 64 *TMR* 75, 76–7.

> "The plant and inventories of The Coca-Cola Company could go up in flames overnight. Yet on the following morning, there would not be a bank in Atlanta, New York or anywhere else that would not lend the company the funds necessary to re-build, accepting as security the inherent goodwill in the trade marks COCA-COLA and COKE."[3]

This book is an attempt to make a systematic examination of the function of trade marks and the purpose of the law protecting trade marks as well as considering certain related issues. It is based to a large extent upon the thesis for which I was awarded the degree of Master of Laws by the University of Bristol. That project in turn was inspired by the impression, gained during my undergraduate study of intellectual property, that Schechter's complaint still held true, at least for modern English trade mark law. Consequently, I have been influenced in seeking a jurisprudential and economic rationale for trade mark law by the work of a number of American and Commonwealth writers in addition to the growing English literature.

In writing I have been conscious of some observations made extra-judicially by no less an intellectual property lawyer than Sir Robin Jacob who commented that "purely theoretical or abstract arguments have no place in forming the rules of intellectual property"[4] and that "lawyers' studies of the problems can become overacademic . . . often they are studied because they are intellectually interesting rather than because they are important".[5] I hope I have succeeded in following this advice—after all, it is inherent in the nature of trade mark law that it has been driven by overwhelmingly practical considerations—nevertheless I would also argue that there is very much a place for theoretical analysis but only to the extent that it brings insights into the practice rather than as a valid influence in itself upon the practice. I would furthermore hope that the important issues now facing trade mark law are also intellectually interesting.

One of the main premises upon which I shall proceed is that the modern trade mark is a creature of the post-industrial consumer society that has been protected for fear of the anticipated consequences of not providing protection; thus trade mark protection is "an entitlement dependent on need".[6] With this in mind, an examination of the use now made of symbols legally protected as trade marks will form the basis of Chapter 2. As well as briefly looking at the historical antecedents of the modern trade mark and the implications for trade marks of brand advertising, this will also involve considering the phenomenon of merchandising and the implications for legal theory of these aspects of commerce.

Having observed the extent and nature of modern trade mark use, Chapter 3 will examine what, if anything, trade marks do to encourage the efficient

[3] Adapted from J. R. Lunsford, "Consumers and Trade Marks: The Function of Trade Marks in the Market Place" (1974) 64 *TMR* 75, 81 quoting from his own article published in 1955.

[4] R. Jacob, "Industrial Property—Industry's Enemy" [1996] *IPQ* 3, 14 (based on the 1996 Stephen Stewart Memorial Lecture).

[5] *Ibid.*, 15.

[6] W. R. Cornish, *Intellectual Property: Patents, Copyrights, Trade Marks and Allied Rights* (3rd edn., London, 1996), para.17–69.

allocation of resources in society through their role in mass-market commerce. On the face of it, their virtual omnipresence in consumer transactions suggests that their influence is considerable. The general question will be approached from the two main perspectives adopted in the literature of law and economics. The first is to consider the monopoly power conferred by trade mark protection. Since the trade mark right is a right to exclude ostensibly no different from those granted in respect of patents and copyright, it would seem that a trade mark owner gains a competitive advantage that is somehow unfair. We must therefore question the correctness of this (apparently common) assumption. The second approach assumes that there is some economically beneficial aspect to trade mark use that would be lost in the absence of legal protection. Therefore it is also worth assessing the extent of this benefit and whether it, at least hypothetically, counterbalances any perceived market distortions caused by legal protection.

Given that market distortions may well result from a failure to protect trade marks from third party interference, Chapter 4 will address within the framework of the Trade Marks Act 1994 the interests, in particular those of consumers and producers,[7] that motivate the prevention of such distortions, as well as whether these interests are at all conflicting. Knowing the primary motivation behind trade mark law is practically significant because it plays an important part in determining the extent of rights available to a trade mark owner in a particular situation. The general purpose of trade mark law will also follow from this, namely whether the law of trade mark protection exists solely to secure the comparatively narrow function of maintaining identity in trade or whether broader "unfair competition" considerations may be admitted.

Finally, Chapter 5 will attempt to put some of the issues discussed in preceding chapters into a more specific, practical context by looking at trade dress protection and the use of a third party's trade mark in comparative advertising. These are relatively unsettled areas on the periphery of trade mark protection, but which nevertheless seem to follow on logically. In the case of trade dress protection this is because trade dress performs such a similar function to that of trade marks; in the case of comparative advertising because a discussion of the underlying issues represents well the whole of trade mark law.

Although I have attempted to state the law as at 31 May 1998, readers should note the following two recent developments. First, the European Court of Justice in its judgment on 16 July 1998 in Case C-355/96 *Silhouette International Schmied GmbH & Co. KG* v. *Hartlauer Handelsgesellschaft mbH* (*The Times*,

[7] Whenever a trade mark is used, it directly affects two parties, the one applying it to a product and the one seeing it in the market place. They will be referred to as the "producer" and "consumer" respectively, although it is admittedly true that a party may apply a trade mark to a product without actually manufacturing it and that a party may encounter a trade mark in the market place without being the ultimate consumer of the underlying product. Note also that it is clear that trade marks may be used in connection with both goods and services with the same practical effect, and indeed modern trade mark law now makes no distinction between the two uses. For this reason and for reasons of verbal economy, "product" will be used throughout to mean both goods and services.

22 July 1998) followed the Opinion of the Advocate General and ruled that the effect of Article 7 of the Trade Marks Directive is to preclude member states from adopting the doctrine of worldwide exhaustion of rights; the doctrine of exhaustion can therefore only apply to goods first marketed within the European Economic Area (EEA). The court largely followed the reasoning of the Advocate General holding that although the Directive did not contemplate full harmonisation, it could nevertheless not allow for variations in the scope of the trade mark right within the Community which varying approaches to worldwide exhaustion would allow. Moreover, such an interpretation, the court held, was the only one consistent with promoting the internal market since allowing varying approaches to worldwide exhaustion would inevitably create barriers to trade within the Community. Finally, it was observed that it is open to the EC to extend the ambit of Article 7 to countries outside the EEA in the same way that the original Article 7 had been extended from simply the countries of the EU to the countries of the EEA as well (Agreement on the EEA of 2 May 1992, OJ [1994] L1/3). That this had not yet been done suggested to the court that Article 7 does not provide for worldwide exhaustion.

Secondly, the Court of Appeal in *Mars & Spencer plc* v. *One In A Million Ltd.* (*The Times*, 29 July 1998) upheld the decision of Jonathan Sumption, QC sitting as a deputy judge of the Chancery Division, that the practice of registering an Internet domain name (such as *marksandspencer.co.uk*) very similar to that of an established business, then attempting to sell the domain name registration to the business for an extortionate amount could constitute both passing-off and trade mark infringement. The main ground contained in the judgment of the court, given by Aldous L.J. after an extensive review of the authorities, was that the defendants' conduct could be subject to injunctive relief where it gave rise to an "instrument of fraud" which could enable passing-off. Clearly the use by a third party of a domain name on the Internet similar to that of a well-known trader could give rise to confusion amongst consumers and hence passing-off. If it were the intention of the defendant to interfere with the traders' goodwill or enable others to do so, the registration of the domain name will create an instrument of fraud. The court was also prepared to find trade mark infringement under s. 10(3) Trade Marks Act 1994. Interestingly, Aldous L.J. commented that he was "not satisfied that s.10(3) does require use to be trade mark use nor that it must be confusing use" but did not go on to express a reasoned opinion. Although an opportunity has thereby been missed to resolve the controversy surrounding the proper interpretation of this "dilution" provision, it also leaves scope for an interpretation other than that favoured by lower courts. Nevertheless, he found that the conduct of the defendant did take unfair advantage of and was detrimental to the distinctive character and reputation of the plaintiffs' trade marks.

I would like to take the opportunity of thanking a number of people who have helped me undertake this work. Particular thanks must go to the University of Bristol, Department of Law, for awarding me a Postgraduate Scholarship which enabled me to carry out the project, to Richard Hart for having such confidence in someone completely untested in legal publishing and to Helen Norman who as my supervisor was an unfailing source of advice, encouragement and inspiration. I must also thank Kate Elliott, Andrew Halpin, Kim Harris, Emma Himsworth, Geoffrey Hobbs, Peter Jaffey, Bronwen Norris, John Parkinson and Phil Russell as well as all my colleagues in the intellectual property litigation group at Denton Hall. Needless to say however, both the views expressed and responsibility for any errors or omissions are mine alone.

C.D.G. PICKERING
London, June 1998

Contents

Table of Cases

Table of Legislation

1

The Background and Scope of Modern Trade Mark Protection

In common with the majority of legal institutions, the trade mark has not been a static phenomenon, but rather has developed in response to the changing socio-economic conditions in which it performs its functions. Ignoring for a moment the variety of functions which a trade mark may be capable of performing, it is worth examining exactly which symbols used in modern commerce are afforded protection. This chapter will examine briefly the evolution of the law of trade mark protection and will culminate in a more detailed account of the law as it now stands governing which commercial symbols are eligible for protection as trade marks. It will also attempt to highlight some of the theoretical issues raised by the current law which will be the subject for discussion in later chapters.

THE HISTORICAL DEVELOPMENT OF TRADE MARK PROTECTION

It is clear that the marking of goods in various ways has been taking place for a considerable length of time,[1] but for reasons which we shall address in the next chapter, trade marks were not generally seen as something *needing* legal protection until around the time of the industrial revolution.[2] Consequently, neither the Common Law nor Equity troubled itself with the issue of trade mark protection until relatively late on, with the result that many writers were originally quite content to presume that the law of trade mark protection was the sole creation of the late eighteenth and early nineteenth centuries.[3] As Schechter moreover has observed, until the seventeenth century trade marks were not really the concern of the general law, but rather were regulated entirely within the trades making use of them according to so-called "guild jurisprudence".[4] When the need for a general protective law did arise, it was met in three ways:

[1] See generally F. I. Schechter, *The Historical Foundations of the Law Relating to Trade Marks* (New York, 1925) (hereinafter Schechter) as well as G. Ruston, "On the Origin of Trade Marks" (1955) 45 *TMR* 127 and B. G. Paster, "Trade Marks—Their Early History" (1969) 59 *TMR* 551.

[2] W. R. Cornish, *Intellectual Property: Patents, Copyright, Trade Marks and Allied Rights* (3rd edn., London, 1996), para.15–04.

[3] See examples in Schechter, n. 1 above, 11.

[4] *Ibid.*, 11–12. The general law's influence was slight and extended through the administrative law courts (*ibid.*, 125–7).

initially at common law alone, then additionally through trade mark registration and finally on an international and Community level.

Protection of Trade Marks at Law and in Equity

The root of trade mark protection[5] in the English common law is generally said to be Dodderidge J.'s (in)famous "irrelevant reminiscent dictum"[6] uttered in 1618 in *Southern* v. *How*[7] concerning an unreported case decided in 1584.[8] After this there came silence in the law reports on the matter until 1742 and the case of *Blanchard* v. *Hill*.[9] Injunctive relief in this case was actually refused because of the fear of allowing an unfair monopoly,[10] and it was only in *Millington* v. *Fox*[11] that a remedy was allowed in Equity even in the absence of any fraudulent intent on the part on the defendant. The essence of liability was a likelihood of public deception arising from the defendant's misrepresentation. The Common Law, on the other hand, starting with the first reported decision of *Sykes* v. *Sykes*[12] allowed an action for damages but based on proof of deliberate deceit. A second line of equitable cases dating from the time of Lord Westbury L.C. indicated that liability actually arose on the basis of the protection of a property right in the mark. However, such a development was ultimately preempted by the advent of registration.[13]

Following the fusion of law and equity, the three bodies of authority[14] allowing trade mark protection by way of an action in tort finally reached their modern synthesis in the House of Lords decision of *Spalding (AG) & Bros.* v. *A.W. Gamage Ltd.*[15] This established that misrepresentation (and so consumer deception) was the true basis of what had then become generally referred to as the tort of passing-off,[16] but that the misrepresentation could be as to one of a number of things, and not merely that the goods of the defendant are those of the plaintiff; and that passing-off indeed protected a property right, the property in the *goodwill* of the plaintiff's business. The effect of the decision also "freed passing-off from being no more than the common law counterpart of trade

[5] See generally C. Wadlow, *The Law of Passing-off* (2nd edn., London, 1995), ch.1 for a more detailed account of the development of judicial trade mark protection.

[6] *Ibid.*, 6.

[7] (1618) Popham 143.

[8] Now identified by Baker and Milsom as *JG* v. *Samford*. See J. H. Baker and S. F. C. Milsom, *Sources of English Legal History* (London, 1986), 615–8.

[9] (1742) 2 Atk. 484.

[10] The case actually involved a mark used in respect of playing cards—the subject-matter of the notorious *Darcy* v. *Allen* (1602) 11 Co Rep 84b—which must have partially influenced the judge.

[11] (1838) 3 Myl. & Cr. 338.

[12] (1824) 3 B & C 543.

[13] See Wadlow, n. 5 above, 18 and the authorities cited therein. Compare this with the potential effect of the decision in *Taittinger SA* v. *Allbev Ltd* [1993] FSR 641 discussed below at n. 234.

[14] Wadlow, n. 5 above, 23.

[15] (1915) 32 RPC 273.

[16] It was referred to as such in *Perry* v. *Trufit* (1842) 6 Beav. 66.

mark infringement"[17] and this fact must be borne in mind when comparing the two contemporary methods of trade mark protection.[18]

The Advent of Registration

In spite of the readiness of judges to recognise and protect trade marks, it was not until 1862 that the matter was first considered by Parliament,[19] and only in 1875 was provision made for the protection of trade marks by registration.[20] The advantages of protection by this method are clear: it is no longer necessary to go through the costly and laborious process of proving that a mark has an acquired reputation connected with the plaintiff.[21] Instead, it is presumed that the mark has some acquired reputation and registration (now) confers exclusive rights on the proprietor of a particular mark.[22] These rights enable him or a registered licensee[23] to prevent certain unauthorised uses of the mark by others.[24] It also gives notice to other traders of which marks are currently in use or to which claim has already been laid. Even in the face of such supporting reasons, the acceptance of a national trade mark law was less than enthusiastic. Legislators, lawyers and merchants alike were unable to characterise a trade mark as an ordinary asset or subject of property:

> "The most dire consequences, such as fraudulent uses and sales of trade marks and the creation of monopolies, it was prophesied, would ensue from the recognition of trade marks as property."[25]

Nevertheless, the 1875 Act was finally passed although the predominant motive for the legislature was thought to be securing reciprocal protection overseas rather than providing a superior domestic law.[26] In fact it is arguable that the

[17] Wadlow, n. 5 above, 27.

[18] See "Protection of Unregistered Marks by way of an Action in Passing-off", below.

[19] Schechter, n. 1 above, 139–40. Even then it was only to criminalise the counterfeiting of marks.

[20] *Ibid.*, 140. Trade Marks Act 1875.

[21] Cornish, n. 2 above, para.15–06.

[22] S.9(1) Trade Marks Act 1994. Unless otherwise stated, all references in the chapter are to this Act. Also, since this book is not in the nature of a textbook, it is presumed that the reader has access to the main statutory provisions which are consequently not set out in full.

[23] Ss.25 and 30.

[24] It does *not*, with respect, confer a monopoly (to use a rather loaded and emotive term) in the use of the mark as some judges seem to think (see, e.g., *Re* COCA-COLA *Trade Marks* [1986] RPC 421, *per* Lord Templeman). More detailed analysis of this point may be found in Ch. 3, below. Contrast this with the effect of a patent or copyright.

[25] Schechter, n. 1 above, 141. An interesting parallel may be drawn between the introduction of trade mark registration and the acceptance of limited liability companies. When such institutions were proposed in the middle of the last century, similarly dire prophesies were made concerning the iniquities which would result, no doubt coloured, e.g., by the infamous South Sea Bubble fiasco. Ultimately incorporation proved to be another highly influential factor in the establishment of the modern economy. See generally L. C. B. Gower, *Principles of Modern Company Law* (5th edn., London, 1992), chs. 2 and 3.

[26] *Ibid.* See also Schechter, n. 1 above, 140 who is quite scathing about this reason for introducing registration. Having said that, with the very considerable increase since the last century in global

first Act was merely procedural; only when a statutory infringement action was introduced in 1905 could the original regime be said to bear the stamp of a special privilege because it created new rights rather than recognised pre-existing ones.[27] The range of registrable marks was increased over successive Trade Marks Acts, including the division of the register into two parts in 1919 to allow the registration of marks which had become sufficiently capable of functioning as a trade mark rather than being inherently so; and the 1938 Trade Marks Act even introduced the (then rather revolutionary) idea of licensing of trade marks.[28] Protection of trade marks by way of registration is now provided for by the Trade Marks Act 1994.

THE SITUATION TODAY: AN OUTLINE OF MODERN TRADE MARK PROTECTION

There are two ways in which trade marks may now be protected[29]: by registering a particular mark with the Comptroller-General of Patents, Designs and Trade Marks and by bringing an action in the tort of passing-off against an unauthorised user of the mark. Whether a particular mark qualifies for protection, the scope of protection and its advantages and disadvantages[30] obviously depend on the method of protection.[31] What, however, cannot be stressed too much is the fact that the absence of protection, by either method, never prevents the use of any particular symbol in trade providing, of course, that it does not conflict with the rights of others. Moreover the use of any marks at all in connection with goods or services is entirely at the option of the trader[32]; but it is of course the most convenient method for identifying his product.

trade, often with various intellectual property rights attaching to the goods which had been granted in the country of origin, trade marks, in common with the subject in general have taken on an important international context. A potential disincentive could have been the absence of reciprocal intellectual property protection in the countries between which trade was taking place. Amongst the treaties entered into to avoid this were the Paris Convention for the Protection of Industrial Property 1883 and the Madrid Agreement for the International Registration of Marks 1891. The United Kingdom is now a signatory to both the former and the new 1989 Protocol to the latter.

[27] See Cornish, n. 2 above, para.15–08.

[28] *Ibid.*, paras.15–09 and 10. Assignment accompanied by goodwill always having been possible.

[29] Although trade mark protection now has a substantial international element, we are concerned only with the provisions which form the English law of trade mark protection as the basis of our discussion. Note, however, that in addition to the international conventions mentioned at n. 26 above, the EC Council of Ministers has adopted a Regulation (40/94/EEC of 20 Dec. 1993 (OJ [1994] L11/1)) providing for a pan-European right in the form of the Community Trade Mark.

[30] See R. E. Annand and H. E. Norman, *Blackstone's Guide to the Trade Marks Act 1994* (London, 1994), 16 and 17.

[31] Note that the two methods are not necessarily concurrent in their ambit and more importantly, the protection of trade marks, unregistered or otherwise, does not define the purposes of the tort of passing-off. See "Protection of Unregistered Marks by way of an Action in Passing-off" below.

[32] This was not always the case: see ch. 2, below.

Registration under the Trade Marks Act 1994

The current registration regime[33] came into force on 31 October 1994 and was introduced because of the pressure for change both domestically and internationally. Areas in need of reform were identified as long ago as 1974,[34] but the sole change made in response was the introduction of a mechanism for the registration of service marks. It was only in a recent White Paper[35] that the government acknowledged, amongst other things, the inability of the 1938 Act to cope with changes in trading practices. The need to meet various international obligations[36] and implement the EC Directive on the harmonisation of trade mark law[37] was also influential. Indeed it is becoming increasingly clear that the Trade Marks Directive is the driving force in English trade mark law. Although it was originally doubted whether the Directive was in fact correctly implemented by the Trade Marks Act,[38] in *Philips Electronics NV* v. *Remington Consumer Products*[39] Jacob J. was prepared to accept that there was no intentional conflict between the two and accepted argument based directly on the wording of the Directive.

Registrability and Maintenance of Registration

Any sign which is "capable of being represented graphically" and moreover "capable of distinguishing goods or services of one undertaking from those of other undertakings"[40] may, *prima facie*, be registered as a trade mark, unless there is some characteristic inherent in the mark which renders it incapable of being registered (the so-called "absolute" grounds of refusal) or it conflicts with

[33] There is a wealth of shorter commentaries such as Annand and Norman, n. 30 above, and also C. Morcom, *A Guide to the Trade Marks Act 1994* (London, 1995). The standard work, T. A. Blanco White and R. Jacob, *Kerly's Law of Trade Marks and Trade Names* (12th edn., London, 1986), however is currently a less than satisfactory source of reference and more of historical interest since the editors have not yet revised the work to incorporate the (sometimes radical) changes made by the new Act.

[34] By the Mathys Committee (*British Trade Mark Law and Practice*, Cmnd. 5601 (London, 1974).

[35] *Reform of Trade Marks Law*, Cm. 1203 (London, 1990); see also Annand and Norman, n. 30 above, 7. An example was the unrealistic provisions (s.28 Trade Marks Act 1938 (the "old Act")) for trade mark licensing, an everyday occurrence in the contemporary world of trade marks.

[36] See Annand and Norman, n. 30 above, 3–5.

[37] First Trade Marks Directive of 21 Dec. 1988 (89/104/EEC, OJ [1989] L40/1). Note also the EC case law governing when trade mark rights may be used to prevent the so-called parallel importation of trade marked goods from other Member States (see text accompanying nnn. 203–207 below) and laying down principles deciding when certain uses of trade marks can be struck down as being contrary to Arts. 85 and 86 of the Treaty of Rome.

[38] Annand and Norman, n. 30 above, 6 and 7. Witness the confusion in *British Sugar plc* v. *James Robertsons & Sons* [1996] RPC 281, 291–293 concerning the relationship between ss. 9 and 10 Trade Marks Act 1994.

[39] [1998] RPC 283, 290–291.

[40] S.1(1). If these requirements are not satisfied, under s.3(1)(a) the mark may not be registered.

the prior rights of a third party (the "relative" grounds). A sign has been said to be "anything which can convey information".[41]

The definition of trade marks that are registrable is intended to be broadly drawn in order to simplify matters for the businesses making use of the right and to encourage greater use of this form of trade mark protection.[42] Registrable marks are said to include "words, designs, letters, numerals or the shape of goods or their packaging".[43] This approach, it is hoped, will help to resolve some of the problems that have occurred in the past with respect to marks which do not fall within the paradigm word or device mark, but which nonetheless are capable of functioning as trade marks. For example in *Smith Kline and French Laboratories Ltd* v. *Sterling-Winthrop Group Ltd*,[44] it was finally accepted that colours applied to products could function as a trade mark when, applied to goods, they had acquired secondary meaning which indicated that they were the produce of a particular manufacturer. Compare this with the Striped Toothpaste cases[45] where Unilever desperately tried to register the stripes on SIGNAL toothpaste as trade marks but was foiled at every attempt. The most perceptive reason for their failure, given by Hoffmann J. in the third round, was that the stripes were not chosen and simply did not function as a symbol of origin nor could any acquired meaning be identified. Similarly in *Philips* v. *Remington*, the sign (a picture of the heads of an electric razor) was found to be incapable of distinguishing because it primarily denoted function rather than anything concerning the product's trade origin.

A second area where the new Act will clarify (in this case expressly) and indeed change the law is with respect to the shapes of goods and their packaging. The leading case on this aspect was the infamous *Re* COCA-COLA *Trade Marks*[46] where the House of Lords refused to allow the registration of the COKE bottle as a trade mark, denouncing it as "another attempt to expand on the boundaries of intellectual property and to convert a protective law into a source of monopoly".[47] This resulted in a "strange metaphysical distinction" between

[41] *Per* Jacob J. in *Philips* v. *Remington* at 298.

[42] E.g. the applicant no longer needs to make out one of the essential particulars under s.9(1) Trade Marks Act 1938 that were necessary for registration in Part A of the old Register. Indeed between when the new Act came into force on 31 October 1994 and February 1996, 636 applications had been made to register marks which could not be protected under the old law. These included 529 applications for marks which included a three-dimensional element, the first of which was the COCA-COLA bottle; 74 colour applications including the colour of BP petrol stations; 12 sound applications amongst which were the DIRECT LINE insurance jingle and Bach's "Air on the G string" for HAMLET cigars; and 14 "olfactory" applications including CHANEL NO.5. The Registry did however suspect that some applications had merely been publicity stunts (Feb. 1996 TW 11–2). See also n. 49, below.

[43] S.1(1).

[44] [1976] RPC 511. Compare this with *John Wyeth and Bro Ltd's Coloured Tablet Trade Mark* [1988] RPC 233 where the colours merely indicated the strength of the tablets and therefore did not function as a trade mark.

[45] *Unilever's Application* [1980] FSR 286; *Re Unilever plc's Application* [1984] RPC 155; and *Unilever Ltd's Trade Mark (Striped Toothpaste No.2)* [1987] RPC 233.

[46] See also n. 24 above.

[47] *Ibid.*, at 275e, *per* Lord Templeman.

colours applied to a product and the configuration of the product itself.[48] It is clear that this decision has now been statutorily reversed.[49] Nevertheless, courts will always be wary of allowing the perpetual trade mark right in the appearance of a product itself and will demand strong evidence that consumers do recognise the product simply by its shape.[50]

Finally one aspect which serves to identify a particular brand of product, but which still does not fall within the new, enlarged definition of what is registrable, is a product's get-up or trade dress. This may well be a collection of often subtle images and devices which in their own right may be common to the trade or insufficiently distinctive, but together form a product's distinctive brand image.[51] It would be difficult however to stretch the meaning of the word "sign" (in section 1(1) of the Trade Marks Act 1994) to include such a combination, and it was for this reason that attempts were made, but without success, to secure protection for this form of trade symbol.[52]

Having considered what may fall within the new definition of a trade mark that is capable of being registered, we now turn to reasons why such a sign, which is perfectly capable of functioning as a trade mark, may nevertheless not be registered. These fall into two categories: the absolute and relative grounds for refusal of registration. In order to establish whether any of the absolute grounds is applicable, the trade mark in question and the circumstances surrounding the application must be examined on their merits. The applicability of a particular ground is a question of fact in each case. Marks that are objectionable include those prohibited by other UK and Community legislation[53]; specially protected emblems[54]; those applied for in bad faith[55]—where there is no *bona fide* intent to use the mark,[56] for example to permit warehousing of marks,

48 Annand and Norman, n. 30 above, 61.

49 By s.1(1) and the Coca-Cola Co. have applied once more to register their bottle as a trade mark. Other three-dimensional trade marks for which registration has recently been sought include the shapes of BIC ball-point pens (in Canada), MONSTER MUNCH crisps (in Spain), KENCO coffee jars and the DIRECT LINE insurance wheeled telephone device (in the UK). See D. A. Daniel, "Can the Shape of Products be Trade Marks? A Brazilian and International Perspective" [1995] *EIPR* 589.

50 See *Philips Electronics NV* v. *Remington Consumer Products* [1998] RPC 283, 304–310.

51 The special case of trade dress protection is considered in Ch.5 below. The difficulty facing producers is illustrated by *Re Proctor & Gamble Ltd's Trade Mark Application*, unreported, Ch.D., 25 July 1997.

52 Annand and Norman, n. 30 above, 61.

53 S.3(4). These may include marks prohibited under e.g. the Trade Descriptions Act 1968 or marks which are chosen because of their tendency to partition the European Economic Area, contrary to Art.30 EEC.

54 S.3(5) and cf. art.6*ter* Paris Convention.

55 S.3(6).

56 There is no requirement in the English law of trade mark registration that prior to registration a mark must have actually been used (there is such a requirement afterwards: see text accompanying n. 107 below); compare this, though, to the protection of marks in passing-off (where one of the elements which must be proven is a trade symbol's acquired reputation: see "Protection of Unregistered Marks by way of an Action in Passing-off", below) and US Federal law before the Trademark Amendment Act 1986.

"ghost" applications,[57] or future merchandising activities; those which are contrary to "accepted principles of morality"[58]; or those which are deceptive.[59]

As the breadth of trade symbols which are recognised as worthy of protection under the Trade Marks Act increases, so the potential for encroachment on the ambit of other I.P. rights[60] becomes correspondingly greater. This is the mischief at which section 3(2)[61] is aimed and represents "an attempt to reconcile the different objectives of fair and free competition with regard to the registration as trade marks of product shapes".[62] It prohibits the registration of a mark if it consists *exclusively* of a shape which either results from the nature of the goods themselves, is necessary to obtain a technical result[63] or gives substantial value to the goods.[64] However, note that the various intellectual property rights are by no means mutually exclusive and that the section is said to apply only to marks which consist exclusively of the objectionable shapes.

Most important are the limitations which relate to the mark's semantic characteristics. This requires some preliminary explanation. If one abstractly considers the meaning of a variety of words used as trade marks, a spectrum of distinctiveness may be perceived which runs from "fanciful or coined" marks which have no meaning other than in connection with the goods or services in question, the classic example being KODAK for photographic equipment; through "arbitrary" marks which have an ordinary meaning, but one which is completely foreign to its trade mark context, such as APPLE for computers; and "suggestive" marks which hint at characteristics of the product without actually describing it, for example CLOVER for margarine; to "descriptive" marks which directly describe the product as is the case with WEETABIX for breakfast cereal or MICROSOFT for computer software; finally come "generic" marks where the mark actually is or has become the common name for an item rather than the goods

[57] E.g. *Imperial Group* v. *Phillip Morris* [1982] FSR 72. The applicant merely wished to prevent the use of MERIT by attempting to register NERIT.

[58] S.3(3)(a) One could speculate whether this would preclude the registration of the French marks SIC and PSCHITT for soft drinks, the Spanish mark BUM for crisps or the Finnish mark SUPER PISS for de-icer! (*The Economist*, "The Year of the Brand" 24 Dec. 1988) More seriously, the operation of this s. is illustrated well by *JARDEX Trade Mark* (1946) 63 RPC 19 where the presence of JARDOX on the register for meat extract prevented the instant mark from being registered in respect of disinfectant.

[59] S.3(3)(b) e.g. *ORLWOOLA Trade Mark* (1909) 26 RPC 683 The goods in respect of which the registration was sought were not "all wool" and if they had been then, in somewhat of a Catch-22 situation, the mark would have been descriptive!

[60] In particular industrial design law and copyright which are true, but limited monopolies and which are justified by the public interest in providing incentives to create æsthetically pleasing designs or various literary, artistic, etc. works.

[61] The provision was considered in several *obiter dicta* of Jacob J. in *Philips Electronics NV* v. *Remington Consumer Products* [1998] RPC 283, 304–309.

[62] White Paper, n. 35 above, para.2.20.

[63] Note that this could have been yet another possible reason why the Striped Toothpaste cases mentioned above at n. 45 were doomed to fail: the red stripes originally contained mouthwash.

[64] It could conceivably be argued that this sub-section would operate to prevent the registration of marks which are used for merchandising purposes (Annand and Norman, n. 30 above, 215), although in *Philips* v. *Remington* Jacob J. (at 309) said that such added value must be considered while disregarding any value attributable to trade mark function, since one of the purposes of a good trade mark is to add value.

or services of a specific trader—the best example is ASPIRIN for acetylsalicylic acid.[65] The level of distinctiveness is of course critical for the success of the mark as a brand name, but also for our present purposes can be decisive in assessing the registrability of the mark. Given the broad scope of the exclusive rights available, there are numerous commercial situations in which registration of a word as a trade mark would allow the proprietor to control use of that word. If the word is fanciful, arbitrary or suggestive, and hence has no meaning in relation to the proposed use, then this does not present any problem. However where the word does refer in some way to the product in question, there exists the potential to disrupt other traders' ability to name and describe their products.[66]

Registration is thus prohibited if the mark either is devoid of any distinctive character[67] or consists entirely of exclusively descriptive[68] or generic[69] signs, *unless* it can be shown that, before the application was made, the mark "has acquired a distinctive (that is, trade mark) character as a result of the use made of it".[70] This last aspect is vital because there is now no prohibition as a matter of law on specific categories of mark,[71] in particular so-called laudatory epithets or geographical names[72]; the sign must simply be shown to function as a trade

[65] It must be stressed that this is merely a convenient set of categories for analytical purposes and does not necessarily have any legal significance. However Carter suggests that the level of distinctiveness *should* determine the level of protection given in *all* contexts (S. L. Carter, "The Trouble with Trademark" (1990) 99 *Yale LJ* 759) in contrast to most commentators who think that such considerations are only relevant in the context of "anti-dilution" protection (e.g. F. I. Schechter, "The Rational Basis of Trade Mark Protection" (1927) 40 *Harv LR* 813). Compare this also with the situation under the old Act whereby differing protection was given to so-called Part A and Part B marks, and see comments made in University of Chicago Law Review, Comment, "The Anti-competitive Aspects of Trade Name Protection and the Policy Against Consumer Deception" (1962) 29 *U Chicago LR* 371, 375–6.

[66] Note that it is the mark's *potential* effect that we are concerned with, that is the possibility that registration would frustrate another trader's legitimate interest in using the mark, not the *actual* effect. Otherwise the court would become involved in an impractical and costly enquiry into, e.g., the public perception of the mark and the structure of the market under consideration. Compare this with the fiduciary duties imposed in company law and the law of trusts whereby company directors and trustees are prevented from entering into certain transaction where there is a risk of self-interest regardless of any actual prejudice since any enquiry into the presence of such prejudice would be similarly impractical (see J. E. Martin, *Hanbury and Martin: Modern Equity* (London, 1993), ch.20 and J. E. Parkinson, *Corporate Power and Responsibility* (Oxford, 1993), ch.7, in particular 206–7).

[67] S.3(1)(b).

[68] S.3(1)(c) these are said to include designations in the course of trade of the "kind, quality, quantity, intended purpose, value, geographical origin, the time of production of goods or rendering of services or other characteristics of goods or services".

[69] S.3(1)(d); this includes signs which are "customary in the current language or in the *bona fide* and established practices of the trade".

[70] Proviso to s.3(1).

[71] This is emphasised by Jacob J. in *British Sugar plc* v. *James Robertson and Sons* [1996] RPC 281, 305.

[72] And so effectively overrules the decisions in PERFECTION *Trade Mark* (1909) 26 RPC 837 and YORK *Trade Mark* [1984] RPC 231. This decision was criticised particularly heavily since it was admitted that the mark YORK for goods vehicle trailers "was 100% factually distinctive", yet it was held that as a matter of law, such geographical names were incapable of being registered as trade marks—other traders were thought always to have a proper motive to use such terms.

mark. For this to happen, compelling evidence is necessary since courts have shown themselves to be wary of "wealthy traders"[73] attempting to appropriate common terms for use on their products:

> "Of course the power of advertising may be able to turn anything into a trade mark, but it must be shown . . . that the mark has really become accepted by a substantial majority of persons as a trade mark—is or is almost a household word."[74]

Such evidence must be of more than mere use.[75]

A problem which manifests itself here is the relationship between section 1(1), which requires that, for a sign to be registrable, it must be capable of distinguishing and section 3(1)(b), which denies registration to marks devoid of any distinctive character; two phrases with ostensibly similar meanings. In *British Sugar*[76] Jacob J. was of the opinion that section 1(1) adds nothing significant to section 3(1)(b) and that the two phrases were essentially synonymous. However, it is submitted that the "better view", which is supported by the observation made in *A.D.2000 Trade Mark*,[77] is to interpret section 1(1) as requiring a minimum standard for registration (below which section 3(1)(a) will prevent registration), that the sign in question may be *potentially* capable of functioning (by distinguishing goods or services of one trader from those of another[78]) as a trade mark and section 3(1)(b) in conjunction with the proviso as requiring that the sign *actually* performs such a function[79]; this will only happen if consumers become aware that it is used as a trade mark. The essence of the complaint is therefore the immaturity of the sign as a trade mark.[80] Using Jacob J.'s approach, on the other hand, there is a danger that the two clearly separate issues will become confused. Examples of marks likely to fall foul of this provision include the colours which merely denoted the strength of the product as seen in *John Wyeth and Bro Ltd's Coloured Tablet Trade Mark*,[81] the Striped Toothpaste cases, in which the stripes in question performed a variety of functions but not those of trade marks,[82] or indeed the mark TREAT in *British Sugar*

[73] *Per* Jacob J. in *British Sugar*, n. 71 above, at 306.

[74] *Ibid.*

[75] *Ibid.* This case involved the mark TREAT for dessert sauces which the plaintiff sought to assert against the defendant's product TOFFEE TREAT (a jam-like product). The action failed for various reasons, amongst which was the invalidity (under s.47) of the plaintiff's mark which was found to be a laudatory epithet falling within s.3(1)(b), (c) and probably (d). The plaintiff was unable to produce any satisfactory evidence that TREAT was recognised as a trade mark.

[76] *Ibid.* This view was not departed from almost two years later in *Philips* v. *Remington*, n. 61 above.

[77] [1997] RPC 168, 173–4 (Geoffrey Hobbs QC, hearing an appeal as an Appointed Person from the decision of the Registrar under s.76 Trade Marks Act).

[78] Something the white colour of tablets was said to be incapable of in *CIMETIDINE Trade Mark* [1991] RPC 17.

[79] This view is also supported by structure of the Directive since "capacity to distinguish" and the absolute grounds are separate elements of validity.

[80] See [1997] RPC 168, 173.

[81] See n. 44, above.

[82] N. 45 above. Also worthy of note here is *HAVE A BREAK Trade Mark* [1993] RPC 217 which, as well as illustrating the excessive measures to which some producers go in order to gain unmerited

itself which, as a laudatory epithet, Jacob J. found to be inherently devoid of any distinctive character.

Secondly, there exists the prohibition on descriptive marks. This is a recognition of the public interest in keeping trade descriptions in the public domain (since such indications can be used with equal truth by other traders) whilst at the same time recognising that certain descriptions have become indicative of a particular manufacturer through use made in the market place.[83] The principle which emerged under the old Act and could well continue to apply to section 3(1)(c) was that a mark was *prima facie* not registrable if it was so descriptive of the goods or services that some section of the business community would regard it as such and *legitimately* wish to use it.[84] Protection cannot attach when the mark denotes something other than the trade origin of the product.[85] If the mark had come to signify the goods of only one trader, then the need of others to use it ceased to be legitimate. A concluding observation to be made is quite how fine and always a question of degree the line is between descriptive marks, which are *prima facie* objectionable, and so-called suggestive marks, which generally will be sufficiently distinctive. Finally, generic or customary marks are excluded. This restriction is necessary because otherwise a proprietor *would* gain a monopoly in a word for which there would be no acceptable synonyms, for example who would generally know that acetylsalicylic acid was the scientific name for ASPIRIN, let alone be able to pronounce it?

It is therefore possible to conclude that there is a discernible but not expressly articulated policy in the law of trade marks in favour of encouraging new words into the language to be used as brand names rather than merely adopting common words already in use. This seems a quite reasonable goal given that it may be argued that the number of fanciful marks available is potentially infinite.[86] If a producer feels it necessary to make use of a descriptive or generic term under which to market his product, he must make certain that it has crossed the Rubicon of distinctiveness before attempting to control others' use of it through the trade mark laws. In other words, a trade mark must, as Geoffrey Hobbs QC aptly said in *AD2000 Trade Mark*, be "endowed *by nature and/or nurture* with the capacity to communicate the fact that the

I.P. protection, was a case where the application to register a slogan was rejected as incapable of functioning as a trade mark. Contrast this with the rather dubious decision in *I CAN'T BELIEVE IT'S YOGHURT Trade Mark* [1992] RPC 533 (registration allowed) which illustrates the extreme fineness of such a distinction.

[83] Annand and Norman, n. 30 above, 82 and 83, or as the White Paper, n. 35 above, chose to put it at para.2.10, "the proviso to s.3(1) was doing no more than recognise *de facto* monopolies". Was it indeed? See the writer's other comments on this topic at n. 24 above.

[84] *Per* Lloyd-Jacob J. in *SMITSVONK Trade Mark* (1954) 72 RPC 117. See also the observation of Lord Parker in *Registrar* v. *W. & G .Du Cros* (1913) 30 RPC 660, 672, recently approved in the context of the 1994 Trade Marks Act by Chadwick J. in *Re Proctor & Gamble Ltd's Trade Mark Application*, unreported, Ch.D., 25 July 1997.

[85] As Geoffrey Hobbs QC put it in *AD2000 Trade Mark*, n. 77 above, at 174.

[86] See W. M. Landes and R. A. Posner, "Trade Mark Law: an Economic Perspective" [1987] *J Law & Econ.* 265, 271–3, on the economics of language.

goods or services with reference to which it is used recurrently are those of one and the same undertaking".[87]

As well as being refused because of an absolute ground, registration may also be prevented if it would conflict with a prior third party right—a relative ground for refusal. The structure of the Act is a lot clearer in this respect, and, logically, the relative grounds mirror almost exactly the provisions describing when infringement occurs, the other occasion when rights may conflict.[88] Section 5(1)–(3) outlines the circumstances in which an "earlier trade mark" will prevent registration, and then section 6 goes on to describe which marks constitute such an earlier mark. This is quite a wide-ranging list and includes international marks, applications for marks, well-known marks (in the Paris Convention sense) and even recently expired marks. Furthermore a registration will be blocked if the applicant's mark either conflicts with an *unregistered* mark which would otherwise be protected by way of an action in passing-off[89] or where a three-dimensional or pictorial element of the mark conflicts with a registered design, design right or copyright belonging to a third party.[90] The circumstances when a prior right will be effective to block a registration and the considerations to be taken into account are identical to those relevant with respect to infringement, and so they will be more conveniently discussed below.[91] Suffice it to say that provision is made for when identical marks for identical goods conflict, when identical or similar marks for identical or similar goods or services conflict (thus giving a range of possible permutations) and when identical or similar marks for *dissimilar* goods or services conflict. Finally, note that all this becomes academic if the owner of the prior right consents to the registration.[92]

At the moment, the onus is on the registrar when examining new applications to find and raise any relative grounds.[93] However provision is made for an opposition-based system to be eventually introduced when this is thought appropriate.[94] Related to this is something of a historical anomaly, the "honest concurrent use" provision[95] whereby registration is allowed in the face of sec-

[87] [1997] RPC 168, 175 (emphasis added). Note that there are marks which are so descriptive that they can never acquire secondary meaning: Jacob J. gives the example of SOAP for soap in *Philips* v. *Remington*, n. 51 above.

[88] As acknowledged by the European Court of Justice at para.13 of its judgment in Case C–251/95 *Sabel BV* v. *Puma AG* [1998] RPC 199.

[89] S.5(4)(a) However note that it is not yet clear whether passing-off would have to be shown in all circumstances or merely between the prior mark and the mark applied for.

[90] S.5(4)(b).

[91] S.10(1)–(3). See "Which Unauthorised Uses may be Prevented?", text accompanying nn. 152 *et seq*. below, in particular with respect to likelihood of confusion and reputation.

[92] S.5(5).

[93] Although it has been said that there is now no presumption either for or against registration: see the decision of Geoffrey Hobbs, QC (hearing an appeal as an Appointed Person from the decision of the Registrar under s.76 Trade Marks Act) in EUROLAMB *Trade Mark* [1997] RPC 279, 288.

[94] S.8. This is likely to be after the Community Trade Mark office has become well established—it was felt that the burden would currently be too great for small businesses to cope with under present conditions (Annand and Norman, n. 24 above, 93).

[95] S.7. See Annand and Norman, n. 30 above, 106–11 for a more detailed account and criticism of the provision, which includes allegations that the s. is in clear breach of the Directive.

tion 5 relative grounds if the applicant can satisfy the registrar that such use has been made. The necessary use has been defined in a series of cases[96] which have emphasised that the relevant interest to be considered is that of the public and does not provide the means for merely overcoming the recalcitrance of a prior right owner. When the register first came into being, trading conditions were rather different from today's and it was quite conceivable that the same mark may be used and goodwill accrued in two geographically diverse locations, so easily justifying a provision of this kind. Now that most products are marketed nationally, it seems anomalous, to say the least, that such a provision is still thought necessary. It will disappear however when a pure opposition-based system is finally introduced.

Once registration has been obtained, this is not the end of the matter. Although the duration of the registration may be without limit of time (in contrast to the other I.P. rights with completely different rationales from trade marks) so long as renewal fees are paid,[97] the proprietor must ensure that the mark does not become liable to be removed from the register in consequence of his actions or omissions, or indeed those of others. There are two groups of reasons why a mark may be removed: supervening events which could result in revocation[98] from the time that the registration became defective, and pre-existing faults which mean that the registration will from the start be invalid.[99] It is open, in contrast with the old law, to anyone[100] to challenge the registration, but it is most likely to be by way of counter-claim from someone threatened with or defending infringement proceedings. The grounds for *invalidity* are straightforward: a trade mark may be declared invalid if it was registered in breach of one of the absolute[101] or relative[102] grounds unless, in the case of absolute grounds, section 3(1)(b)–(d) has been overcome by proof of acquired distinctiveness or with respect to the relative grounds, the owner of the prior right has consented.

A trade mark may be *revoked* for lack of genuine use,[103] because it has become the generic name for the product in the relevant trade due to the proprietor's acts or inactivity,[104] or because it has become deceptive particularly as to the product's nature, quality or geographical origin.[105] These grounds raise

[96] E.g. *Alexander Pirie and Sons Ltd's Application* (1933) 50 RPC 147 and *Bainbridge and Green's Application* (1940) 57 RPC 248. They are expressly stated still to be good law in the new Act, about which see the comments made obiter by Jacob J. in *Origins Natural Resources Inc.* v. *Origin Clothing Ltd.* [1995] FSR 280, 287.

[97] The example is often given of registered trade mark no.1 for the BASS red triangle which is still a current registration.

[98] See s.46.

[99] See s.47.

[100] S.46(4) or s.47(3) respectively.

[101] S.47(1).

[102] S.47(2).

[103] S.46(1)(a), (b).

[104] S.46(1)(c).

[105] S.46(1)(d).

interesting theoretical questions and, for the purposes of this book, the most interesting is what constitutes "genuine use". Although the English law of registered trade marks allows for registration *without* proof of any use actually having been made,[106] and so without the mark first necessarily having attained any commercial significance (and it will be argued that this significance is fundamental to the trade mark right's rationale),[107] use must be made in order to maintain registration. Otherwise the presence on the register of an unused mark with no particular acquired significance would frustrate another's legitimate wish to use that mark or a similar one, and furthermore vest the registrant with substantial rights of no justifiable basis. The issue of what constitutes trade mark use is in fact not only of theoretical interest and indeed, as will be seen in the context of infringement, is of crucial importance to the whole of the law of trade marks. The provision covers a multitude of sins, including bad faith applications, minimal use and other cases considered under the old law which still seem to apply now: the word "genuine" appears to equate with the old phrase "*bona fide*", which was interpreted extensively under the old Act;[108] but the issue of greatest significance is use in respect of promotional goods,[109] as exemplified by KODIAK *Trade Mark*.[110]

This concerned the prior mark KODAK for clothing blocking the applicant's mark KODIAK in respect of the same goods. The applicant therefore sought the cancellation of the earlier mark on the ground of the predecessor to section 46(1)(b), arguing that since the proprietor of KODAK simply used the mark on T-shirts and the like to promote its main line of business, photographic equipment, no genuine use had been made. It had not been used to indicate the trade source of the goods, the essential trade mark function at least to the minds of the majority of English courts. Judge Paul Baker QC was no exception to this and the mark was duly revoked in respect of clothing. In all fairness, the judge did acknowledge the distinction between use to indicate origin and use to promote other goods,[111] but further acknowledged[112] that even if the use was as a trade

[106] Although a statement that the applicant or his licensee intends to use the mark must be filed (s.32).

[107] See Ch.2 below.

[108] See examples cited in Annand and Norman, n. 30 above, 123–4.

[109] It will be submitted in Ch. 2 that modern trade mark use may be analysed in two categories: branding and merchandising. Branding is used to describe the classic use of the trade mark to indicate that goods, in connection with which the trade mark is used, are the responsibility of a particular manufacturer; whereas merchandising refers to the use of a trade mark to decorate or otherwise embellish goods which may have no other connection with the proprietor of the trade mark. (This second category then breaks down into two further sub-categories: promotional goods and character or personality merchandising. The former occurs when the decorative mark has previously acquired a reputation as a brand, e.g. COCA-COLA pencil cases or GUCCI watches; while the latter indicates use of a mark which has *never* functioned as a brand and is instead being used as a convenient way of protecting the design or decoration, e.g. STAR WARS T-shirts or, of course, TEENAGE MUTANT NINJA TURTLES lunch boxes). This distinction is developed further in the next chapter and the challenges it poses to the current legal model are discussed.

[110] [1990] FSR 49.

[111] At 56 and 57.

[112] At 61.

mark, it still would not have been substantial enough to be "*bona fide*" which he held to be question of degree. That is to say, it could have performed a dual function, but the promotional function would have had to be coincident with the origin-denoting function and would not have been deemed to be the necessary trade mark use in its own right. The implications of this decision are considerable. As well as serving to re-enforce the conviction that trade marks merely indicate origin (and it will later be submitted that this is mistaken), trade mark proprietors using their registered marks for character merchandising purposes may well find their registrations challenged by others attempting to "cash in" on the particular fad which they created and are successfully exploiting. Further discussion of this (possibly unfortunate) judicial attitude will be reserved until the next chapter.

The next possible fate potentially to befall a registered trade mark is that it becomes the generic name for a product or service. Note however that it must become generic through acts of the proprietor or with his consent—common usage by the general public, as in America, will not suffice. This may happen by the proprietor's failure to control infringement or by his use of the mark as a noun rather than as an adjective in conjunction with a generic name.

Finally, a mark may become deceptive. This provision is again important for our immediate purposes because it is the only *obligation* imposed upon the trade mark owner regulating how he deals with his mark. Generally a trade mark is seen as a commercially valuable, legally protected asset to the proprietor and he is free to deal with the mark as he pleases[113]—the law will protect the trade mark as long as certain, mainly procedural requirements are complied with—however here we see a substantive limitation[114] on this freedom. Furthermore this provides evidence which seems to dispute the presence of any complete property right in the conventional sense in the trade mark, and we in fact see (for once) the interests of the consuming public taking precedence over those of the trade mark owner.[115] As with the non-use ground, a variety of conduct may lead to revocation, and two examples serve to highlight the practical importance of the problem of establishing what function trade marks perform. If the emphasis on orthodoxy (exemplified by KODIAK *Trade Mark*) is retained, then this has implications for the effect of this provision. First, if a mark becomes deceptive as to the nature or quality of the goods, then cancellation may ensue. This seems to enforce, by a rather circuitous route, a form of "guarantee" (in the loosest possible sense) that the product or service will conform to a particular standard or quality to which consumers have become accustomed.[116] This is nevertheless a rather blunt instrument in this context and the deception would have to be of

[113] Compare this with the historic marks which, as we shall see in the next chapter, were a positive liability.

[114] And moreover one deriving from *within* the law of trade marks rather from some external source such as Competition Law, EC Law or Consumer Protection Law.

[115] See Ch.4 below, as to whether the trade mark confers power without responsibility.

[116] E.g. CHINA-THERM *Trade Mark* [1980] FSR 21 which became misleading when applied to *plastic*, thermally-insulated tumblers.

the grossest kind.[117] Secondly, if the proprietor indulged in uncontrolled licensing of the mark,[118] or "trafficking"[119] as it was referred to in the old Act, then this was certainly sufficient to render the mark liable to mislead the public under that Act. Although the section does not now refer to deception as to trade origin,[120] it may be argued, depending on the emphasis given to trade origin in interpretation, that this will remain the case.[121] Of course there still remains the danger that such behaviour will result in the mark becoming misleading as to quality. This becomes all the more significant given the "deregulation" of formal dealings in trade marks, since section 46(1)(d) will be the only *legal* restriction on how marks are dealt with in this context, to which we will now turn.

Dealings in the Trade Mark: Assignment and Licensing

There is the potential for a great deal of ink to be spilt in an attempt to ascribe a conventional label, such as "property" or "proprietary right", to trade marks without actually casting any light on the real issues of the function or proper scope of protection.[122] Certainly the exclusive rights in a mark have to be attributed to someone, and this person may well change during the trade mark's life, through, for example, the assignment of the mark or the grant of a licence to use the mark. For these reasons a trade mark could be said to behave in a manner similar to tangible property, and this is in fact done in section 22 of the Act. We shall later return to the accuracy of this assumption.

One of the most radical changes in the law made by the Trade Marks Act 1994 is what may be termed the "deregulation" of such formal dealings in registered trade marks.[123] By this we mean that it is now possible to license[124] as well as freely assign[125] registered trade marks with only a minimum in procedural requirements,[126] which ensure that the transaction is good against the whole

[117] It is debatable whether, for example, COCA-COLA would have become liable for expunction following the CLASSIC COKE débâcle in the early 1980s when the drink's formula was changed without publicity (see N. S. Economides, "The Economics of Trade Marks" (1988) 78 *TMR* 523, 530).

[118] As in *JOB Trade Mark* [1993] FSR 118.

[119] See *Re American Greetings Corp.'s Application* [1984] RPC 329 (the HOLLIE HOBBIE case).

[120] And indeed Annand and Norman, n. 30 above, 133 see this as more evidence that "trade origin has been subsumed by the wider functions of trade marks in the 1994 Act".

[121] A good example here is the conduct of the Virgin organisation which uses the mark VIRGIN on a remarkably diverse range of goods and services, not all of which are now linked to the brand's founder, Richard Branson.

[122] I am certainly of the opinion that it is not possible to establish the proper scope of trade mark protection by simply analysing it as "property" since this begs the question what is property. See comments in Ch.6 below.

[123] See K. Parks, "'Naked' Is Not a Four Letter Word: Debunking the Myth of the 'Quality Control Requirement' in Trade Mark Licensing" (1992) 82 *TMR* 531, which, albeit in an American context, calls for such deregulation and addresses the unreal and impractical nature of the old law.

[124] S.28.

[125] S.24 that is, both with goodwill attaching or in gross *without* any related business or goodwill.

[126] The transaction must be in writing and duly registered with the Trade Marks Registry: ss.28(2) or 24(3) and 25(2) respectively. Until this happens, in respect of any infringement, the assignee or licensee is not entitled to any pecuniary remedies: s.25(4).

world[127] and, in the case of a licence, that use may accrue to the proprietor and that the full protection[128] of the Act is available to the licensee.

Previously, whilst assignment had always been possible, licensing was heavily regulated by a scheme of "registered users". This entailed formal scrutiny by the registrar of any agreement for the use of a trade mark by someone other than the proprietor, to ensure that adequate quality control obligations were specified. Such a person would then be entered on the register as a registered user. In other words, in order for what was effectively a licence to be granted, *substantive* as well as procedural requirements had to be met. These provisions had always been problematic and open to abuse, and indeed the legal effect of abuse was unclear. Furthermore franchising[129] and merchandising[130] are now widespread practices with which the consuming public is quite accustomed[131]; the old Act provisions proved to be merely a hindrance to them. These substantive measures have therefore now been completely abolished, leaving regulation to what may be best described as "market forces". That is to say, the onus lies with the trade mark owner to ensure that the consuming public does not, through the owner's dealings in the mark, lose faith in the trade marked goods or services and so as a result devalue the mark.[132]

Although the control of trade mark licences is now a matter for the freedom of contract subject to the principles of EC law governing competition and the free movement of goods within the EEA, a proprietor is still not completely free simply to indulge in arbitrary and uncontrolled licensing, since this may well expose the mark to revocation on the grounds of lack of genuine use or deceptiveness[133]—but a more appropriate balance between commercial interests and public protection seems now to have been struck.

Finally, a registered trade mark is freely alienable, in that a full or partial assignment of exclusive rights in it may be made. As was the case under the old Act, this is possible with or without any of the goodwill which may attach to the mark. However, there is no provision corresponding to that contained in the old Act[134] which rendered ineffective any assignment which, being against the public interest, could be deceptive or confusing. Consequently, any such dealings in a mark which alter the mark's character in this way will either have to be the

[127] S.25(3)(a) indicates that a person without notice will not be bound until the transaction is registered.

[128] Ss.30 and 31.

[129] "A business situation where a franchisee pays the franchisor for the use of the latter's name, reputation and get-up, the exploitation of which will normally remain under the franchisor's control and supervision": J. Holyoak and P. Torremans, *Intellectual Property Law* (London, 1995), 438.

[130] See n. 109 above.

[131] White Paper, n. 35 above, para.4.36; though the legal effect of such familiarity is not yet clear: cf. *Mirage Studios* v. *Counter-Feat Clothing* [1991] FSR 145 and *ELVIS PRESLEY Trade Marks* [1997] RPC 543.

[132] *Ibid*. See Landes and Posner, n. 86 above, 270 on the effect of market forces in ensuring the consistent quality of trade marked goods.

[133] Annand and Norman, n. 30 above, 201.

[134] S.22(4) and (6) Trade Marks Act 1938.

result of any such dealings by a revocation action (only likely in the context of an infringement action) or else fall to the mercy of the market forces now thought to be essential to this area of the new law.

Which Unauthorised Uses of the Mark may be Prevented?

The essence of the right deriving from a trade mark registration is that it allows the proprietor to object to certain uses of marks identical or similar to the registered mark; it bears repeating that it *does not* confer a monopoly in the particular word, device, shape, colour or whatever. In Chapter 4, we will attempt to rationalise this conduct in order to establish the true basis of trade mark protection. The infringement provisions contemplate both the use of marks in relation to goods or services[135] as well as contributory infringement.[136] Such conduct may however be justified on a number of grounds.[137]

The Trade Marks Act contemplates a series of factual matricies in which a trade mark owner's exclusive rights are enforceable. These concern circumstances where a third party uses a sign in the course of trade which is either identical or similar to the registered mark in relation variously to goods and/or services which are identical, similar or dissimilar to the goods and/or services in respect of which the mark is registered.[138] On the face of it, this is a very broad range of circumstances in which objection may be made to a third party's use of a particular sign. Although it is not immediately apparent, this raises the important preliminary issue of *the manner* in which the offending sign must be used, such that objection may be made since common sense alone, without further investigation at this stage, suggests that the purposes of trade mark protection cannot justify objection in every case. The underlying question has already been touched upon with respect to revocation for lack of use: is the purpose of the law to protect trade marks as advertising, promotional or even decorative tools in merchandising ventures, and moreover in contexts other than the markets for the products in respect of which marks are registered? Or is it merely to protect trade marks as brand names? It is worth examining this issue in more detail, since one does not have to look far in the law reports to find such "marginal" situations where disputes have arisen concerning the extent of trade mark rights. These include use of a band's name in a book title[139]; use of an allegedly distinctive laudatory word in the name of a product[140]; incidental use of a logo

[135] S.10(1)–(3); specific acts are particularised in s.10(4)(a)–(d).

[136] S.10(5). This form of infringement is unimportant for current purposes.

[137] Ss.11 and 12.

[138] S.10(1)–(3).

[139] *Bravado Merchandising Ltd* v. *Mainstream Publishing Ltd.* [1996] FSR 205 (Ct. Sess.).

[140] *British Sugar*. It is clearly possible for a descriptive mark (as opposed to a descriptive *use* that is, a use of a trade mark in its trade mark sense *to refer* to the trade mark owner's product rather than *as* a trade mark, in particular in comparative advertising) to be used both in a trade mark sense or not as the case may be, e.g. in *British Sugar* the mark in question was TREAT which could equally be used to signify the plaintiff's product or in the unrelated context of "[a]n irresistible toffee spread

in a photograph[141]; and use of the name of a famous brand to decorate T-shirts.[142]

According to the 1938 Trade Marks Act and cases interpreting it, for there to be infringement the offending mark had to be used "in such a manner as to render the use of the mark likely to be taken . . . as being use as a trade mark".[143] Read in conjunction with the interpretation section of the Act,[144] this was understood to mean that the mark must be used to indicate a connection in the course of trade between the goods and the owner or authorised user of the registered trade mark.[145] There is no such provision or indeed restriction in the 1994 Act, which after all is a "reforming Act" containing provisions "of extraterritorial provenance".[146] Consequently, one could argue that trade mark infringement is now contemplated in a wider range of circumstances, such as those mentioned above.[147] Although the matter has received some recent judicial consideration, it is still difficult to draw any unequivocal conclusion.

In *British Sugar*, Jacob J. seemed to reject any restriction on the scope of the infringement provisions to uses of the offending sign as a trade mark. It was argued (but not accepted) that since section 9(1) says that a proprietor has "exclusive rights in the trade mark which are *infringed by use of the trade mark*", this has the effect of requiring that any sign referred to in section 10

for a treat on any occasion" as suggested by Jacob J. Contrast this with coined and fanciful marks which are arguably always used in their trade mark sense, e.g. KODAK means nothing outside its trade mark context, although consider the concept of American expressive genericity (R. C. Dreyfuss, "Expressive Genericity: Trade Marks as Language in the PEPSI Generation" (1990) 65 *Notre Dame LR* 397) which holds that trade marks which are used in common language because of the qualities they suggest ought to be freed to a certain extent from the clutches of the trade mark owner. The classic example is "it's the ROLLS-ROYCE of its type".

141 *Trebor Bassett Ltd* v. *The Football Association* [1997] FSR 211.

142 KODIAK *Trade Mark* (see text accompanying nn. 110–12 above.

143 S.4(1)(a) Trade Marks Act 1938.

144 S.68(1) Trade Marks Act 1938.

145 In the leading Court of Appeal decision, *Mothercare UK Ltd.* v. *Penguin Books Ltd.* [1988] RPC 113, Dillon L.J. said (at 118) that "it stands to reason that a Trade Mark Act would only be concerned to restrict the use of a mark as a trade mark or in a trade mark sense" and Bingham L.J. (as he then was) added (at 123) that "to conclude otherwise . . . would be to hold (where a trade mark consists of an English word or words) that parliament intended to grant the proprietor of the trade mark what would in effect be commercial copyright in that word or those words". Other cases have used this reasoning, so in *Mars (GB) Ltd.* v. *Cadbury Ltd.* [1987] RPC 387 the mark TREETS for confectionery was not infringed by the words "treat size" on the packaging of miniature chocolate bars, whereas in *News Group Newspapers Ltd.* v. *Rocket Record Co. Ltd.* [1981] FSR 89 PAGE THREE for audio and video recordings was held to be arguably infringed by a record entitled "Page Three Girls". This second decision is often cited as being anomalous, but I would submit that the decision is consistent with Dillon L.J.'s requirement that use must be "in a trade mark sense"; the secondary meaning conveyed to your average, *Sun*-reading punter by the mark concerns exactly the subject-matter of the record, namely so-called glamour models appearing undressed in newspapers published by the plaintiff.

146 T. Martino, *Trade Mark Dilution* (Oxford, 1996), 92.

147 Certainly the supposedly influential Benelux trade mark law did not require use by the alleged infringer as a trade mark to be shown where the use was in any "economic intercourse . . . without a valid reason under circumstances likely to be prejudicial to the proprietor of the mark" (*Coca-Cola/Alicia* [1977] Ned. Jur. 59). This case concerned the obscene use of a Coke bottle in a pornographic film.

must be used as a trade mark. However, he stated that "s.9(1) is really no more than a chatty introduction to the details set out in s.10, itself adding no more than that the acts concerned must be done without consent", that is to say, it is a broad statement of principle certainly not intended to restrict the natural meaning of what may fall within the infringement criteria laid down in section 10. In support of this one may further argue that since section 10 refers neutrally to what the third party uses as a "sign", the implication seems to be that it does not strictly have to be used *as* a trade mark. On the other hand, in *Bravado Merchandising Ltd* v. *Mainstream Publishing Ltd*[148] it was conceded that use as a trade mark or in a trade mark sense *was* necessary in order for infringement to be established.[149] This case concerned the use of a band's name (Wet Wet Wet) in the title of a book about the band (in respect of which the mark was in fact registered) which was in the event held to infringe, because the use of the mark was *in its trade mark sense* in order to identify the book's subject-matter, even though it was not used *as a trade mark*. It is, with respect, suggested that the correct approach is that adopted by Jacob J., since to do otherwise would be to apply a gloss to the statutory provisions not even alluded to on the face either of the Act or the Directive.[150] If there is an intention to limit the proper ambit of the statutory trade mark right, it must be found by other means.

Should the courts nevertheless decide that infringement must be restricted to situations involving trade mark use, a possible solution to this problem may be found by the courts in the requirement that the offending sign must be used in relation to the goods and/or services in respect of which the mark is registered. In *British Sugar*, Jacob J. went on to comment (obiter) that although the sign Wet Wet Wet was used in its trade mark sense as part of a book title, the mark WET WET WET was not infringed because the sign was not used in relation to the goods in respect of which the mark WET WET WET was registered. In the later case of *Trebor Bassett Ltd* v. *The Football Association* Rattee J. held that the English football three lions logo was not even arguably infringed by use of an identical sign incidentally in a photograph, because again it was not used in relation to the relevant goods. The judge declined to comment on whether use as a trade mark was necessary to make out infringement.

There is undoubtedly confusion surrounding this aspect of the Trade Marks Act which will only be resolved by reference not to intuitive responses (however

[148] Note that a defence was available under s.11(2)(b) (see n. 198 below and accompanying text).

[149] This was supported by a reference to the government view expressed in Parliament that it was implicit in trade mark law that the use made of a sign must be as a trade mark before the exclusive rights may be enforced and to the 10th Recital of the Preamble to the Directive, the central theme of which was that a trade mark is intended to guarantee the origin of goods. This approach was rejected by Jacob J.

[150] In *Philips* v. *Remington*, n. 61 above, Jacob J. hinted that he may reconsider this view because of the danger presented of legitimate non-trade mark uses not being caught by the s.11 defences, but declined to express a definitive view (at 311–312).

correct)[151] to novel situations, but to the underlying questions of principle already outlined. It may well not matter whether situations such as those found in *Bravado Merchandising* or indeed *British Sugar* are excluded from ambit of infringement by section 10 or section 11(2), but it is clear that the interpretation of section 10 does impinge on the protection of merchandising ventures. There is a danger of "throwing the baby out with the bath water" by restricting the scope of section 10 if the intention of the new trade mark law was to make the range of objectionable conduct broader than that actionable under the 1938 Act.

The specific infringement provisions mirror almost exactly the relative grounds for refusing registration, and so the following discussion is equally valid in that context. The actual scope of conduct is quite wide-ranging. If the objectionable sign is identical to the registered mark and is used by the third party in connection with goods or services identical to those in respect of which the mark was registered, then the use may always be prevented.[152] This is straightforward trade mark piracy where the rogue trader effectively represents that his goods are those of the trade mark owner. More likely is the situation where either the offending sign and/or product are merely similar rather than identical. In *British Sugar*[153] Jacob J. identified a series of factors which are relevant when comparing goods so as to establish similarity and which he intended to take into account modern marketing methods; these were based on the factors considered under the old Act,[154] so presumably the same approach will be taken with respect to comparison of marks.[155] Such use may be prevented only if the similarity results in "a likelihood of confusion on the part of the public,

[151] E.g. in *British Sugar*, Jacob J said that "it would be fantastic if the new trade mark legislation had the effect of enabling a quasi-censorship of books about people or companies just because these people or companies had registered their names as trade marks for books" (293).

[152] S.10(1).

[153] See n. 71 above.

[154] The judge basing himself on *Jellinek's Application* (1946) 63 RPC 59. The factors identified (use, users and physical nature of the product, trade channels, display of items available by self-service and manner in which trade would classify the product) have been described as "objective" factors—factors which are related solely to the product itself. However in Case C–39/97 *Canon KK* v. *Pathe Communications Corp.* (unreported, 2 Apr. 1998, ECJ—note that transcripts of all unreported ECJ judgments and opinions are available on the ECJ website at http://www.curia.eu.int), Jacobs A.G. delivered an Opinion in which he appears to submit that a court must moreover consider the reputation of the earlier mark. The problem with this approach is that it tends to elide the clearly separate questions of whether products are similar (to which it is not apparent from the wording of the Directive that the recognition on the market of the mark is relevant) and whether by reason of such similarity there exists a likelihood of confusion (10th Recital of the Preamble makes it clear that recognition/reputation is relevant). As Jacob J. pointed out himself in *British Sugar*, this would result in a "strong" mark getting protection for a greater range of goods than a "weaker" mark; as the A.G. expressed the situation, "[it] is permissible to consider goods or services to be similar in relation to particularly distinctive marks when such goods or services would not be considered to be similar in relation to other, less distinctive marks". It may be that the A.G. is confusing similarity as an absolute concept which must satisfied for the allegedly infringing sign to fall within s.10(2) with the degree of similarity (in relative terms) which the court is directed by the 10th Recital to consider when assessing the presence of a likelihood of confusion.

[155] That is *The Pianotist Co.'s Application* (1906) 23 RPC 774 will be relevant. See comments made by Jacob J. in the *Origins* case (n. 96 above) concerning the use to be considered when comparing marks (at 284).

which includes the likelihood of association with the trade mark".[156] Finally if an identical or similar sign is used in connection with *dissimilar* goods or services, then the owner of the earlier mark may object if this mark has acquired a "reputation" in the UK and the third party's conduct takes unfair advantage of or is detrimental to the mark's repute or distinctive character.[157] This is basically a dilution provision which is different in essence from confusion-based protection[158] and represents a radical new departure for English trade mark law. Notice however that such protection (on the face of the provision at least) is not given where the goods in question compete, but where there is no likelihood of confusion, thus giving potentially stronger protection in respect of non-competing goods.

The bases of protection, the concepts respectively of potential confusion and injured reputation, are completely new. These ostensibly derive from the Benelux trade mark law which was influential in the drafting of the Directive,[159] and so reference to the Benelux case law was expected by way of an aid to interpretation.[160] It was thought to start with that likelihood of confusion would be appreciably wider than the equivalent consideration under the old Act.[161] It would take into account evidence of actual public perceptions of the registered mark, as well as the more traditional examination in the abstract, since the Directive indicates that the "degree of similarity" between the mark and the sign and the "recognition of the trade mark on the market" are relevant in assessing the likelihood of confusion.[162] This possibility received an initial set-back through Jacob J.'s comment in *Origins* that section 10 "requires the court . . . to assess a likelihood of confusion . . . *discounting external added matter or circumstances*".[163] Such a proposition was rejected by the European Court of

[156] S.10(2).

[157] S.10(3).

[158] This distinction will be enlarged upon in Ch.4 below.

[159] See Annand and Norman, n. 30 above, 154–8.

[160] *Ibid*. Both Laddie J in *Wagamama Ltd.* v. *City Centre Restaurants plc* [1995] FSR 713, 723–8, and Jacob J. in *Philips Electronics NV* v. *Remington Consumer Products* [1998] RPC 283, 299 thought otherwise. Laddie J refused to admit evidence of a widely known Council Minute relating to the adoption of the Trade Marks Directive (which was then confidential but which has now been published by the Office for Harmonisation in the Internal Market (Trade Marks and Designs): see OHIM *Official Journal*, May 1996, 607 and 609) which indicated that the provision in question was based on and seemed to be intended to adopt this aspect of pre-harmonisation Benelux law. The decision has been controversial due both to Laddie J.'s approach to interpreting the statute and to his eventual conclusion: see opinions expressed by P. A. Harris, "UK Trade Mark Law: Are You Confused?" [1995] *EIPR* 601; C. Gielen, "Likelihood of Association: What Does it Mean?" Dec. 1995/Jan. 1996 TW 20; A. Kamperman Sanders, "The Wagamama Decision: Back to the Dark Ages of Trade Mark Law" [1996] *EIPR* 3; P. Prescott, "Think Before You Waga Finger" [1996] *EIPR* 317; and A. Kamperman Sanders, "The Return to Wagamama" [1996] *EIPR* 521. However, it is clear that the Trade Marks Directive has established a new order in European trade mark law, and it must be right that interpretation of national law deriving from it must be guided solely by the jurisprudence of the ECJ: "We now have a new European law and one cannot get any help from the details of the old law of any particular European country" (*per* Jacob J. in *Philips* v. *Remington* at 299).

[161] Annand and Norman, n. 30 above, 154.

[162] See the 10th Recital of the Preamble to the Directive.

[163] Emphasis added.

Justice in the *Puma* decision in which it was affirmed that "likelihood of confusion must . . . be appreciated globally, taking into account all factors relevant to the circumstances of the case".[164]

Furthermore, and this is where Benelux jurisprudence was anticipated as having the strongest influence, it seemed that consumers do not necessarily have to be confused as to the source of the product: they merely had to make a mental link between the marks, the likelihood of association, for the requirement to be made out.[165] The extent of confusing similarity was therefore expanded, "aimed at protecting the wider integrity of a trade mark".[166] Or so it was thought until the decision in *Wagamama Ltd.* v. *City Centre Restaurants plc.*[167] Whilst refusing to take into account evidence of the genesis of the section in Benelux practice and the *travaux préparatoires* of the Directive,[168] Laddie J. concluded that section 10(2) covers *only* "classic infringement" (that is, what would have infringed under the 1938 Act) and *not* the "non-origin association" (as he termed it) described above. This was done by applying purely English principles of construction,[169] and then by his attempt to support the correctness of his belief through (unsubstantiated) assertions concerning unjustified monopolies and restraint of trade.[170] Although the correctness of this latter reason will be questioned later,[171] the fomer reason, namely that in the sentence "there exists a likelihood of confusion on the part of the public, which includes the likelihood of association with the trade mark", likelihood of association comes after likelihood of confusion and so, Laddie J reasoned, must be a sub-set of the latter, was in fact seized upon by the European Court in *Puma*.[172] The court held that the semantic association between sign and mark was only one of "numerous elements" which could result in the finding of a likelihood of confusion—the "specific condition"[173] for finding infringement under section 10(2). In theory, we are not therefore completely "back to square one", able to prevent only third

[164] Para.22 of the judgment. This case actually concerned the interpretation of Art.4(1)(b) Trade Marks Directive, which concerns the relative grounds for refusal of registration, but the principles are of identical application in the context of Art.5 from which s.10 Trade Marks Act is derived.

[165] Annand and Norman, n. 30 above, 155 where examples are given of how Benelux courts approached the question.

[166] *Ibid.*

[167] See n. 160 above.

[168] Note that the Council Minute which Prof. Gielen exhibited to the court suggesting that a wider meaning of "likelihood of association" was intended by the Directive has now been published by the Office for Harmonisation in the Internal Market (see n. 160 above), thus disposing of one of Laddie J.'s objections (see 724–8).

[169] *Ibid.* at 722–3.

[170] *Ibid.* at 731.

[171] See Chs.3 and 4 below.

[172] At para.18 of the judgment. In contrast, s.43(a) US Lanham Act has been interpreted such that a wide range of confusing conduct has been admitted, even though this has resulted in a wider scope being accorded to the trade mark right than the umbrella term "likelihood of confusion" would initially imply (see S. H. Hartman, "Subliminal Confusion: the Misappropriation of Advertising Values" (1988) 78 *TMR* 506).

[173] *Ibid.*, at para.19.

party trade mark use which causes confusion as to actual source,[174] because Laddie J.'s very narrow interpretation was not wholly adopted by the European Court. On the other hand, neither was the wide Benelux interpretation. Realistically though, it is submitted that the English courts will see *Puma* as a vindication of their position until further guidance from Europe is provided.

The concept of unfair advantage being taken or detriment being done to a mark's distinctive character or repute is a manifestation of the dilution doctrine first put forward by Frank Schechter.[175] This contemplates the "gradual whittling away or dispersion of the identity and hold upon the public mind of the mark . . . by its use upon non-competing goods".[176] There is still not academic agreement as to which marks ought to receive this protection, which specific acts the doctrine contemplates or how damage is actually shown,[177] but in English law, reputation must first be established. Obviously it still remains for the court to interpret the concept, but it seems that it is generally aimed at "famous" marks such as COCA-COLA, MARLBORO or ROLLS-ROYCE.[178] Furthermore, unfair advantage or detriment without due cause must be shown—it is not precisely clear what is contemplated by this provision.[179] Given the attitude of Laddie J.[180] in *WAGAMAMA* towards any basis of trade mark protection not founded on source confusion, it seems that this aspect of the trade mark right might prove to be still-born. The first potential stumbling-block to this provi-

[174] See e.g. *Portakabin Ltd* v. *Powerblast Ltd.* [1990] RPC 471 (PORTAKABIN/PORTABLAST). Compare this also with the decision in *Harrods Ltd.* v. *Harrodian School* [1996] RPC 697, where it was held that, in order for passing-off to be made out, the connection which members of the public must be at risk of making due to the defendant's misrepresentation was that the plaintiff was at least responsible for the quality of the defendant's goods; a mere association of brand names was apparently insufficient.

Note also the comments made in B. Sherman, "Patent Claim Interpretation: The Impact of the Protocol on Interpretation" (1991) 54 *MLR* 499 who, in commenting on the lessons that may be learned from the experience of the European Patent Convention, notes that:

> "it is necessary to understand the practices, language and concepts which shape the legal discourse in the respective countries. In short what is needed is an approach that attempts to take into account, rather than to ignore, the diversity of legal cultures that fall within the umbrella of the countries to be harmonised." (*ibid.*, 510).

It is questionable whether this has taken place with respect to trade mark infringement; Sherman also comments that any harmonisation which has taken place with respect to patent claim interpretation owes more to the "spirit of co-operation, understanding and education rather than to the Protocol itself" and that there must be a profound awareness of the differing legal traditions (*ibid.*); e.g. compare the contrasting attitudes here and on the continent to unfair competition law.

[175] See F. I. Schechter, "The Rational Basis of Trade Mark Protection" (1927) 40 *Harv LR* 813.

[176] *Ibid.*, at 825. See A. F. Simonson, "How and When do Trade Marks Dilute: A Behavioural Framework to Judge 'Likelihood' of Dilution" (1993) 83 *TMR* 149 and also Annand and Norman, n. 30 above, 156 for examples of how this may occur.

[177] See Ch.4 below, and also n. 65 above.

[178] The American and Benelux experience with this form of protection is summarised by Annand and Norman, n. 30 above, at 157.

[179] Although Martino, n. 146 above, at ch.12 attempts to predict the scope of this provision based on American experience.

[180] An attitude apparently shared by the senior patents judge, Jacob J., who made disparaging comments about the necessity of expanding trade mark protection beyond that provided for by the 1938 Act when speaking extra-judicially at the University of Bristol on 29 Feb. 1996.

sion is the contention that there is an implicit requirement in section 10(3) of a likelihood of consumer confusion between the offending sign and the registered mark, a problem that has dogged U.S. courts for years.[181] The interlocutory decision in *Baywatch Production Co. Inc.* v. *Home Video Channel*[182] found such a requirement while manifesting a lack of judicial enthusiasm for section 10(3). On the other hand, an observation of the court in *Puma* contradicts this approach.[183] In *Marks & Spencer plc* v. *One In A Million*,[184] Jonathan Sumption QC did not express a view, but was unable to accept the ECJ's opinion unreservedly. Section 10(3) is another situation where the issue, discussed above, of use as a trade mark is critical. Some of the more celebrated dilution cases, such as the novelty condom card with the message NEVER LEAVE HOME WITHOUT IT[185] would not fall under the provision since this is clearly not use as a trade mark. In any event,[186] since it is clear that this form of protection is again not strictly necessary to facilitate the mere indication of the origin of trade marked goods, we will have later to examine quite what this does set out to achieve.[187]

Obviously a third party may use a trade mark other than by attaching it to a product. He may also use it to *describe* or refer to the goods or services of the mark's proprietor. Such conduct is also potentially subject to the exclusive rights in the mark,[188] and this enables the trade mark owner to control, in particular, the use of his mark in comparative advertising.[189] Whether trade mark owners should be able to influence comparative advertising is an especially controversial issue[190] and discussion of the merits will be reserved until a later chapter.[191] The Act achieves an interesting compromise in this context by stating that any descriptive use is *prima facie* legitimate by requiring that it must be "in accordance with honest practices in industrial or commercial matters" and

181 See B. W. Pattishall, "The Dilution Rationale for Trade Marks and Trade Identity Protection: its Progress and Prospects" (1977) 71 *North Western ULR* 618.

182 [1997] FSR 22, 30–31, and see also *BASF plc* v. *CEP (UK) plc.*, LEXIS Transcript, 26 Oct. 1995, Ch.D.

183 At paras. 20 and 21.

184 [1998] FSR 265, 272–273.

185 *American Express Co.* v. *Vibra Approved Laboratories Corp.*, 22 USPQ 2d 1009 (E.D.N.Y. 1991).

186 The presence or absence of this requirement is debated in the pages of the *European Intellectual Property Review* by Messrs. Kamperman Sanders and Prescott (see n. 160 above).

187 See Ch. 4 below.

188 S.10(6).

189 Compare this with blatantly false advertising positively denigrating the product in question which may always be objected to by way of an action for malicious falsehood or trade libel.

190 And one upon which an EC Directive has just been adopted (European Parliament and Council Directive amending Directive 84/450/EEC concerning misleading advertising so as to include comparative advertising (97/55/EC, OJ [1997] L290/18). Although the wisdom has been questioned of the UK Parliament legislating on such a subject when the EC was contemplating similar legislation (see Annand and Norman, n. 30 above, 159), it does seem that the impact of the new Directive will be greatest in those EC Member States has hitherto been taboo rather than in our own rather more aggressive markets.

191 See Ch.5 below.

should not harm or take unfair advantage of the repute or distinctive character of the mark.[192] These rather nebulous concepts were first tested in *Barclays Bank plc* v. *RBS Advanta*.[193] Laddie J. saw the test of honesty as objective in that "if the use is considered honest by members of a reasonable audience, it will not infringe" and added that such an audience would be aware of the "trade puffery" and "hyperbole" which is evident in advertising. However, and contrary to the opinion expressed by counsel and elsewhere,[194] assessing whether the use was in accordance with honest practices in industrial and commercial matters does not involve reference to the various statutory or voluntary codes of practice, although the judge did concede that "the nature of the products or services in question will affect the degree of hyperbole acceptable". Finally, Laddie J. was of the opinion that the requirement of unfair advantage or detriment added "nothing of significance" to the test of honesty; he could not envisage a situation where a less than honest use would not take unfair advantage thus sweeping the requirement "under the carpet". These views have since been endorsed and elaborated upon by Jacob J. and Michael Crystal QC in *Vodaphone Group plc* v. *Orange Personal Communication Services Ltd*.[195] and *British Telecommunications plc* v. *AT&T Communications (UK) Ltd*.[196] respectively. The effect of these rulings seems to restrict the ambit of the trade mark right in this context and further liberalise comparative advertising compared with the situation under the old Act, such that any comparative advertising involving a registered trade mark is now possible unless it is "substantially misleading".

In addition to the provision regulating use of a trade mark in comparative advertising, there are also specific savings for other descriptive uses, namely the use of a third party's name and address[197]; the use of matter describing the various attributes of goods and services[198]; and the use of a trade mark to indicate the intended purpose of goods or services.[199] These limitations on the trade mark right are all subject to a similar proviso prescribing use in accordance with honest practices in industrial or commercial matters, thus ensuring that the mark is used only for descriptive purposes rather than to derive any benefit from association.[200] Given the wide range of conduct falling within the ambit of section 10 following *British Sugar*, it is clear that these provisions have an impor-

[192] Proviso to s.10(6).

[193] [1996] RPC 307.

[194] See Holyoak and Torremans, n. 129 above, 320; Annand and Norman, n. 30 above, 160.

[195] [1997] FSR 34.

[196] [1997] EIPR D–134.

[197] S.11(2)(a).

[198] S.11(2)(b), e.g. to indicate that a fabric contained LYCRA or a soft drink contained NUTRASWEET (Annand and Norman, n. 30 above, 166).

[199] S.11(2)(c), in particular in the motor parts industry.

[200] See e.g. *British Northrop Ltd* v. *Texteam Blackburn Ltd*. [1974] RPC 57 ("every part shall be inspected and approved by engineers with many years experience in the manufacturer of NORTHROP parts"). Note however that in Case C–63/97 *BMW AG* v. *Deenik* (unreported, 2 Apr. 1998), Jacobs A.G. submitted in his Opinion that the offending sign would not be in accordance with honest practices if it was used either to mislead consumers (e.g., by leading them to believe that a garage is an 'authorised distributor') or seriously damage the reputation of the trade mark, but it would *not* be

tant role, as illustrated in the WET WET WET case,[201] in protecting uses of a sign when used in its trade mark sense in order to identify the product (in that case a service) concerned rather than *as* a trade mark.

The Conflict Between Trade Mark Law and the Principles of the EC

A final, separate situation where *prima facie* infringing conduct, in particular the import or export of goods under an infringing sign,[202] may be legitimate is where the goods in question are so-called parallel imports from within the EEA. This is because of the inadvertent clash between the promotion of the free movement of goods within the EEA and the fact that trade mark rights, in common with all intellectual property rights, result from the exercise of sovereignty within a defined area of the EEA, namely the Member State. The relevant provision is section 12 and encapsulates several decades of case law of the European Court of Justice. This essentially decides that where trade marked goods are marketed within the EC (and now the EEA) by the trade mark proprietor or with his consent, then the proprietor's rights in the trade mark have been "exhausted" and are therefore ineffective to prevent the import and sale of the goods in another EEA country by alleging trade mark infringement. The ability to object to further dealings in trade marked goods is not regarded as essential to the trade mark right.[203] What must be stressed is the presence of consent. If the trade mark proprietor has not consented, then the trade mark use is obviously infringing and the imports may be prevented.[204] This much is uncontroversial since ultimately the consumer will recognise the goods as being from the trade mark owner, but also that they have arrived by a more circuitous route. There is however an exception to these principles contained in sub-section (2) and is effective where "there exist legitimate reasons for the proprietor to oppose further dealings in the goods". This exception was developed in the context of the re-packaging of drugs,[205] but a recent ECJ decision[206] held that

contrary to honest practices merely to derive advantage from use of the mark. This gloss seems to be at odds with the wording of s.10(6).

[201] See nn. 139 and 148–9 above, and accompanying text.

[202] S.10(4)(c).

[203] Case 15/74 *Centrafarm BV* v. *Winthrop BV* [1974] 2 CMLR 480.

[204] See most recently Case C–9/93 *IHT Internationale Heiztechnik GmbH* v. *Ideal Standard GmbH* [1994] FSR 59.

[205] Case 102/77 *Hoffmann-La Roche & Co. AG* v. *Centrafarm GmbH* [1978] ECR 1139. Hence sub-s.(2) goes on to state that it applies "in particular where the condition of the goods has been changed or impaired after they have been put on the market". The ECJ confirmed the relevance of the principle outside the field of pharmaceuticals in Case C–349/95 *Frits Loendersloot* v. *George Ballantine & Sons Ltd* [1998] Fst 544.

[206] Case C–337/95 *Parfums Christian Dior SA* v. *Evora BV* [1998] RPC 166. Building upon this principle, the Opinion of Jacobs A.G. in Case C–63/97 *BMW AG* v. *Deenik* (unreported, 2 Apr. 1998) submits that "in cases where there is a . . . likelihood of advertising leading the public to believe that the re-seller is an 'authorised distributor', it should be permissible for the trade mark owner to rely upon the trade mark . . . in order to prevent the public being misled in this way, even if, because the undertaking is competent and respectable, there is *no damage thereby to his reputation*" (emphasis and quotation marks added).

although a parallel importer is also free to use the goods' trade mark to promote them, a further legitimate reason to oppose the use of the trade mark in connection with parallel imports is that the use of the mark for promotional purposes seriously damages the reputation of the trade mark. This acknowledges that there is something about the trade mark which derives from the manner in which the goods are marketed. While this comtemplates an extreme situation and one that is quite marginal in terms resolving the conflict between national intellectual property rights and the principle of the free movement of goods, it nevertheless makes assumptions about the nature and protection of trade marks which will important for our purposes in later chapters.

Note finally that the rules governing parallel importation within the EEA derive from Article 30 of the EEC, the free movement of goods provision, as well as Article 7 of the Trade Marks Directive. The corollary of this is that parallel imports from non-EEA countries (where the Treaty of Rome does not apply) *can* be prevented by the assertion of trade mark rights, and indeed this is supported both by *Colgate-Palmolive Ltd.* v. *Markwell Finance Ltd.*[207] as well as the more recent decision under the 1994 Act in *Microsoft Corporation* v. *Computer Future Distribution Ltd.*[208]

Protection of Unregistered Marks by way of an Action in Passing-off

Registration is not the only method of preventing third party interference with a trade mark, and indeed its use is not obligatory; existing in parallel to the statutory scheme of registration is the common law action of passing-off[209] which may always be used by the owner of a trade mark *in use* to achieve an effect similar to that of the statutory infringement action. Having said this, the modern law of passing-off is now of a fundamentally different basis and has developed into much more than merely a form of common law trade mark infringement although it does share historical roots at Common Law and in Equity with straightforward trade mark protection.[210] Whereas the proprietor of a registered trade mark has specific statutory rights, which derive from formal state grant as a result of registration, to prevent certain kinds of conduct

[207] [1989] RPC 497.

[208] Unreported, 25 Feb. 1998, Ch.D. (note however this decision was on an application for summary judgment). In fact Jacobs A.G. has recently delivered an Opinion in the ECJ to the effect that Art.7 of the Trade Marks Directive *precludes* Member States from adopting a principle of "international exhaustion" (Case C–355/96 *Silhouette International Schmied GmbH & Co. KG* v. *Hartlauer Handelsgesellschaft mbH* [1998] FSR 474). He argued that both the legislative history of the provision as well as the fact that leaving a discretion to individual Member States would disrupt the single market and having unilateral international exhaustion would be unwise in the absence of reciprocal provision in non-EEA states militated against international exhaustion.

[209] Which is preserved by s.2(2) and not expressly affected by anything within the registered trade mark regime. Cornish (n. 2 above, para.15–09) observes that the reason for the concurrence of the two means of protection lies with the choice at the end of the last century of a registration system involving substantive examination rather than mere deposit.

[210] See nn. 15–18 above, and accompanying text.

involving his mark, the essence of passing-off is the protection of a trader's "goodwill"[211] from tortious interference through another trader's misrepresentation. It is worth considering briefly the tort's ambit before turning to its relevance to our discussion generally.

In order for passing-off to be made out, certain judicially determined conditions must be fulfilled. The action has been considered twice by the House of Lords in recent years,[212] and for present purposes the most convenient analysis is that of Lord Oliver of Aylmerton in *Reckitt and Coleman Products Ltd.* v. *Borden Inc.*[213] who stated that the plaintiff must prove that his goodwill or reputation has been damaged (or is likely to have been) through the defendant's misrepresentation (which need not be intentional).[214] Notice that it is reputation which need be proved and not merely ownership of a trade mark, and that the defendant's actions must actively cause at least a risk of confusion amongst a relevant section of the public. The requirement of *goodwill* generally means that the plaintiff must prove that his trade symbol has acquired a secondary meaning, such that the public will recognise goods or services bearing the mark as something for which he is responsible.[215] A variety of factual elements are taken into account when assessing this including volume of sales and advertising, duration of use and geographical area in question.[216] Interestingly, in *Chocosuisse Union des Fabricants Suisses de Chocolat* v. *Cadbury Ltd.*[217] Laddie J. identified a specific line of authority where it is possible for the goodwill to be shared between producers of a similar and moreover famous product as illustrated by the various alcoholic drink cases.[218] These cases all involved necessarily descriptive terms, but where a higher standard of reputation can be shown, as will be seen below, a broader scope of damage is admissible.

Misrepresentation is the essence of the tort, that is to say conduct on the part of the defendant that is likely to cause confusion amongst consumers as to the provenance of the product in question.[219] This was established in *Spalding* v. *Gamage* where it was said that the misrepresentation may be made expressly or

[211] "The attractive force which brings in custom", *per* Lord Macnaghten in *IRC* v. *Muller & Co.'s Margarine Ltd.* [1891] AC 217.

[212] In *Erven Warnink BV* v. *J Townend & Sons (Hull) Ltd* [1979] AC 731 and *Reckitt and Coleman Products Ltd.* v. *Borden Inc* [1990] 1 all ER 873.

[213] *Ibid.* See Holyoak and Torremans, n. 129 above, 341–3 who describe the confusion that resulted from what they see as Lord Diplock's "over-convoluted" formulation in *Warnink* v. *Townend* (n. 213 above, at 343).

[214] [1990] 1 All ER 873, 880.

[215] The public must be "moved to buy by source," *per* Jacob J. in *Hodgkinson and Corby Ltd* v. *Wards Mobility Ltd.* [1995] FSR 169, 178.

[216] See Annand and Norman, n. 30 above, 21 and cases cited therein.

[217] [1998] RPC 117, 124–129.

[218] Starting with *J. Bollinger* v. *Costa Brava Wine Co. Ltd.* [1961] RPC 116 (champagne) and including *Vine Products Ltd.* v. *MacKenzie & Co. Ltd.* [1969] RPC 1 (sherry), *John Walker & Sons Ltd.* v. *Henry Ost & Co. Ltd.* [1970] RPC 489 (Scotch whisky) and of course *Warnink* v. *Townend*, n. 213 above (Advocaat—which was not even required to have to come from the same region as long as the product was distinctive).

[219] This was recently re-stated in most emphatic terms by Jacob J. in *Hodgkinson & Corby Ltd* v. *Wards Mobility Services Ltd.* [1995] FSR 169, 175. See generally Wadlow, n. 5 above.

more commonly by implication, but must, for example through the defendant's imitation of the plaintiff's trade symbol, produce an association in the minds of the public between the products of the two parties.[220] There exist a large number of ways in which the misrepresentation may be made[221] and they include the following. The defendant may use the plaintiff's trade name or trade mark. This was especially useful in the past when a trade mark was insufficiently distinctive to be registered, for example because it was descriptive or geographical,[222] or where the two sets of goods involved were unrelated.[223] However with the new criteria for registrability, this area will probably decline in importance unless a mark is deliberately not registered.[224] More important is imitation of the plaintiff's get-up or trade dress. This is in the main not registrable because the nature of the trade dress (as an especial combination of images) will not fall within the Act's criteria and must be protected in passing-off in the absence of any other unfair competition law. The classic example where the plaintiff succeeded is the *JIF lemon* case. Generally, though, in pure get-up cases the plaintiff faces a high evidential burden.[225] This problem is especially prominent where a supermarket produces an own-brand look-alike of the plaintiff's product[226] but then places its own trade name on the goods, thus negating any actionable public confusion.[227] Finally recent cases[228] suggest that passing-off may be used to protect merchandising activities. By this we mean the situation where an undertaking attempts to exploit the success of a particular fad, for example a film or rock band, by producing goods bearing images of the characters or personalities in question. The value for the person responsible for their popularity lies in having the right to prevent others from producing such goods. This is often achieved through trade mark registration[229] or copyright, but in the absence of such pro-

[220] (1915) 32 RPC 273, 284.

[221] Not all involving the use of trade marks. Other ways include false suggestion of superior quality, particular geographical origin of goods, false suggestion of professional endorsement, advertising campaigns and "reverse" passing-off.

[222] See e.g. *Powell* v. *Birmingham Vinegar Brewery Co. Ltd.* [1891] AC 710 (HL).

[223] See *LEGO System A/S* v. *Lego M. Lemelstrich* [1983] FSR 155. This case is also particularly significant because it demonstrates how goodwill may extend outside the original field of business and may be protected in a similar way to that of anti-dilution provisions.

[224] Annand and Norman, n. 30 above, 26.

[225] Jacob J. explains why in *Hodgkinson & Corby* (n. 216 above) at 178–9.

[226] A good example recently was in *United Biscuits (UK) Ltd.* v. *Asda Stores Ltd.* [1997] RPC 513 where Asda was found liable in passing-off for selling PUFFIN biscuits, an own-label version of the plaintiff's PENGUIN biscuit. Another notorious example was the Sainsbury's CLASSIC COLA case where the supermarket was forced by the Coca Cola Company to change the get-up of the own-brand product which it considered to be too similar to its market-leading product.

[227] Note however that in the JIF lemon case such a label was found, in evidence, *not* to be effective.

[228] *Mirage Studios* v. *Counter-Feat Clothing* [1991] FSR 145 and *ELVIS PRESLEY Trade Marks* [1997] RPC 543.

[229] If the image can fulfil the registration criteria and such use can be said to be "genuine (trade mark) use" (see n. 109 and accompanying text, above). A previous, now inapplicable, objection to this form of protection was that it resulted in "trafficking" of trade marks. See the HOLLIE HOBBIE case and s.28(6) Trade Marks Act 1938. *Re American Greetings Corp's Application* [1984] 1 WLR 189.

tection passing-off has the potential to fill the lacuna.[230] However the issue of whether potential should be exploited is controversial and I will address this further in the next chapter.

The necessary *damage* (or likelihood) is classically diversion of custom as well as injury to the reputation of the plaintiff's business or, in the case of unauthorised merchandising activities, loss of royalties from licensing the image and possible damage to reputation where the image is used on sub-standard goods. If a tort is actionable without proof of actual damage, then it must involve the interference with some property right: this is usually thought to be the goodwill of the plaintiff's business.[231] All the forms of damage listed above relate to just this point. However, the decision in *Taittinger* v. *Allbev*[232] seems to challenge this orthodoxy by allowing the plaintiff to recover for what was effectively the dilution or tarnishment of the word "Champagne" in the presence of only a minimal likelihood of public confusion.[233] One view of this is to suggest that a consequence of this is a shift in favour of recognising property in the trade mark itself rather than merely the goodwill (or at least that a trade mark may have a significance wider than simply indicating a product's source) and that this also anticipates the provisions contained in section 10(2)(3) of the Trade Marks Act.[234] A less radical view is that put forward in the *Chocosuisse*[235] case which suggests that damage of this nature is only actionable in the case of famous yet descriptive marks, such as those in the Champagne cases. In any event, we may certainly discern a broadening of the scope of passing-off.[236]

Given the recent upheavals in the law of trade mark registration, it is difficult to know the exact relationship between the tort of passing-off and trade marks,

[230] Representations were made during the passage of the new trade marks legislation in favour of a separate character merchandising right, but these were ultimately dismissed: see White Paper, n. 35 above, para.4.43.

[231] Annand and Norman, n. 30 above, 24. It does not *confer* any property right, but merely recognises and protects pre-existing ones.

[232] [1993] FSR 641.

[233] This tends to go against Jacob J.'s assertion in *Hodgkinson & Corby* (n. 216 above) at 175 that "[n]ever has the tort shown even the slightest tendency to stray beyond cases of deception". See also the similar decision, albeit on a thoroughly bizarre set of facts in *Rolls-Royce* v. *Dodd* [1981] FSR 517 and the LEGO case (n. 224, above) where damages were granted for the loss of opportunity to franchise. The recent decision in *Harrods Ltd.* v. *Harrodian School* (n. 174, above) muddies the waters to the extent that it requires that even under this head of damage, risk of consumer confusion must still be shown in spite of the fact that the erosion of a mark's distinctiveness is quite possible in the absence of such confusion; Millett LJ seems to misunderstand the nature of the dilution doctrine recognised in *Taittinger* v. *Allbev*. Furthermore, Millett LJ apparently attempts to restrict the ambit of *Taittinger* v. *Allbev* to cases where the defendant's action may result in the risk of the plaintiff's mark becoming generic: one of the plaintiff's concerns in *Taittinger* v. *Allbev*, but certainly not the only occasion the dilution doctrine is applicable. See S. Lai, "The Erosion of Goodwill" (1996) 146 *NLJ* 874.

[234] Annand and Norman, n. 30 above, 24.

[235] See n. 218 above.

[236] Annand and Norman, n. 30 above, also suggest (at 32) that s.56 Trade Marks Act in conjunction with the trend just described *may* provoke the reformulation of passing-off since that provision seems to rely on reputation in the sense of mere notoriety, and this seems again to indicate that property lies in the mark itself.

both as essential features of the market place and as a legal institution. As long as trade mark protection in general is not conditional on some form of deposit or registration, passing-off is of great practical importance to traders since it will always protect the "goodwill" underlying a trade mark in use. Up until now, it has often been wider in ambit than the law of pure trade mark protection (based on registration) due both to its essentially differing foundations and the flexibility of its elements, but at the same time narrower due to the requirement that actual goodwill acquired through use be shown (it is presumed in registration). Its importance has therefore derived from its ability to fill gaps in the landscape of protected trade symbols.[237] However, following the introduction of the new statutory regime, a large number of situations covered by passing-off are now subject to the exclusive rights conferred upon a registered trade mark owner by the Trade Marks Act and the new scheme is intended to encompass a far greater range of registrable marks. Consequently, it has been predicted that this will cause the decline of passing-off's importance with respect to trade marks.[238] A fundamental re-assessment of passing-off in light of all this is therefore necessary.

It may continue to serve as a second line of defence against unauthorised use of a registered trade mark or could be used instead where statutory protection is unavailable. Not every symbol used on goods in the course of trade will reach the registrability threshold, and even if this is satisfied, then the registration process is still quite time-consuming (in commercial terms).[239] The *Taittinger* v. *Allbev* and indeed *Mirage Studios* v. *Counter-Feat Clothing*[240] decisions are indicative of the potential for further development present in passing-off: although it has always been possible to describe passing-off as a form of "unfair competition law", albeit a rather attenuated one, it may now be argued that the tort could be progressing in the direction of a general principle against unfair competition.[241] Several difficulties stand in the way of this goal,[242] not least of which is the question of what is meant precisely by "unfair competition"[243] but,

[237] Particularly with respect to collective goodwill, insufficiently distinctive marks, trade dress protection and merchandising activities.

[238] Annand and Norman, n. 30 above, 18 and 19.

[239] A good example of a trade symbol falling outside the registration scheme is the combination of images, etc. forming the get-up of goods.

[240] See n. 229 above, and accompanying text.

[241] Given the large number of discrete embodiments of passing-off. See n. 222 below and accompanying text. There is in fact a growing English literature calling for such a law to be introduced: see generally comments made in Wadlow, n. 5 above, and, amongst others, G. Dworkin, "Unfair Competition: Is the Common Law Developing a New Tort" [1979] *EIPR* 241 and A. Terry, "Unfair Competition and the Misappropriation of a Competitor's Trade Values" (1988) 51 *MLR* 296, as well as recently D. Harms, "Hark! There Goes a Tort" [1995] *EIPR* 453 and A. Robertson and A. Horton, "Does the UK or EC need an Unfair Competition Law?" [1995] *EIPR* 568 and cf. M. Spence, "Passing-off and the Misappropriation of Valuable Intangibles" (1996) 112 *LQR* 472. The transformation may take place with or without the intervention of the legislature. Hopes were raised but subsequently dashed by the Privy Council decision in the Pub Squash case (*Cadbury-Schweppes Pty Ltd.* v. *Pub Squash Co. Pty. Ltd.* [1981] RPC 429).

[242] See in particular those identified by Spence, n. 241 above.

[243] See Wadlow, n. 5 above, 32.

given the increasingly comprehensive nature of the law of trade mark registration, it seems that passing-off may be freed to pursue this ambition.

Returning, though, to the immediate concerns of this book, it is arguable that registration is the *primary* method of trade mark protection since it is involved solely with protecting trade marks for their purpose in commerce; it starts from the premise that trade marks are an institution in themselves rather than merely being a means by which a trader's "goodwill" may be manifested. It follows then that passing-off must only be of subsidiary interest, but we can by no means ignore it completely since it is still a significant method by which trade marks may be protected, it compensates for the lack of a more satisfactory means of trade dress protection and finally, as will be seen, it may provide a more appropriate context for dealing with unfair competition questions currently falling within pure trade mark law.

CONCLUSION

As well as setting out the legal context of the subject-matter of this book, the preceding survey has attempted to identify some unresolved problems in the law of trade marks as applied in practice. For example, are trade marks really monopolies? Do any obligations attach to the ownership of a trade mark? Should a trade mark be protected as an advertising, promotional or even a merchandising tool? Does the law protect some wider significance of trade marks? Should trade dress be protected in the law of trade marks and ought a trade mark owner be able to control the use of his mark in comparative advertising? These are problems upon which light may be shed in the course of discussing some of the more theoretical issues underlying the legal protection of trade symbols, the first such issue being the purposes to which legally protected trade marks are put.

2

Modern Phenomena in Trade Mark Use: Branding and Merchandising

INTRODUCTION

From the previous chapter, it is clear that the law is prepared to protect certain symbols from unauthorised interference. However a comparatively abstract examination of the law paints only half the picture and certainly does not supply us with a justification or purpose for such a substantial body of law. In order to establish such a justification, we must turn first to how this protection is used and ask what functions are performed by the symbols which may be protected under the Trade Marks Act 1994 or indeed by way of an action in passing-off. Consequently, this chapter will examine the significance of modern trade mark functions and their consequences for legal theory; it will seek to question judicial assumptions and the validity of orthodox beliefs concerning the role of trade marks.

The reason for starting with the practice and deducing from this the underlying theory is to be found with the fact that it is impossible to define the supporting rationale of trade mark protection without reference to the practical functions of trade symbols. Compare this with the other main intellectual property rights,[1] copyright and patents, which are of a fundamentally different nature from trade marks. Those two rights can be seen as being granted in order to stimulate creativity or provide incentives to ingenuity, that is to say, they are artificial legal constructs premised on the fact that, were it not for the availability of legal protection, the subject-matter of the rights would be less likely to have been brought into existence; people would still invent, but not with the same enterprise. Trade mark protection, on the other hand, is arguably an intervention with respect to a pre-existing social phenomenon, the marking of goods, but one which was in need of legal support in order to secure most effectively its continuing benefits. Copyright and patents are therefore creatures of the law, brought into being with a specific purpose which may be *defined in the abstract*, whereas the trade mark is a creature of commerce and hence the reason for its protection may only be *defined by reference to its function*.[2]

[1] The other intellectual property rights, registered designs and design right as well as rights in performances may be seen for these purposes as sub-species of patents and copyright respectively; confidential information and "know-how" are juridically rather more ephemeral and do not, as yet, have any firm rationale with which trade marks may be contrasted.

[2] This conclusion was supported by Laddie J. in *ELVIS PRESLEY Trade Marks* [1997] RPC 543, 547.

The assumption, then, upon which we shall proceed is that the trade mark, supported by legal protection, has evolved into an important instrument of the modern consumer society such that the relationship between the two may be described as essentially symbiotic. It is apparent that the marking of goods is a direct response to the practical needs of the organisation of modern commerce, and one could even go so far as to argue that it is a hallmark of capitalist society.[3] The corollary of this is that the rationale for trade marks or their legal protection is something which could not exist in the abstract, that is to say, detached from the context of a late twentieth century exchange economy based on the principles of the free market, trade marks would cease to have a meaning. Consider the hypothetical example of a primitive society, the members of which are generally self-sufficient, but which has some form of legal system. It does not seem inconceivable that property rights would be granted, since people would need to be able to reserve to themselves the means off which they live. More specifically, it is also possible to envisage the idea of copyright protection in this context in order that people may enjoy the exclusive right to the fruits of their intellectual labours or even of granting monopolies in new inventions (although the utility of such a right would appear to be severely limited). However, trade marks, legally protected or otherwise, seem entirely irrelevant to this situation: no trade is taking place, let alone over great distances, and so there is simply no need to indicate by way of marking anything at all about goods present in this society.

With this in mind, we must first examine the function of what is actually being protected (since after all, "the life of the law has not been logic; it has been experience"[4]) so that we may later examine the interests served by trade mark protection. Although, as will be seen in greater detail below, trade marking as a social phenomenon gave rise to trade marks as legal instruments in the shape of legally protected symbols, when we now seek to find the rationale of their protection in the use made of such protection, not all symbols potentially capable of being protected as trade marks function as a trade mark in the traditional sense. A cursory examination of how almost any of the majority of products[5] on the market today is presented for sale is likely to reveal two things: a prominently placed symbol, be it a name, logo or image of some description as well as an adjacent "®" or "™" sign and perhaps a statement to the effect that the particular symbol is regarded as a trade mark of a particular organisation.[6] It is

[3] Although this is not to say that they do not have a place in a purely socialist economy: see A. Dietz, "Intellectual Property and Desocialisation in Eastern Europe" [1995] *IIC* 851, 860, where the use of trade marks in erstwhile communist economies to enforce the total state regulation of markets is discussed.

[4] O. W. Holmes, *The Common Law* (Boston, Mass., 1881), 1.

[5] The exception being certain staple commodities.

[6] Note however that "™" cannot be said to have any legal effect other than to put competitors on notice as to how the producer regards the sign: in *Philips Electronics* NV v. *Remington Consumer Products* [1998] RPC 283, 296 Jacob J. thought that use of such a symbol was not likely to make a sign any more eligible for protection than otherwise.

submitted that such a symbol is there for one of two reasons: either the producer is using it to impart information to consumers about the product or the producer has identified a demand for products which consumers will buy simply because they wish to own a product decorated with that particular symbol. These two reasons may be referred to as branding and merchandising respectively, and together they broadly describe the two modern uses of trade mark protection. The fact that producers consistently take such pains to assert intellectual property rights in what they see as their trade symbols begins to indicate the importance attached to securing such protection. It also leads one to enquire into the reasons why this form of intellectual property is so vital to producers. We will therefore examine both of these phenomena in turn and assess in the light of this the implications for how the subject-matter of trade mark protection may now be rationalised.

TRADE MARKS AS THE FOUNDATION OF PRODUCT BRANDING

It can largely be said that trade marks have always been used in some shape or form to convey information about the goods in conjunction with which they are used. It is submitted that the primary contemporary function of trade marks is the result of the evolution of trade marks since product marking was first conceived into what can be now seen as the basis for the branding of products. Indeed to most people trade marks are synonymous with brand names. We shall first consider the contrasting roles of historic marks, then the changes necessitated by the transformation in the distribution of goods since the industrial revolution, including in particular the inception of branding accompanied by mass-media advertising, and finally the new rationales to emerge from this fundamental shift. This will lead us to examine the contemporary importance of trade mark function and how this has subtly altered even since the use of legally protected trade marks became widespread.

Historic Trade Marking

The practice of marking goods[7] for various purposes has been known since prehistoric times, and indeed for centuries before legal protection was even an issue. Examples are cited of cattle branding[8] and pottery bearing markings from

[7] See generally F. I. Schechter, *The Historical Foundations of the Law Relating to Trade Marks* (New York, 1925). Schechter's seminal work is the result of that writer's extensive exploration of a multitude of non-legal, historical sources. As he observes in ch.1, this was necessary because of the courts' relative lack of interest in trade marks until fairly late on and also the presumption which prevailed at the time of writing that trade marks originated first in late 18th century jurisprudence.

[8] T. D. Drescher, "The Transformation and Evolution of Trade Marks—from Signals to Symbols to Myth" (1992) 82 *TMR* 301, 309.

as long ago as 5000 BC.[9] Trade marks (in the general sense) attained particular importance as a result of widespread trade in the ancient world,[10] especially from Egypt,[11] and later within the Roman Empire.[12] Because of the long distances over which trade took place and the hazards of such journeys, these ancient trade marks functioned in the main as proprietary marks which conclusively indicated the ownership of goods, for example in cases of shipwreck and piracy, as well as assisting the illiterate who came into contact with these goods. However with the fall of the Roman Empire in the fifth century, save for a few exceptions,[13] evidence of the marking of goods disappeared.

The twelfth and thirteenth centuries, though, saw a resurgence in trade and revival in the use of marks on all manner of goods.[14] Two distinct, but not necessarily mutually exclusive, types of mark could be identified[15] during this time: the proprietary mark and the regulatory or production mark.[16] The former was very similar in function to the type of mark just described and an important ancestor to the modern trade mark[17]; but it is the latter which is of especial historical interest.

In order to appreciate the nature of these medieval production marks, we must first of all examine the organisation of trade in the middle ages. At the same time as the improvement in trading came the rise of towns as autonomous urban units, and within towns came the guilds.[18] Essentially, each trade or form of manufacture was supervised by a guild, to the extent in fact that the whole of industry was at one time organised in this manner.[19] Each guild was a federation of master craftsmen, frequently established by some form of charter, and had two main aims: to monopolise its trade in a particular town or city and to promote the interests of the guild as a whole. This was done by seeking equality in all matters between members, in particular with respect to the standards of workmanship and the amount which could be charged for goods, and at the same time prohibiting any form of advertising or competition, either between

[9] G. Ruston, "On The Origin of Trade Marks" (1955) 45 *TMR* 127, 128. Pottery marking is often given as an example simply because of its durability over the centuries.

[10] Drescher, n. 8 above, 309–10 gives examples of several other uses of trade marks during ancient times including applications which come close to present day usage.

[11] See Ruston, n. 9 above, 130.

[12] *Ibid.* 135. Interestingly, it is not clear whether marks were legally protected under Roman law. However compare the findings of B. G. Paster, "Trade Marks—Their Early History" (1969) 59 *TMR* 551, 554–5, who claims also to have identified a primitive marketing function of Roman trade marks: *ibid.*, 554.

[13] Ruston, n. 9 above, 134–5. See also Paster, n. 12 above, 555 with respect to the lack of satisfactory reasons for this decline.

[14] *Ibid.*, 135.

[15] F. I. Schechter, "The Rational Basis of Trade Mark Protection" (1927) 40 *Harv LR* 813, 814.

[16] Note that any particular mark could simultaneously perform both functions (see Schechter, n. 7 above, 21) and Ruston, n. 9 above, 128 gives the colourful example of a cattle brand which indicates ownership whilst on the live animal but origin of its hide after slaughter.

[17] Schechter, n. 7 above, 34. Schechter is of the opinion that this type of mark still colours judicial thinking with respect to trade mark function (*ibid.*).

[18] Drescher, n. 8 above, 311.

[19] Schechter, n. 7 above, 40.

members or with other guilds.[20] Trade in the goods produced by members of each craft then took place locally, with the result that consumer was always in close contact with producer.

Each producer, that is to say guild member, was *obliged* to attach his mark, which had previously been recorded with the guild, to his goods. Its purpose was to identify the craftsman who had manufactured the goods so that the origin of any sub-standard produce could be easily traced. It was a form of medieval consumer protection, albeit a relatively unimportant one given the close proximity of consumer and producer. A far more important consequence was that the production mark became an instrument of the guild's monopoly power. It enabled the guild to identify and exclude goods of those foreign to its territory and at the same time regulate legitimate traders. Since the very use of a mark indicated that the product bearing it conformed to a uniform standard, there was no reason why the mark should symbolise any individual excellence. It represented the producer, not the product. That would otherwise have promoted personal enrichment at the expense of other members which, of course, was anathema to the organisation of trade at that time.[21] The medieval production mark, the use of which was entirely compulsory, can therefore be seen as positive *liability* to its owner, a "police mark" as Drescher terms it,[22] and which served only the interests of the guild.[23]

In this tightly regulated environment, though, lay the germ of what is today recognised as a trade mark. Schechter identified two trades, cloth and cutlery, where trade mark use was shifting in a more modern direction.[24] It was in the cloth industry that the concept of collective goodwill first originated.[25] This was a natural consequence of the products of a particular municipality or guild becoming known for their excellence and this quality being identified and repeatedly purchased through the attached trade symbol[26]; the symbol had a pre-sale significance to consumers. Furthermore conciliar law (if not the common law courts) began to recognise that such marks were worthy of protection because of their function in pointing up the desirable qualities, as well the defects, of the products to which they were attached.[27] Secondly evidence can be seen in the cutlery trade of trade marks being treated as something akin almost to tangible personalty, another characteristic of the modern trade mark. Schechter cites evidence which he sees as demonstrating a clear shift in the nature of marks from liability to asset, with specific legal rights of ownership, in

[20] Drescher, n. 8 above, 312–3.

[21] Schechter, n. 7 above, 39–42. In the course of ch. 3, Schechter gives a comprehensive description of the operation of this system of trade regulation. Drescher, n. 8 above, illustrates this with a fictitious account of a medieval trader at 313–20.

[22] *Ibid.*, 319.

[23] Schechter, n. 7 above, 78.

[24] *Ibid.*, chs. 4 and 5 respectively.

[25] Collective goodwill which has again become prominent in the modern law of passing-off (see the champagne cases mentioned in Ch.1, n. 219 above) is therefore nothing new.

[26] Schechter, n. 7 above, 78 and 79.

[27] *Ibid.*, 94–6.

particular transferability, attaching.[28] By the seventeenth century, this process seemed to be complete, certainly in the cutlery trade.[29] Even though these modern features were evident in the way trade marks came to be regarded, their use was still in the hands of the guilds' regulation of trade.[30] The event that produced a crystallisation in the evolution of trade marks, resulting in them being regarded for the first time as true *assets*, came in the eighteenth and early nineteenth century: the industrial revolution.[31]

This saw the "triumph of capitalism and secularism over the Christian world order of the middle ages"[32] and that "any qualms about the godliness of the pursuit of individual wealth had long since been swept away".[33] Changes were wrought on the whole basis of manufacturing and trade:

> "Capital had been accumulated on a vast scale in the major urban centres [and] the factory had long since replaced the craftsman's workshop. . . . As for regulation of trade and industry, *laissez-faire* and market forces could surely perform that task more efficiently than the officers of the guild."[34]

Even more significant was the separation of the producer from the consumer. The coming of the canals and then the railways as fast and efficient means of distribution, coupled with the mechanisation of production, resulted in goods being mass-produced at a central location and then marketed nationally. Equally important for our purposes was the acceptance of the ideal of competition in a free market in the manner still characteristic of the organisation of commerce today. This necessitated some form of marking on goods identifying the producer who might have been some distance from the consumer and distinguishing the goods from those of competitors.

The implications of all this for the development of trade mark use were simple. It became the link between the producer and the consumer, the valuable symbol of "goodwill" which had previously been associated with a local, known trader.[35] The two strands of trade mark evolution mentioned above, and which Schechter identified, had therefore been thrust to the fore. Modern trade marks became established as assets of some commercial value and economic significance, which traders now gladly used in connection with their goods. If such markings were to have any meaning to consumers, a means was necessary to prevent others from imitating this marking; Schechter cites evidence of this need in the American sail cloth industry from as long ago as 1788.[36] Consequently

[28] *Ibid.* 101 ff.
[29] *Ibid.*, 121.
[30] *Ibid.*, 125–7.
[31] See Schechter, n. 7 above, 129–34 and Drescher, n. 8 above, 320–2.
[32] Drescher, n. 8 above, 320.
[33] *Ibid.* p.321.
[34] *Ibid.*
[35] Schechter, n. 7 above, 129. See also Schechter, n. 15 above, 818 where he quotes from H. G. Wells to illustrate this newly discovered significance.
[36] Schechter, n. 7 above, 130–3. He also mentions first a petition to Congress of 1791 from the same industry seeking the exclusive right to use a particular mark on goods and secondly a letter

attention shifted to protecting marks and the considerable worth that could potentially attach to them. As was seen in Chapter 1, the courts of Common Law and Equity became willing to prevent such imitation of the marks then being used on goods. The courts adopted various jurisprudential bases in protecting trade marks,[37] but exactly what function did this new trade mark use perform to justify the protection that was given, and could this function be said to be the same as that of contemporary trade marks?

The early cases in which protection for marks was sought involved merely the use of the plaintiff's name, for example in *Sykes* v. *Sykes*[38] the mark in question was SYKES PATENT. The mark was arguably performing a function scarcely different from that of the former production marks. The only difference was the owner's motive: here he voluntarily and willingly alerts others to the fact that he is responsible for the goods and seeks protection to prevent others from passing their goods off as being of similar quality to his own.[39] Clearly if a producer marks his goods with his name, for example KELLOGG'S corn flakes, this will serve to indicate to the consumer at the other end of the chain of distribution (which has since arisen) that originally W.K. Kellogg and now the Kellogg Company was the source from which the breakfast cereal emanated. This much is generally undisputed since the mark is doing what trade marks have always done: link the product with a particular individual. The turning point was when producers began to sell their goods under a brand name which was not necessarily their personal name.

The object of this brief historical overview is to demonstrate the fact that trade marking has already served a variety of historic purposes and that the functions of trade symbols are constantly evolving. It is also possible to see the historical roots of preconceptions[40] which have arguably coloured contemporary thinking on trade mark functions[41]: consider, for example, the fact that the medieval production mark was an instrument of monopoly and that proprietary marks' *sole* purpose was to indicate ownership or origin of goods. Finally, we can see the emergence of the trade mark as a discrete form of intellectual property at the time of the industrial revolution and relatively late on compared with patents and copyright.[42] From this starting point, it is possible to trace the con-

dating from the same year to a newspaper warning of the dangers of not preventing counterfeiters from taking advantage of the goodwill attached to a producer's mark (*ibid.*).

[37] *Ibid.* Courts saw themselves as variously protecting the plaintiff's property in the trade mark or preventing fraud on consumers.

[38] (1824) 3 B & C 543.

[39] See the discussion of the pleading in this case in Schechter, n. 7 above, 138.

[40] Consider the cases cited in n. 79 below.

[41] Schechter, n. 7 above, 147.

[42] As early as 1474, Venice was granting privileges similar to patents aimed at stimulating invention and the infamous English Statute of Monopolies of 1624 preserved the right to grant monopolies for such purposes (W. R. Cornish, *Intellectual Property: Patents, Copyrights, Trade Marks and Allied Rights* (3rd edn., London, 1996), para.3–04). Equally, copyright had achieved its modern form by the beginning of the 18th century (*ibid.*, paras.9–01–05). Since then both have enjoyed reasonably settled rationales in contrast with the law of trade marks which, having crystallised only at the beginning of the 19th century, is still arguably in a state of evolution.

tinual evolution of the modern trade mark into something with far greater significance than a mere label or "shadow of goodwill".

The Advent of Branding and Advertising

Two concepts are fundamental to appreciating the nature of modern trade mark use. The first is the brand, the name used to identify a type of product made by a particular manufacturer which can in fact be seen as the final stage in the process whereby goods or services are presented to consumers:

> "Take water and sugar: they are *commodities*. Process them into cola drinks, and you have *products*. Market and promote them into COCA-COLA and PEPSI-COLA: you have *brands*."[43]

The second phenomenon which has shaped the evolution of the modern trade mark is the advertising of goods, especially on a national scale. Newspaper advertising has been widespread since the end of the eighteenth century, and the first pictorial poster dates from 1871.[44] As Drescher points out, advertising was simply "unnecessary and irrelevant" to the medieval organisation of trade[45]; in contrast, mass-produced and nationally marketed goods competing for the same custom are very much in need of a means to alert consumers of their availability. It is therefore an essential adjunct to the branding process.

Until approximately 100 years ago, goods were generally sold in the form of bulk commodities and consumers were assured of their quality through the local reputation of the merchant selling the goods or by actually testing the goods before purchase[46]; it was in the retailer that consumers placed their trust that the goods would be suitable for their needs. However, in late-nineteenth century America this was to change. A good example is QUAKER oats. Oats are a paradigm fungible commodity previously sold by retailers in bulk, but what one Henry Parsons Crowell did was to package them in boxes and attach a trade mark, QUAKER, which encaptured the characteristics which he wished to

[43] *The Economist*, "The Year of the Brand", 24 Dec. 1988, 101.

[44] Schechter, n. 7 above, 130.

[45] N. 8 above, 321.

[46] Drescher, n. 8 above, 321; in Schechter, n. 15 above, 818 a passage from *The World of William Clissold* by H. G. Wells is identified which illustrates this and is worth quoting in full:

> "In the days of our youth, an enormous number of things were sold anonymously that are now sold under the brands of makers and packers. Our father had been one of the pioneers in this christening of goods with his Partington's Packet Teas. When I was a child every grocer had his own sorts of teas, his tea-chests with different qualities, and he weighed the tea out and packed it up for each customer. . . . Almost everything he sold them . . . he sold from stocks of his own buying and his own individual reputation. He had pickled onions and cabbage in a great tub, as they still have them here in France. . . . And the oilman sold his own lamp oil, and no one asked where he got it. But even in our childhood there was already a number of vigorous firms *reaching their hands over the retail tradesman's shoulder, so to speak, and offering their goods in their own name to the customer*" (Schechter's emphasis).

associate with the product. Furthermore he guaranteed the oats, through the use of this device, to be of consistent quality and quantity and indulged in an advertising campaign to promote his particular brand of oats.[47] Similarly, soap was formerly a generic product often of inconsistent quality due to the lack of understanding of the process by which soap was manufactured, but once this difficulty was overcome, William Procter and James Gamble set about marketing IVORY soap—so-called again because of the images its producers felt it conjured up—under the famous (in America, at least) slogan that it was "99 and 44/100 percent pure".[48] The equivalent development took place in Britain when W.H. Lever first marketed his SUNLIGHT soap.[49]

Along then with that other pioneering brand COCA-COLA,[50] we see for the first time goods being sold in a packaged form under a brand name. This is the (modern) product's trade mark and consequently the subject-matter of the trade mark right. It could be the personal or corporate name of the producer, but equally often it may not be. What is significant is the huge expansion in trade mark use at the turn of the century,[51] the departure from the practice, dating from the middle ages, of marking goods *solely* in order personally to identify the producer (other characteristics are indicated in addition and sometimes instead) and the shift from trade in commodities from known suppliers to trade in known goods.[52] A largely technical distinction could be identified between trade names, which referred to marks used in a more historic manner[53] and trade marks which were essentially brand names, but, as Handler and Pickett argued,[54] this distinction was artificial and, in securing protection, it has long since ceased to matter whether a mark was one or the other; they both performed the same function. A final factor which has been influential in modern trade mark development has been the sheer diversity of products available and in particular novel, technologically advanced goods, for example electrical products or pharmaceuticals, which were by their nature differentiated and for which the trade mark under which they were marketed was their only means of identification.[55]

[47] Cited in Drescher, n. 8 above, 322–3.

[48] *Ibid.* 326–7; D. A. Aaker, *Managing Brand Equity: Capitalising on the Value of a Brand Name* (New York, 1991), 1–5.

[49] Drescher, n. 8 above, 327.

[50] Originally marketed as a brain tonic (!), *The Economist*, 43 above.

[51] An illustration of this is the fact that in America in 1870 only 121 trade mark registration were made, whereas in 1923, 15,000 were registered. See Schechter, n. 7 above, 134.

[52] With the result that producers of goods found themselves in a much stronger position in relation to the retailers. As we shall see in Ch.5, below, a shift is again taking place, this time in favour of the retailers who, through the marketing of "own-brand" substitute product, their ability to control the way in which products are offered for sale to the public and the use of technology in this process, are becoming as influential as their suppliers, the producers.

[53] See comments by Drescher, n. 8 above, 322, who notes that the historic production mark was rather like the modern corporate name, e.g. Proctor and Gamble, which appears on a variety of products in conjunction with the products' brand names.

[54] M. W. Handler and C. Pickett, "Trade Marks and Trade Names: an Analysis and Synthesis" (1930) 30 *Columbia LR* 186, 759.

[55] J. M. Murphy, "Branding and Trade Marks", Apr. 1987 *TW* 12, 13.

Rationalising Trade Mark Functions

In spite of this upheaval,[56] the US Supreme Court, amongst others, was still content in 1916 to state in *Hanover Star Milling Co.* v. *Metcalf*[57] that "the primary and proper function of a trade mark" is "to identify the origin or ownership of the goods to which it is affixed".[58] Frank Schechter, however, was of the opinion that this statement, which would not have appeared incongruent to the parties in *Sykes* v. *Sykes* almost a century earlier, was simply out-dated and untrue.[59] He outlined his fear in the 1927 *Harvard Law Review*[60] that the conventional views of trade mark theory failed to take into account new commercial practices (discussed above). He was adamant that "the true functions of the trade mark are . . . to identify a product as satisfactory and thereby to stimulate further purchases by the consuming public".[61]

The first aspect of this is the idea of anonymous source, that is to say the connection indicated by a trade mark is not between the goods and a particular, known source but between the trade marked goods and a source from where previously satisfactory goods emanated.[62] This much has long been evident and judicial support of this view may be cited from the 1923 decision in *McDowell's Application*,[63] where Warrington L.J. thought that it did not matter "whether the public do, or do not, know what the source is".[64] Moreover, marks are often incapable of indicating any source other a single anonymous one because they denote the product not its producer,[65] for example MARMITE is undoubtedly a (registered) trade mark used to identify yeast extract spread, but on examining the small print, we are told that the product is "produced *for*" a company called

[56] See generally in addition to references already cited G. W. Goble, "Where and What a Trade Mark Protects" (1927) 22 *Illinois LR* 379; E. W. Hanak, "The Quality Assurance Function of Trade Marks" (1975) 65 *TMR* 318; A. Michaels, "The Function of Trade Marks: The Law and the Reality" [1980] EIPR 13; G. R. Stewart, "The Source Theory and Trade Mark Law Reform: A Functional Analysis" (1982) 20 *U Western Ontario LR* 337; L. Akazaki, "Source Theory and Guarantee Theory in Anglo-American Trade Mark Policy: A Critical Legal Study" (1990) 72 *J Patent & Trademark Office Society* 255; T. Martino and P. Groves, "Trade Marks: Deliver Us From Days of Old" [1991] *EIPR* 355; K. Parks, " 'Naked' is not a Four Letter Word: Debunking the Myth of the 'Quality Control Requirement' in Trade Mark Licensing" (1992) 82 *TMR* 531.

[57] (1916) 240 US 403.

[58] *Ibid.* at 412. See also Bowen L.J. in *Powell* v. *Birmingham Vinegar Brewery Co. Ltd.* (1896) 13 RPC 235 (CA) who stated that "the function of the trade mark is to give an indication to the purchaser of . . . of the trade source from which the goods come".

[59] Schechter, n. 15 above, 814–6.

[60] *Ibid.*

[61] *Ibid.*, 818.

[62] *Ibid.*, 816.

[63] (1926) 43 RPC 323. See also the earlier case of *Powell* v. *Birmingham Vinegar Brewery Co. Ltd.* (1896) 13 RPC 235 (CA) in which Lindley L.J. commented that "people may be mislead and may mistake one class of goods for another, although they do not know the names of the makers of either," and comments in Martino and Groves, n. 56 above, 356. Contrast this with the view of Bowen L.J. in the same case at n. 58 above.

[64] *Ibid.*, at 337.

[65] Drescher, n. 8 above, 323.

CPC (UK) Ltd.; there is no way of establishing who physically manufactured as opposed to marketed it. Who cares? Perhaps a consumer who has purchased a defective jar of MARMITE does, but the information only becomes material *after* the purchase; beforehand, he is arguably only interested in purchasing a jar of MARMITE, not "a jar of yeast extract spread marketed by CPC (UK) Ltd." (although MARMITE is of course a convenient shorthand[66]). The fact is that MARMITE only indicates the source of the product in the loosest sense which in any event is irrelevant to the actual purchasing decision, the point of first contact with the trade mark. This proposition is supported by a comparison[67] of *Bowden Wire Co. Ltd.* v. *Bowden Brake Co. Ltd.*[68] with *BOSTITCH Trade Mark*.[69] In the former, earlier (1913) case, both the plaintiff and defendant had used the mark, so depriving it of the ability to indicate the source of the goods in question and thus rendering it invalid, whereas in the latter, factually similar case decided 50 years later, the mark was held to be valid because it still served to indicate the identity of two products which were the same; the law had advanced to such an extent that it was recognised that "the public interest is sufficiently protected when the products are the same, not only when they have a common origin".[70] It is in fact common and indeed advantageous for a producer to create product identities distinct from his own.[71] This is illustrated by Proctor and Gamble who produce brands ranging from ARIEL detergent to PRINGLES crisps, yet it is the trade marks ARIEL and PRINGLES which are given far greater prominence in comparison with the corporate name.[72] Insisting that trade marks primarily denote the source of goods also ignores the contemporary prevalence of trade mark licensing.[73] Although the common law takes a less than tolerant view of the practice, the Mathys Committee report,[74] the preparatory White Paper[75] and the Trade Marks Act 1994[76] itself all regard it as an acceptable, widespread and of course lucrative[77] part of modern commerce, for example as part of a franchising agreement or where a firm's international subsidiary manufactures goods bearing the parent's trade mark. Trade mark licens-

[66] See W. M. Landes and R. A. Posner, "Trade Mark Law: An Economic Perspective" [1987] *J Law & Econ*. 265, 269.

[67] Michaels, n. 56 above, 14.

[68] (1914) 31 RPC 385.

[69] [1963] RPC 183.

[70] Michaels. n. 67 above.

[71] Drescher, n. 8 above, 324.

[72] This is termed a "brand dominant system" and has the advantages of insulating the reputation of a particular mark, allowing diversification without the risk of diluting established marks either because of product failure or blurring of the established product's identity and also allowing competition between different products of the same manufacturer. See Drescher, n. 8 above, 324 and references cited in n. 76 above. Note, however, that the trade marks are not product marks in the sense that they *only* identify the product regardless of manufacture. See Stewart, n. 56 above, 349–53.

[73] Parks, n. 56 above, 533–5; Michaels, n. 56 above, 14–16.

[74] *British Trade Mark Law and Practice*, Cmnd. 5601 (London, 1974).

[75] *Reform of Trade Marks Law*, Cm. 1203 (London, 1990), paras. 4.34–9.

[76] As we saw in the previous ch., subject to certain procedural requirements, a trade mark owner is completely free to assign or license his registered mark in full or in part.

[77] Parks, n. 56 above, 558–9.

ing undermines the source theory because it allows the mark to be used by someone other than the owner with whom the mark was originally associated. If this is the case, the mark must indicate something other than product's origin.

In spite of all this, some commentators[78] and judges[79] continue to argue that the most effective way in which to rationalise trade mark function is by reference to trade marks' source-denoting quality. If one is content to concentrate solely on the objective information communicated by trade marks as to the manufacture of products, it could at least be said that the most basic function is rather to differentiate the product of one producer from that of another. For example, by labelling their clothes ST. MICHAEL, Marks and Spencer indicate to the consumer that they are the particular producer of the clothes rather than British Home Stores or Littlewoods. This is admittedly a rather subtle distinction, and apparently the corollary of source indication, but one which has the virtue of shifting the emphasis away from absolute indication of the provenance of goods towards the positioning of goods relative to those of other producers. Furthermore this emphasis reflects the basic criterion for registrability in section 1(1) of the Trade Marks Act 1994 that a trade mark is "any sign . . . which is capable . . . of distinguishing goods of one undertaking from those of other undertakings"[80] and, as will be seen in the next chapter, it is the ability of trade marks to differentiate ostensibly identical products that is seen by economic theory as one of the primary factors from which the economic consequences of protection are seen to flow.

The second aspect of Schechter's argument is that the trade mark has an active role to play in the "creation and perpetuation of good will"; its role is more than as merely a passive symbol. To illustrate this, Schechter quotes from H. G. Wells, observing that through his trade mark a producer "'reaches over the shoulder of the retailer' and across the latter's counter straight to the consumer".[81] Although this formulation drew attention to the expanding role of trade marks in modern marketing practices of the type discussed above, it also gave rise to misconceptions as to the exact nature of this expanding role; the surrounding uncertainty and indeed controversy may be seen as a manifestation of legal theory attempting to come to terms with the fact that legally protected

[78] Parks, n. 56 above, 553–7; Stewart, n. 56 above; cf. Akazaki, n. 56 above.

[79] See comments by Laddie J. in *Wagamama Ltd.* v. *City Centre Restaurants plc* [1995] FSR 713, 730 that "the primary function of trade marks is to indicate origin of goods or services" and in *British Sugar plc* v. *James Robertson and Sons* [1996] RPC 281, 298 Jacob J. talks of the mark in question as a "badge of origin" and says that

> "it is noteworthy that the Directive notes the function of a trade mark is 'in particular to guarantee the trade mark as an indicator of origin'. No other purpose is mentioned. I think this sole purpose permeates the whole Directive and hence our 1994 Act."

[80] See R. E. Annand and H. E .Norman, *Blackstone's Guide to the Trade Marks Act 1994* (London, 1994), 15 who contrast this with s.68(1) Trade Marks Act 1938 which states that a trade mark is "used in relation to goods for the purpose of indicating . . . a connection in the course of trade between the goods and some person having the right to the use the mark".

[81] Schechter, n. 15 above, 817–9; see also n. 46 above.

trade marks tend to be used as brand names rather than simply to identify the producer. Schechter's observations have been elaborated upon by the identification of two new functions of modern trade marks: the so-called guarantee and advertising functions. Given that it is unlikely that consumers will perceive a trade mark as indicating a direct link between a product and a specific physical source, the guarantee theory represents attempts to establish what the trade mark does indicate or "guarantee", namely that the product in question will be of a certain quality. One reason, according to Brown, why misconceptions arose was due to proponents of this view "(overstating) the case by christening it the 'guarantee' function". He continues by arguing that

> "since the user of the symbol probably guarantees by it nothing more than his hope that the buyer will come back for more, the term smacks strongly of the ad-man's desire to create the illusion of guarantee without making more than the minimum warranty of merchantable quality."[82]

This may seem overly cynical, but illustrates the difficulty in reaching consensus as to the meaning of the guarantee function. Another reason, it has been argued, was the way in which the guarantee theory was used to render the practice of trade mark licensing legitimate.[83] Until the 1938 Act, such conduct would have been fatal to a mark's registration, but with the passing of this Act:

> "the law was updated through the adoption of an expanded, quality assurance theory of trade marks, which held that although consumers may not be justified in relying on a mark as a symbol of a single physical, the mark could nevertheless be relied on as an accurate indicator of the quality of trade marked goods."[84]

This change was effected by the former registered user scheme whereby the licensee was registered as someone other than the trade mark owner authorised to use the mark in question, provided that the registrar was satisfied that the licensee was subjected to adequate quality control requirements in the licence agreement. In this way it was ensured that the licensed mark continued to signify the level of quality that it originally represented. Encouraged by this substantive emphasis on quality *within the legal framework* (American law still makes an analogous requirement), certain commentators nevertheless sought to argue that the "guarantee" provided by the trade mark was in fact generally an enforceable warranty,[85] although such a right has never been recognised in this

[82] R. S. Brown, "Advertising and the Public Interest: Legal Protection of Trade Symbols" (1948) 57 *Yale LJ* 1165, 1186–7 (footnotes omitted). The equivalent English provision is s.14 Sale of Goods Act 1979.

[83] See Parks, n. 56 above, 533–5.

[84] *Ibid.*, 534. The passage quoted actually refers to US law, but describes with equal validity the shift in English law.

[85] See Michaels, n. 56 above, 16 who calls for the "unexploited potential" to be invoked against trade mark proprietors who allow their product quality to drop and Parks, n. 56 above, 546–53 who discusses U.S. cases where this was argued along with the literature (in particular Hanak, n. 56 above) seeking such an interpretation of trade mark function. As Parks demonstrates (n. 56 above) at 554–5, Schechter himself certainly did not intend this consequence.

country. Indeed the case for there being any substantive obligations on trade mark users was weakened when the registered user scheme was subsequently abolished by the 1994 Act, to be replaced by a far more liberal regime. The express ground for this reform was that the arrangements proved to be technically unsatisfactory[86] with the result that trade mark licensing was left to be regulated by the market[87] and the fact that a grossly deceptive trade mark is liable for revocation under section 46(1)(d) of the Trade Marks Act 1994. In effect it also brought registered trade mark law into line with the view that the guarantee function is no more than a "broadened restatement of the source theory", that a trade mark merely "guarantees" that it is subject to a single source of quality control,[88] and hence it is theoretically inconsistent to make any greater substantive demands in relation to a licensed trade mark than with respect to a non-licensed trade mark.

Although it is quite easy to argue that the guarantee theory does not represent a particularly fundamental shift in the analysis of trade mark function and that it does not justify using the law of trade marks to insist that trade mark users adhere to certain quality standards, there still remains an aspect that vindicates Schechter and highlights an aspect of trade mark function which cannot be directly explained by the source theory: that trade marks signify *consistent* quality. As we shall see in the next chapter, it is this aspect of trade marking which economists see as economically beneficial because if consumers recognise trade marks as signifying consistent quality, producers will be given the incentive to create and maintain brands of that particular standard.[89] Furthermore, Schechter's position is vindicated because goodwill in its classic sense of "the attractive force which brings in custom"[90] is created and retained when consumers realise that the trade marked product will always conform to their expectations.[91]

Schechter's belief that trade marks possessed "an agency for the actual creation and perpetuation of goodwill"[92] likewise drew attention to their ability actually to promote the goods concerned—what has been characterised as the advertising function.[93] Since producers are concerned with creating identities for their brands, it is natural that this should take place through using the trade mark in advertising: "the advertising copy creates a context which informs and

[86] See Annand and Norman, n. 80 above, ch.11 and the White Paper, n. 75 above.

[87] Consumers who are dissatisfied by the quality of goods which they purchase need simply stop buying the product. See comments by Parks, n. 56 above, 559 and more generally Landes and Posner, n. 66 above.

[88] Parks, n. 56 above, 553.

[89] See again Landes and Posner, n. 65 above.

[90] *Per* Lord Macnaghton in *IRC* v. *Muller & Co's Margarine Ltd.* [1897] AC 217, 222.

[91] Drescher, n. 8 above, 326. A good example of this is the soap industry following the discovery of how to make soap of a uniform standard. See nn. 48–9 above and accompanying text. Schechter's position was anticipated over 50 years earlier by Lord Westbury LC in *Hall* v. *Burrows* (1863) 4 De G J & S 150.

[92] Schechter, n. 15 above, 818

[93] See, e.g., Annand and Norman, n. 80 above, 14–15.

begins to obsess the mark".[94] The mark still identifies products, "but not with source, nor with prior purchases. It is identification with advertising."[95] This is illustrated by the example of QUAKER OATS encountered earlier:

> "Early QUAKER OATS packaging and advertising copy exploited the QUAKER symbol with its connotations of moral and physical strength in order to lend those attributes to the oats themselves: 'Women who exercise, men who walk—are the QUAKER OATS enthusiasts'."[96]

This also alludes to the inherent desirability of symbols, the alleged ability of certain trade marks to attract custom solely because of some semantic characteristic,[97] which was a fact not lost on Schechter[98] or Brown.[99] In our example of QUAKER OATS, we are told that the mark was chosen because a picture of a Quaker appears to be "earnest, hard-working and virtuous".[100] Of course, if one does accept that some marks are inherently more desirable than others, one must ensure that a producer has a legitimate interest in being allowed exclusive use of a particular mark before it is accorded protection.[101] It is by attaching various images and values to the trade mark through advertising or by selecting "a symbol which independently predisposes the consumer to buy"[102] that marks may take on a persuasive function; whether the law should

[94] Drescher, n. 8 above, 325.

[95] Brown, n. 82 above, 1187. He expresses it with the following metaphor:

> "If the advertising is successful, it directs demand to the article bearing the symbol. The symbol itself then becomes a vital link. It is a narrow bridge over which all the traffic powered by the advertising must pass. If an imitator can seize the bridge, he can collect a rich toll; and so it is commonplace that the more highly advertised is a branded product, the more attractive is its symbol to imitators."

[96] Drescher, n. 8 above, 324–5. It is interesting to note the manner in which even advertising techniques and their use of trade marks have developed over the course of the century. Initially, advertisements went to great lengths to educate consumers as to the virtues of a product (e.g. "WRIGLEY'S chewing gum is good for you for five reasons: it steadies nerves, allays thirst, aids appetite, helps digestion and keeps teeth clean"; "COCA-COLA is the ideal brain tonic for headache and exhaustion as knowledgeable pharmacists can testify"). Contrast these with the "primarily visual, sensual appeals of today" and the fact that their efficacy "was challenged early on by those who favoured suggestion over logic as a motivating force". Drescher suggests that these "didactic appeals to logic" were a transitional phase from when consumers did literally see trade marks as an indicator solely of the goods' manufacture to their contemporary perception of the rather more symbolic value of marks; this is a transformation from "explanation to suggestion". (*ibid.* 325–6).

[97] See L. O. Brown, "Advertising Requirements of Trade Marks" (1954) 44 *TMR* 794 who considers the process of selecting an appropriate mark according to its inherent characteristics.

[98] Schechter, n. 15 above, 826–30.

[99] Brown, n. 82 above, 1188.

[100] See Drescher, n. 8 above, 323.

[101] S.3(1)(c) Trade Marks Act 1994, e.g., denies registration to a descriptive mark unless it can be shown that the mark is recognised by the public as a trade mark, and for an unregistered mark to be protected in passing-off, it must always be demonstrated that the mark is recognised as a trade mark. Note also the increasing trend towards using slogans as trade marks, e.g. Microsoft's WHERE DO YOU WANT TO GO TODAY?, which will be protected so long as it is distinctive and does not generally raise new issues, but does also illustrate a new layer of meaning attributed to the brand.

[102] Brown, n. 82 above, 1189.

encourage this aspect is controversial and we shall return to this in the next chapter.[103]

It is obvious that establishing a general rationale, first explaining how consumers have been conditioned to perceive trade marks and hence secondly characterising trade mark functions, is a controversial undertaking. However, it is vital that we be clear about what is being protected, so that when we are confronted by a symbol in respect of which a claim for protection is made we may confidently say whether it may be protected as a trade mark or not.[104] To this extent these descriptions of "discrete functions" are necessary for practical clarity when applying the law. We must distinguish, though, between the minimum function which all trade marks must perform, such that the law will recognise them as such and the significance of trade marks beyond this threshold.

The problem that we encounter is that even when Schechter was writing, trade marks had not fully crystallised into their modern form.[105] As a result, the traditionally perceived trade mark functions do not reveal the complete significance of contemporary trade mark use and so have their limitations as analytical tools. Jacob J. has stated that he felt that Benelux law (and indeed what has been termed the Netherlands school[106]) treated trade marks as "something precious and important"; he could not seem to understand why such status was accorded to something that to him was a mere "badge of origin".[107] With respect, to comprehend the significance of modern trade marks from such a narrow perspective is to do them a disservice.[108] Modern, legally protected trade marks are such multi-faceted creatures that to appreciate adequately their contemporary importance, we must further analyse their function from the point of view of their role in providing the foundation for the process of branding products. It is through this process that modern trade marks have taken on an even more sophisticated significance than that contemplated by the Schechterian analysis. Any particular trade mark could still, depending on the manner in which it is used, be performing only one or alternatively all of the discrete functions at once, so source indication and the like are subsumed within this framework. These factors must be kept in mind when considering why the law will protect trade marks, for it is only in this way that the connection may be

[103] The most scathing critic of this area of trade mark function was in fact Prof. Brown: see generally n. 97 above.

[104] Annand and Norman (n. 80 above, 14–15) point to clues within the Trade Marks Act which seem to indicate what functions a symbol could perform in order that it may secure the Act's protection, e.g. s.1(1) requires that a mark must be "capable . . . of distinguishing goods of one undertaking from those of other undertakings" and s.10(3) seems to be able to protect the advertising values which may attach to a mark.

[105] J. B. Swann and T. H. Davis, "Dilution, an Idea Whose Time has Gone; Brand Equity as Protectable Property, the New/Old Paradigm" (1994) 84 *TMR* 267, 284.

[106] See P. Prescott, "Think Before You Waga Finger" [1996] *EIPR* 317.

[107] The senior patents judge in the Chancery Division speaking extra-judicially at the University of Bristol on 29 Feb. 1996.

[108] It also has the potential to ignore the role, that we shall consider in Ch.3 below, of trade marks in allocating society's resources through the mechanism of the free market economy.

discerned between functions of trade marks in the abstract and their wider social context.

The Contemporary Importance of Branding

> "[A] survey last year by the Henley Centre revealed that the public trust brand names such as Kellogg's, Heinz and Marks and Spencer more than parliament, the police and the legal system."[109]

In light of this comment and judging by the efforts made by producers to secure intellectual property protection for their products including,[110] in this case, the associated brand names, it is clear that the ability to prevent others from interfering with the branding of their particular product is important to producers. Although this fact of itself is not a sufficient basis upon which to found claims for trade mark protection, further examination of the significance of the branding process will reveal and illustrate why it is a matter of such concern to producers.

Branding is essentially concerned with how products, be they goods or services, are presented to consumers, and consists of "the development of sets of product attributes and values which are coherent, appropriate, distinctive, protectable and appealing to consumers"[111] and which will relate to a trade marked product. It can be seen as a particular aspect of the broader activity of marketing "which concerns the development and implementation of strategies for moving products . . . from the producer to the consumer in a profitable fashion"[112] and which also includes advertising or "the use of media to inform and stimulate consumers that products . . . are available for them to purchase".[113] In this world of "marketing-speak" and the "brand manager", the trade mark features in a pivotal role because it identifies the underlying product as well as providing the focus for the branding exercise. Note that whereas the product's brand name will generally be its trade mark, the two are not necessarily synonymous, since the trade mark is a legally protectable symbol, but the brand is the features of the product, its name, packaging, etc., used regardless of trade mark protection though the trade mark will normally form a fundamental part of the brand. Consequently, although the trade mark may form the foundation of a brand, the trade mark is still separate since legal protection relates to the mark and not

109 *Sunday Times*, "A can of worms is a bad diet", 5 Apr. 1998.

110 See comments made above concerning the marking of products with "TM" and "®" symbols and consider also the trade mark cases of *I CAN'T BELIEVE IT'S YOGHURT Trade Mark* [1992] RPC 533; *HAVE A BREAK Trade Mark* [1993] RPC 217; and *British Sugar* [1996] RPC 281, as well as, e.g., the copyright case of *Interlego* v. *Tyco* [1989] AC 217 and the patent case of *Merrell Dow* v. *Norton* [1996] RPC 76 (HL) where the bounds of credulity are stretched by the producers' actions in their attempts to secure intellectual property protection.

111 Murphy, n. 55 above, 12.

112 *Ibid.*

113 *Ibid.*

product as whole, but of course the mark only has any value in use to the producer as long as it has commercial significance deriving from the associated brand. The worth of trade marks as commercial symbols was recognised as long ago as 1942 by Frankfurter J. in his famous observation that:

> "The protection of trade marks is the law's recognition of the psychological functions of symbols. If it is true that we live by symbols, it is no less true that we purchase goods by them. A trade mark is a merchandising short-cut which induces a purchaser to select what he wants, or what he has been led to believe he wants. The owner of a mark exploits this human propensity by making every effort to impregnate the atmosphere of the market with the drawing power of a congenial symbol. Whatever the means employed, the end is the same—to convey through the mark, in the minds of potential customers, the desirability of the commodity upon which it appears. Once this is attained, the trade mark owner has something of value."[114]

Consequently, branding relates to how values of various types may be attached to a name, the congenial symbol, and hence associated with a product which the branding exercise strives to sell; it relies on how the meaning of symbols is open to manipulation.

Understanding how this takes place requires a brief digression into the philosophy of language,[115] but this will enable us both to appreciate the multi-faceted nature of trade marks and further illustrate their recent development. The basis of linguistic communication is signs which are generally thought to be composed of a signifier and a signified. For example the word "tree" is a sign consisting of the signified, the concept of a large plant with roots, a trunk with bark and branches with leaves as well as the signifier, the letters "t-r-e-e".[116] Note that signs cannot exist in isolation, but must relate to some overall cultural language in order to have meaning. They can also vary in complexity, with some triggering a single, automatic response and others being able to evoke a wealth of meanings and associations. It is possible to categorise these as signals and symbols respectively. A road sign with the word "STOP" on it is almost universally recognised as requiring a motorist to halt and is thus a signal,[117] but what if the sign is detached from its familiar context?

> "[W]hat if we use STOP in connection with ammunition? Looking at STOP on an ammunition box, we might think of stopping, obey, authority, police, guns policeguns, enforce, shoot-to-kill, and so on. Once we free a sign, in this case a signal, . . . all sorts of harmonies and discords are set up and everything becomes possible. . . . [W]e have wrenched the sign away from its function as a signal and given it a new life by pushing it towards becoming a symbol."[118]

[114] *Mishawaka Rubber and Woollen Mfg. Co.* v. *SS Kresge Co.* (1942) 316 US 203, 205.

[115] This discussion is based on the description given by Drescher, n. 8 above, 303–8 where references may be found to the literature in this subject.

[116] *Ibid.*, 303.

[117] *Ibid.*, 304.

[118] *Ibid.*, 304–5.

It is clear that meaning can be created and manipulated by context and that symbols, given their multi-layered meanings, can evoke associations perceived as attributes of a product.[119] By the use of an "obsessing technique", the use of advertising in various ways, a modern trade mark can be associated with certain images which may influence consumers' perception of the underlying product[120]; it is truly a symbol in the sense which we have just described. Contrast this with historic trade marks which merely served to identify the person responsible for the manufacture of the product. These marks functioned unambiguously as *signals*.[121] It is the modern trade mark's apparent ability instead to function as a *symbol* capable of such a range of meaning that demonstrates further evidence of its evolution into something much greater than a mere label.

Returning to Frankfurter J.'s proposition that a trade mark's value derives from the "drawing power" of being a "congenial symbol", it seems that this results from the use of advertising techniques to cause the mark to refer not only to the product itself, but also to broader cultural themes[122]; the ability of a symbol to convey varying levels of meaning is being exploited. Drescher describes this as "a historical overlap in trade mark function. At one level, the mark signals the product; at another level, it symbolically advertises the product." He gives the example of PEPSI-COLA where the trade mark is used to denote the objectively observable features of the product, but it arguably also connotes youth culture because it has been advertised through its endorsement by figures such as the Spice Girls.[123] The mark therefore becomes thoroughly "congenial": it is congenial to the values apparently sought by the intended consumer.[124] Another example is the fine fragrance industry where the image that the consumer "buys" is almost secondary to the actual composition of the fragrance in question. The perfume houses' efforts to secure their brand image of the exclusive world of *haute couture* are such that they seek to regulate all aspects of the retail of their products, even down to the outlets.[125] In many situations, therefore, trade marks "serve the function of court jesters of yore: they make consumers feel good and regal".[126] All this serves to demonstrate that trade marks, when considered as

[119] *Ibid.*, 305.

[120] *Ibid.*, 306–7.

[121] *Ibid.*, 308.

[122] *Ibid.*, 328.

[123] *Ibid.* See also R. C. Dreyfuss, "Expressive Genericity: Trade Marks as Language in the PEPSI Generation" (1990) 65 *Notre Dame LR* 397 who discusses the implications of the fact that certain trade marks have become so highly charged with such meaning that they have entered everyday language and in themselves deserve to be set free from their creators' control.

[124] Drescher, n. 8 above, 329.

[125] This resulted in a Monopolies and Mergers Commission enquiry: *Fine Fragrances: A Report on the Supply in the UK for Retail Sale of Fine Fragrances*, Cm. 2380 (London, 1993). See in particular paras.3.52–3.74 which provide an insight into how the manufacturers seek to maintain their brands. The recent ECJ decision in Case C-337/95 *Parfums Christian Dior SA* v. *Evora BV* [1998] RPC 166 is illuminating in this respect since it featured a French perfume house which sought to prevent the use of its trade mark in the promotional material of a Dutch firm that was selling parallel import perfume in its rather less prestigious stores!

[126] Swann and Davis, n. 105 above, 273. Consider also Aaker, n. 48 above, 161.

symbols, may be used to carry several layers of meaning dependant on the context in which they are used. Although this has been illustrated with the example of the intangible imagery which producers hope will appeal to consumers, there is a huge range of objective, more tangible information which may be conveyed by trade marks in symbolic form. It may concern product attributes, for example that a VOLVO is durable, a JAGUAR is elegant or a BMW is "the ultimate driving machine"; it may refer to consumer benefits such as CREST, which fights cavities, or AQUAFRESH, which freshens breath; or it may even indicate price range: compare SWALLOW ROYAL, MARRIOTT, FORTE POSTHOUSE and TRAVELODGE.[127]

Much has been made of the trade mark as a "symbol of goodwill". After *Spalding* v. *Gamage*,[128] it was thought to be a masterstroke when Lord Parker characterised the producer's proprietary interest which was subject to protection as lying in the goodwill attaching to the product rather than in the trade mark itself, and indeed at the turn of the century such a formulation was helpful in resolving the conflicting conceptions of the interest protected.[129] However the decision also, by implication, accepts the view that "the goodwill is the substance, the trade mark is merely the shadow"[130]; it ascribes a *passive* role to the trade mark and arguably perceives it as nothing more than a signal of the type described above. A more fundamental problem is the exact nature of "goodwill". Martino goes so far as to say that:

> "it is [his] conjecture that two factor inhibited early on the maturation of the trade mark into adulthood, namely, the orthodox juridical conception of goodwill and symbiotic relationship between goodwill and trade mark."[131]

It is a highly nebulous concept[132] from the point of view of analysing trade mark function and is, it is submitted, nothing more than another way of expressing the fact that trade marks are only protected in relation to the products upon which they are used and will not be protected "in gross", in other words "goodwill" means the business surrounding the product directly related to the trade mark. On the contrary, it is clear that the trade mark's role has become increasingly active[133] and that nowadays when we say "goodwill" we in fact mean a product's "brand equity", what may be described almost as an ecosystem surrounding the trade marked product. It has been defined as a set of assets such as name awareness, customer loyalty, perceived quality and associated images linked to a brand name.[134] The distinction with goodwill is admittedly a rather

[127] Swann and Davis, n. 105 above, 276.

[128] (1915) 32 RPC 273.

[129] C. Wadlow, *The Law of Passing Off* (2nd edn., London, 1995), 27.

[130] E. S. Rogers quoted in Schechter, n. 15 above, 818.

[131] T. Martino, *Trade Mark Dilution* (Oxford, 1996), 24.

[132] See Lord Macnaghton's definition in the text accompanying n. 90 above.

[133] This seems (almost) a foregone conclusion to Martino: "That a trade mark does more than merely symbolise goodwill is both trite and essential" (n. 131 above).

[134] See Aaker, n. 48 above, 4 and at Appendix A, below, a table from Aaker's work is reproduced to illustrate the web of meaning surrounding a branded product. See also generally Swann and Davis, n. 105 above.

subtle one, but one which at the very least emphasises the trade mark's more central, *active* role in the presentation of the product, its features and intended market; it expresses better how the trade mark is more than a mere label: it is an integral part of product. The ability of trade marks to "evoke a range of images beyond the quality and variety characteristics of the products themselves"[135] has been variously referred to its "persona",[136] "commercial magnetism",[137] and "reputation".[138] However, it is suggested that the more neutral term "commercial significance" is a better label to apply to the meaning conveyed by the trade mark to those who encounter it in the course of commercial dealings, the consumers.

Of course such an analysis is by no means uncontroversial. It is open to the criticism that by adopting the "vocabulary and, what pass for the methodologies, of the trade name creators", the future rational development of trade mark jurisprudence will somehow be stunted because such analysis encourages commentators to "abandon trains of enquiry which might ultimately yield verifiable models with discernible limits and has persuaded them instead further to mystify a process which they obviously believe to be a mystery".[139] Whilst it goes without saying that legal principles must be developed with regard to objectively verifiable factors,[140] I would nevertheless submit that it is essential to consider trade marks in the context of advertising and marketing, both because advertising is the natural environment of trade marks and because the full significance of trade marks in the market place can only be appreciated fully by throwing off the restraints of legalistic analysis.

Once a trade mark's meaning, its commercial significance has been established through means such as advertising and consumer experience of the mark's associated brand, it is clear that the producer will possess a valuable corporate asset. This has been a comparatively recent realisation,[141] but evidence can be found in two areas. First, several commentators have noted the spate of brand-driven take-overs, in particular during the late 1980s.[142] In all these cases, although the usual motivations concerning, for example, economies of scale were mentioned, given the huge premium paid in each instance over and above the value of the target's tangible assets, the conclusion drawn was that the buyer

[135] Swann and Davis, n. 105 above, 272–3.

[136] E. P. Winner, "Right of Identity: the Right of Publicity and Protection for a Trade Mark's Persona" (1981) 71 *TMR* 193.

[137] F. W. Mostert, "The Parasitic Use of the Commercial Magnetism of a Trade Mark on Non-competing Goods" [1986] *EIPR* 342.

[138] It may be argued that this is what the word "reputation" in s.10(3) Trade Marks Act 1994 refers to. See Annand and Norman, n. 80 above, 156–8.

[139] Martino, n. 131 above, 98–9.

[140] One cannot discount the contribution of disciplines other than law simply by arguing that "it takes one's eye off the ball".

[141] *The Economist*, n. 43 above, 101.

[142] *Ibid.*, 102; Swann and Davis, n. 105 above, 275–6; Drescher, n. 8 above, 302–3. The most famous of these is Nestlé's £2.5 billion bid for Rowntree Mackintosh, but they also include the fight over RJR Nabisco, the take-over of Kraft by Phillip Morris and of Pillsbury by Grand Metropolitan.

felt that it could manage the target's brands more effectively, and moreover that the buyer itself would, for various reasons,[143] have difficulty in establishing its own rival brands.[144] Secondly, although it is nothing new,[145] recent years have also seen the growth of the practice of brand valuation[146] on company balance sheets. Despite the intangible nature of trade marks and their associated brands, producers are still highly conscious of their value and therefore feel compelled to reflect this fact by balance sheet valuation.[147] Of course it is possible critically to view branding as no more than a method by which one may manipulate a product's worth,[148] thereby encouraging brand loyalty or, as Akazaki expresses it, "[n]o article of property could be as valuable as one which distorts equilibrium market price levels in its favour",[149] although, as we shall see in Chapter 3, this conception is based on a controversial and partially discredited economic analysis of trade mark law. What is also clear is that once the mark's significance in commerce has become established, it is not something that will endure automatically; if the mark is to continue to serve as an asset to the producer, it is agreed that he must make continual investment in the underlying brand.[150] A trade mark's value is intimately connected with the meaning it carries to consumers, and whilst a miscalculation on the part of a producer[151] may not be ultimately damaging to the mark's status as a trade mark, it could be fatal to any potency it may possess as a marketing symbol.

Branded products are an elementary feature of modern commerce. Central to this marketing process is the product's brand name which is protected as a trade mark and which is undeniably important in determining people's perceptions of a product—consumers will buy on the strength of a brand name. Therefore, if one analyses trade mark use as the foundation of branding and the branding process is seen as conveying information to consumer, then the effective subject-matter of protection is a trade mark's commercial significance.

[143] See e.g. F. Hone, "The Decline and Fall of New Brands in the US", Oct. 1989, *TW* 13.

[144] *The Economist*, n. 43 above, 102.

[145] Drescher, n. 8 above, 302.

[146] See W. Anson, "Placing Market Values on Trade Marks and Brands", Sept. 1995, *TW* 27 for a discussion of the various indices that may be used in this process.

[147] The motivations for this are multifarious. Consider the examples of Guinness adding £1.695 billion, News International adding $600 million and Rank Hovis McDougall adding £678 million to their assets in this way (discussed in Swann and Davis, n. 105 above, 275; *The Economist*, n. 43 above, 106).

[148] *The Economist*, n. 43 above, 101.

[149] Akazaki, n. 56 above, 260.

[150] This is one of the main arguments put forward in Aaker, n. 48 above. See also A. Kamperman Sanders, "The Wagamama Decision: Back to the Dark Ages of Trade Mark Law" [1996] *EIPR* 3, 4.

[151] Swann and Davis give the example of the American beer SCHLITZ which saw its brand equity reduced from $1 billion to $75 million through changes in advertising and cost cutting measures (n. 105 above, 277).

The Implications for the Theoretical Basis of Trade Mark Law

Trade mark protection originally grew out of the need to safeguard marks first used around the time of the industrial revolution to indicate the identity of the producers of the goods in connection with which the marks were used. As will be seen further in Chapter 4, the motivation for such protection was to prevent the injury done to consumers and producers alike by counterfeit goods. However, over the course of the last one and a half centuries, trade marks came in many cases to be used in an ever more sophisticated manner, and so came to bear an ever more sophisticated meaning with the result that they could become "up-rooted" from their "semantic foundation", their indication of product source. In parallel to this evolution, the law developed in a way such that it was willing to recognise as protectable an increasingly broad range of symbols and contexts of use. This much has become clear during this and the previous chapter. What must now be addressed is the need for a new rationale to describe the subject-matter of trade mark protection.

Trade Mark Law is Seen to Protect Symbols of Commercial Significance

Since the emergence of branding as the primary context of trade mark protection, it has become the case that many trade marks "simply cannot be viewed as mere abstract indications of source"[152] because they "evoke a range of images beyond the quality and variety characteristics of the products themselves".[153] On the other hand, it is also true that many trade marks have a more limited scope of meaning due perhaps to their owners' smaller marketing operation or advertising commitment. Consequently we find small, regional brands, which may be no more than the producer's name, "rubbing shoulders" on the trade marks register with the likes of COCA-COLA and MARLBORO, about which it has been said that "the trade mark has a value independent of the goods it identifies and itself is a good".[154] These contrasting positions may, however, be reconciled by the notion that the trade mark law operates by protecting the commercial significance of trade marks or their meaning to those who encounter them which they acquire by *use in commerce*. This meaning can range from an indication that a particular organisation was responsible for the related product to the way in which the trade mark imparts a certain intangible attractiveness to the underlying product. The common factor in every instance is that some message is communicated to the person encountering the mark. However, this message must be acquired through use—a mark, like any sign, means nothing in the abstract—hence the theoretical necessity of the section 46(1)(a), (b) of the Trade Marks Act requirement of "genuine use". Although this provision has the

152 Swann and Davis, n. 105 above, 297.
153 *Ibid.*, 272–3.
154 Landes and Posner, n. 66 above, 32.

important practical effect of preventing traders from "warehousing" marks (registering, to the detriment of competitors, apparently desirable marks for later use or licensing), its theoretical importance is more fundamental because it recognises "the conception that trade mark registration is an entitlement dependent upon need"[155]; the need to protect a trade mark's commercial significance which can only arise through the trade mark's use in the market place. After all, trade mark registration originated as merely an evidential shortcut allowing a trade mark owner to bring a passing-off action without the need to prove the reputation of his mark.

Characterising the subject-matter of trade mark protection as a trade mark's commercial significance frees the law from arguably out-dated conceptions of "goodwill". At common law following the decision in *Bowden Wire*, a trade mark was effectively inseparable from the "goodwill" of a particular product or business that it represented. As we saw earlier in this chapter,[156] the label "goodwill" cannot adequately express or rationalise the true meaning of many trade marks. Moreover, limiting trade mark use in the manner contemplated in *Bowden Wire* is inimical to the modern practices of licensing and franchising. The explicit reasoning concerning avoidance of deception in the *Bowden Wire* decision has now been rejected,[157] but another fear implicit in the case still remains: that of conferring trade mark rights "in gross" or treating a trade mark as something over which its owner has an absolute right distinct from the reason why it was originally protected. Requiring that a trade mark could not be separated from its associated "goodwill" artificially restricts the scope of a trade mark's use, and hence the scope of the owner's rights, but even on this basis, could this approach strictly be said to be necessary?

The spread of franchising is not the only modern trade practice to overtake trade mark law.[158] Brand extension is another common marketing practice, which illustrates how a modern trade mark may possess a commercial significance that on the one hand is not rooted entirely in a single product of one manufacturer, but on the other has discernible limits. It is the practice whereby a producer seeks to diversify by introducing a new product under the same trade mark as an existing product in the hope that consumers will identify the new product with some or all of the desirable characteristics of the original product, with the result that promotional costs are saved and the new product may become established more quickly.[159] By implication then, a trade mark can be

[155] Cornish, n. 42 above, para.17–69.

[156] See text accompanying nn. 128–38, above.

[157] Cf. White Paper, n. 75 above, para.4.36 and the licensing provisions contained in the Trade Marks Act.

[158] Even the normally radical Schechter took the conservative view that "[developing] a trade mark as a guarantee of quality . . . then . . . '[farming out]' the use of that mark apart from his business" (Schechter, n. 15 above, 822), i.e. franchising, was unacceptable.

[159] Murphy, n. 55 above, 13–14. E.g., the mark DORITOS attained recognition in connection with Mexican-style crisps and so was later used by Walkers to market a range of complementary salsa dips.

seen to have a meaning beyond the product with respect to which it originally acquired such meaning; otherwise the process simply would not be effective. That this practice takes place, and indeed its legitimacy, is acknowledged by sections 5(2) and 10(2) of the Trade Marks Act, which contemplate preventing a new entrant's use of a mark in respect of products similar to those for which the mark was originally registered. However, brand extension is not simply a matter of applying an existing trade mark to a new product. Successful brand extension is constrained by what consumers have come to associate the mark and the nature of the underlying product[160]: its brand equity. For example, the Jack Daniel Distillery was able to market profitably barbecue charcoal in the same trade dress as its more famous whisky because of the cultural connections between the two; on the other hand JACK DANIEL'S baby food seems unlikely, given the incompatibility of the imagery of alcohol with young children.[161] Brand extension therefore demonstrates first that a trade mark is not strictly appurtenant to the trade in respect of which it originally gained recognition. It also seems that any particular trade mark is self-restricting as to the contexts in which the mark may realistically be used since the risk of damaging the brand equity and thus the commercial significance attaching to a trade mark through a badly judged attempt at brand extension is a practical limitation on trade mark owners; moreover, it limits the ability of trade marks to exist as a protectable interest "in gross".

Modern trade mark law still demands a degree of appurtenance between the trade mark and the values that it represents. However this is best expressed not by reference to "goodwill" and all its accompanying doctrinal baggage, but through the notion that a trade mark is inseparable from its commercial significance acquired through use. Therefore protection is conditional on continued commercial significance secured through use of the mark in relation to goods or services. With the abolition of the registered user regime, a major substantive restriction on the use of a registered trade mark, it is furthermore clear that there is nothing inherently wrong in treating a trade mark as an asset to be exploited by its owner.

THE MERCHANDISING PHENOMENON

However, are there limits on the extent to which a symbol protected as a trade mark may be treated as an asset ripe for exploitation?[162] Exactly what motivates consumers to choose one product over another is still very difficult to establish, however it is possible to speculate in broad terms on why product A is apparently more desirable than product B and why there should be a demand for

160 Drescher, n. 8 above, 330.

161 *Ibid.*, 331.

162 This section has benefited from the comments of Peter Jaffey; responsibility however for the views expressed remains mine.

product X but not product Y. One reason is because of a symbol of some description applied to or used in conjunction with the product in question. This symbol may be the product's brand name and, as already indicated, it will influence the consumer's purchasing decision because of the associations it creates between various attributes of the product and the product itself. On the other hand, it may be the name of a sports team or rock band, the image of a famous personality, real or fictional, or even the name of a famous manufacturer of an unrelated type of product. In this case, the consumer's motivation is thought to be entirely different: the inherent desirability of owning a product bearing that symbol.[163] Although it might not be clear precisely what motivates consumers to buy a product in any particular instance, two observations can nevertheless be made. First there is an obvious demand amongst consumers for products solely because they bear certain symbols[164]; and secondly, although there are several examples of products falling into this category because of their "attractive" brand names,[165] many products are purchased bearing symbols which from a branding point of view are meaningless[166]; the symbol has become a product in its own right.

This, in essence, is the marketing phenomenon known as merchandising. Expressing it in such abstract terms can obscure what is in actual fact a highly lucrative industry. To illustrate the sheer profit potential, one may point to the fact that there are shops world-wide selling spin-off merchandise from the Disney films, and the 1994 Rolling Stones world tour anticipated making a profit

[163] C. W. Grimes and G. J. Battersby, "The Protection of Merchandising Properties" (1979) 69 *TMR* 431, 432–4, have identified three different categories of symbol or "merchandising property" which may influence consumers' choice. (The term "properties" is used in a general sense rather than to imply that the creator has an specific proprietary right in the image). They may purchase a product because of the symbol's status and what being seen to own such a product says about its owner, for example, ROLEX watches or VERSACE clothing (See *Sunday Times*, "On the Bratwalk", 8 May 1996, sect. 8, 10 for recent evidence of consumers (in this case teenage children) purchasing goods simply for their prestigious brand names). They may also purchase a product because the symbol identifies "desirable characteristics" and "the purchasers of [these] products seek to psychologically associate themselves with such desirable characteristics" (Grimes and Battersby, 432–3). They may even purchase a product because of the symbol's widespread popularity:

> "[The symbol] achieves public recognition in a variety of ways, although generally as a result of mass-media promotional 'hype' of . . . a 'primary' product or service, for example, television shows, movies, sports, musical groups, etc. As a result of such recognition, [the symbol] can then be used on 'secondary' products to create demand therefor" (*ibid.*, 433).

[164] Cornish, n. 42 above, para. 16–34.

[165] See n. 163 above. Consider also the example of COCA-COLA or HARLEY DAVIDSON stationery. HARLEY DAVIDSON is a particularly interesting example. I have seen stationery and toiletries marketed under the mark which was of course first made famous in relation to motorbikes. It is not at all clear whether the manufacturer has radically diversified or just licensed its name almost indiscriminately. It seems a bizarre marketing strategy since it is difficult to envisage why anyone should want to buy toiletries from a motorbike manufacturer (this seems to fall classically within Learned Hand J's lipstick and steam shovel situation (*L. E. Waterman* v. *Gordon* (1934) 72 F 2d 272, 273)) or alternatively why a fan of their motorbikes should necessarily choose to advertise their loyalty through their choice of stationery!

[166] I.e. they cannot convincingly be demonstrated to indicate matters such as the underlying product's quality.

from merchandise almost eight times that of the already considerable direct earnings from the concerts.[167] Even in 1978, the merchandising revenue of *Star Wars* was 22 million dollars compared with the 25 million dollar box office takings.[168] Indeed it is not possible to travel very far when shopping without being invited to buy a product and pay a premium for it because it bears an image of or is connected with a particular character or personality of the moment. A high profile example of a good merchandising opportunity in recent years was the EURO '96 football championship,[169] and since the death of Diana, Princess of Wales, there has been a huge market for merchandise commemorating her life. Nor is merchandising a new phenomenon. The first instance could be said to be toy Noah's arks sold in Germany during the seventeenth century and examples are cited from the nineteenth century of children's china decorated with scenes from the works of Charles Dickens, and Beatrix Potter's awareness of the merchandising potential of her characters.[170] However, merchandising's first major success came in the mid-1930s with the arrival of Mickey Mouse, from which time the increasing popularity of films, comic strips and televisions meant that the merchandising industry was set to grow to such an extent that by the mid-1960s, character merchandising agents had established themselves as a distinct professional group.[171] It must however be noted that the ability of manufacturers to profit from this consumer demand will always only be secondary to the means by which the images, and hence their associated merchandise, came into demand in the first place[172]; the symbol or image used must have gained some significance to its purchasers, for example from its use in a film, book or television programme,[173] even though this may not be of the type familiar to brand managers. Consequently, despite the fact that the focus in a merchandising context seems to be on the mark or symbol for its own sake, treating it as a commodity, the significance for purchasers derives from how it has been used previously.[174] In any event and in light of this, Frankfurter J.'s statement that,

[167] Annand and Norman, n. 80 above, 210–11.

[168] J. Adams, *Merchandising Intellectual Property* (London, 1987), p.xxvi.

[169] See *The Times*, "Roll up, roll up and sell the game", 22 May 1996, sect.2, 46; *The Times*, "Euro '96 coins enjoy royal approval", 22 May 1996, sect.2, 48; and *The Times*, "Euro '96 is a big draw for small firms with the right sales pitch", 18 June 1996, sect.1, 22. Indeed amongst the products of the 110 "official" EURO '96 merchandise manufacturers are said to be computer mouse mats, commemorative medallions, football-shaped postcards and posters.

[170] Adams, n. 168 above, xxv–xxvi. The first reported case involving a merchandising property seems to be *Re Holt* (1896) 1 RPC 16.

[171] *Ibid*., p.xxvi.

[172] R. C. Denicola, "Institutional Publicity Rights: an Analysis of the Merchandising of Famous Trade Symbols" (1984) 62 *North Carolina LR* 603, 635.

[173] Adams, n. 168 above, p.xxvii. This is of course central to the argument that the activities of the merchandisers is not worthy of protection.

[174] Furthermore, given the requirement that genuine use must be made of a registered trade mark (s.46(1)(a) Trade Marks Act 1994), one cannot set about registering marks indiscriminately on the off chance that consumers may at some point in the future find them attractive, but bearing in mind the cost of registration, it unlikely that this will in any event happen. As Jacob J. said in *Origins Natural Resources Inc.* v. *Origin Clothing Ltd.* [1995] FSR 280, 285, "[p]eople do not make trade mark applications for the fun of it. It costs money".

"[i]f it is true that we live by symbols, it is no less true that we purchase goods by them",[175] can be seen to take on a new dimension and so we must examine the challenges that this creates for the existing law protecting trade symbols.

The Overlap Between Trade Marks and Merchandising Objects

Two aspects of merchandising are interesting from the point of view of contemporary trade mark use: where an image has achieved a certain popularity and its creator wishes to use the law protecting trade symbols to gain the right to control its commercial exploitation[176]—which we shall examine shortly—and where a trade mark has become "famous" in some way as a brand name and its owner wishes to exploit this fame by using the mark in conjunction with a product unrelated to the mark's original context.[177] The mark is only one step removed from being a merchandising object proper in the sense of a symbol that has never been used to convey information about the underlying product. This distinction can be important when assessing merchandising objects' claims for protection because the source of the symbol's fame may or may not fall within the more orthodox concern of trade mark law. If it is eventually decided as a matter of policy that merchandising objects should not be protected by the law of trade marks or, alternatively, the law as it stands will not accord protection, then a cut-off point must be drawn somewhere. It is however not always an easy distinction to draw:

> "it is virtually impossible to construct a legal framework which would distinguish between straightforward character merchandising . . ., the practice of decorating goods . . . with a trade mark having a reputation in connection with quite different goods, and cases where a trade mark simultaneously decorates the goods and distinguishes their source."[178]

Consider the marketing phenomenon known as brand extension whereby what have been termed "mythically related"[179] new products are marketed under the same brand name as existing products in the hope that consumers will identify the positive attributes of the existing brand with the new product. This is obviously branding use of the trade mark. There is also the widespread practice of selling goods decorated by the trade mark of the manufacturer of an unrelated product so that purchasers of the goods may, for example, signify their approval of the unrelated product. This is merchandising use and is exemplified by BUDWEISER T-shirts. Finally, goods may be distributed again bearing the trade mark of an unrelated product, but this time it is not because anyone realistically

[175] N. 114 above.

[176] The image never previously having been a concern of trade mark law.

[177] That is to say the owner is merely seeking to extend the influence of the right which he already possesses over the mark.

[178] Trade Mark White Paper, n. 75 above, para.4.43.

[179] Drescher, n. 8 above, 331.

wants to buy such goods but rather to *promote* the primary, unrelated business. The case of KODIAK *Trade Mark*[180] demonstrates this scenario where the goods in question were T-shirts bearing the famous mark KODAK purely to promote the owner's photographic equipment business. It represents a grey area since it is question of degree whether the mark is perceived as a brand name or as a decorative symbol.[181] The point which can be drawn from this is the extent to which brand names and merchandising objects can become enmeshed; is it realistic to attempt to unravel the two? Or would this create arbitrary distinctions?

Legal Problems

The difficulty facing the person responsible for the success or recognition of the image to be merchandised is that its commercial value derives from having the exclusive right to control its use, and hence the ability to license others (for a profit) to produce goods bearing the image (merchandising is rarely undertaken by the originator of the symbol); if anyone could satisfy consumer demand for such goods, the image would effectively be worthless to its creator.[182] Indeed the practice relies on the assumption that someone will in fact have such an exclusive right. However, English law does not recognise any form of merchandising right as such.[183] Instead any merchandising right must found parasitically by use of a right that may subsist incidentally in the merchandising object. It may well be the case that copyright will subsist in the image in question, which could form the subject-matter of the licensing agreement presuming that the image falls within the definition of an "artistic work" in section 4 of the Copyright, Designs and Patents Act 1988. However, there are notable exceptions to this including names (e.g. STAR WARS would not be protected by copyright) and copies which are not derived (in the technical sense) from the original image.[184] The result is that sometimes protection which is the derivative of the law of copyright can be somewhat arbitrary in the context of merchandising.

180 [1990] FSR 49.

181 Mention must be made at this point of products such as VERSACE jeans which consumers are known to buy simply because they have a VERSACE label rather than because of anything the label may indicate concerning their origin or quality. It may therefore be possible to enquire into consumer perceptions of the use made of the mark, but again this is unsatisfactory because, depending on the view taken of merchandising, this may serve to invalidate the branding use of the VERSACE label if this is predominated by the merchandising use. The only feasible way, if necessary, of distinguishing branding and merchandising use is to take each case on merits and examine how the symbol is used in all the circumstances.

182 As argued by A. Kozinski, "Trade Marks Unplugged" (1993) 68 *NYULR* 960, 966–9, the person with the greatest moral claim at least to protection.

183 Along the lines, e.g., of the American publicity right. See generally Winner, n. 136 above and Grimes and Battersby, n. 163 above.

184 See Annand and Norman, n. 80 above 211–3 for details of limitations on the usefulness of copyright for securing protection for merchandising ventures; and also more generally G. Dworkin and R. D. Taylor, *Blackstone's Guide to the Copyright, Designs and Patents Act 1988* (London, 1989).

Alternatively, the prospective licensor may turn to the law of trade mark protection. Even though the merchandising object may well have a decorative significance completely alien to that for which brand names are protected, the law does manifest a certain willingness to accord them protection both by registration and by way of an action in the tort of passing-off. That such protection is utilised in this way is apparent, for example, from the preponderance of "®" and "™" signs visible on goods adjacent to symbols and images whose merchandising value is being exploited, and in recent trade mark cases in which the subject trade mark registration has clearly been made with merchandising in mind.[185] Both routes, however, bring their own problems. Under the first route, the creator of a merchandising object would register it as a trade mark, license the trade mark to the merchandise manufacturer, and in the event that a third party tried to manufacture or sell goods bearing the merchandising object (or indeed one similar), sue the third party for infringement of the trade mark. It is unclear whether he would succeed at any of the three stages outlined. Certainly under the 1938 Act, things would have been quite difficult. The registration may have been refused in the first place both because the object failed to satisfy the definition of a trade mark as being a mark "used . . . in relation to goods for the purpose of indicating . . . a connection in the course of trade between the goods and some person having the right . . . to use the mark"[186] and moreover because the object is not sufficiently distinctive.[187] The problems posed by this second point were apparent in the recent decision in *ELVIS PRESLEY Trade Marks*[188] in which Laddie J. refused to register two marks consisting of the name Elvis Presley on the ground that the more famous the name, the less distinctive it is for the purposes of trade mark law, since Elvis Presley's fame did not identify the applicants' goods (his successors in title) but merely helped to identify their goods with him. If registration was in any event secured, the 1938 Act required trade mark licences to be registered, but section 28(6) directed the registrar to refuse registration if the agreement appeared to facilitate "trafficking" in trade marks or dealing with them as commodities in their own right, as happened in *Re American Greeting Corp's Application (HOLLIE HOBBIE)*.[189] Even if the mark was validly licensed, it could have been liable for revocation under section 26 for lack of *bona fide* use. As was seen in the previous chapter, the case of *KODIAK Trade Mark* indicated that purely decorative use did not constitute the necessary *bona fide* use required by the 1938 Act; the mark in question was not used to indicate a connection in the course of trade between the goods and the manufacturer. Finally it could also have been argued that the third party was not using the merchandising object as a trade mark and so did not fall within the

[185] *Bravado Merchandising Ltd.* v. *Mainstream Publishing Ltd.* [1996] FSR 205 (Ct. Sess.); *Trebor Bassett Ltd.* v. *The Football Association* [1997] FSR 211; and of course *ELVIS PRESLEY Trade Marks* [1997] RPC 543.

[186] S. 68(1) Trade Marks Act 1938.

[187] As required by s.9 of the same Act.

[188] [1997] RPC 543.

[189] [1984] 1 WLR 189. See in particular Lord Brightman at 198.

infringement provisions.[190] Has all this now been relegated to the realms of legal history?

Arguably the situation has changed under the 1994 Act.[191] The criteria for registration under section 1(1) merely require that the symbol protected as a trade mark be capable of product differentiation and being represented graphically. At first glance, it seems then that the merchandising object is protectable because it is doing just that, namely differentiating goods bearing the merchandising object from other goods which does not. Furthermore, this approach can be supported by the argument that the use of the image would serve to indicate that the clothing was manufactured under licence from and with the blessing of the image creator; the trade mark guarantees that it is "official" merchandise.[192] Alternatively, this may be expressed by stating that the trade mark indicates the organisation's endorsement of the product concerned, and this constitutes the secondary meaning necessary for registration.[193] However it is also quite tenable to argue that since a merchandising object will always be recognised by consumers as exactly that, and not a trade mark capable of conveying information about the underlying product, it would always be devoid of distinctive character.[194] Such an approach follows the reasoning of Laddie J in *ELVIS PRESLEY Trade Marks*. As regards licensing, the White Paper expressly stated that section 28(6) of the Trade Marks Act 1938 was to be repealed by the 1994 Act because of the obstacle it placed in the way of character merchandising,[195] while the deregulation of trade mark licensing (through the removal of the quality control requirement in licences[196]) removes a further obstacle.[197] The question whether an image used as a merchandising object is capable of infringing a registered trade mark under the 1994 Act has not yet been fully decided. On the ordinary meaning of the provisions of section 10 of the Trade Marks Act 1994,

[190] As was the case in *Mars* v. *Cadbury* [1987] RPC 387 ("Treat Size" did not infringe TREETS) and *Mothercare* v. *Penguin Books* [1988] RPC 113, although cf. *News Group Newspapers Ltd*. v. *Rocket Record Co. Ltd*. [1981] FSR 89 (record title "Page Three Girls" *did* infringe PAGE THREE).

[191] See n. 80 above, and accompanying text with respect to the shift in emphasis in the Trade Marks Act towards the basic trade mark function.

[192] See Annand and Norman, n. 80 above, 216.

[193] Grimes and Battersby, n. 163 above, 441–2. These creative formulations of trade mark use seem to rest on, and so are to an extent weakened by, the presumption that consumers buy the product because it has been licensed by the symbol's creator, and hence is "official" merchandise. However, on the basis of observation, it would seem that while merchandised images and symbols do have a significance to consumers, such that they convey whatever meaning that consumers find attractive, this does not necessarily extend to always indicating that the product is approved in some way by the film maker, football team, rock band, etc. This is not to say that consumers have no preference whether the merchandise is "official" or not, but rather that this is not always a consideration in the purchasing decision whereas the fame of the symbol is essential.

[194] I am grateful to Peter Jaffey for putting forward this view.

[195] N. 75 above, para.4.40.

[196] See Ch.1, text accompanying note 123, *supra*.

[197] Since consumers do not buy the goods for the indication of quality control that the trade mark would bring in a branding context, requiring quality control provisions in the merchandising licence agreement seems to bring an element of consumer protection of which consumers in fact have no need (Parks, n. 56 above, 563). On the other hand it is not in the interest of licensor to have his image or symbol associated with shoddy goods.

it seems that it is, however as we saw in Chapter 1[198] observations made in *Bravado Merchandising* v. *Mainstream Publishing*, *British Sugar* and *Trebor Bassett* v. *The Football Association* suggest that the section may be taken to require that for infringement to be made out the offending sign must be used as a brand name; use as a decoration would not suffice.

Equally problematic is the second route, whereby the creator of the merchandising object would argue that the actions of the third party merchandiser in making "unauthorised" use of the merchandising object constitute passing-off. It will be recalled that passing-off generally protects a business' goodwill from being damaged by the misrepresentation of another trader. Until 1991, the weight of authority did not accept that unauthorised use of a merchandising object would fall within this formula. In the case both of fictitious characters[199] and personalities[200] the courts took the view that the necessary misrepresentation would only be made out where consumers, on seeing the defendant's goods bearing the merchandising object, would infer that the plaintiff licensed and exercised some form of quality control over the defendant's goods and that consumers bought the product in reliance upon such quality control; in other words, if the public viewed the merchandising object as a trade mark used in the branding sense. This burden of proof was almost impossible to discharge. An additional obstacle was the requirement of goodwill: since the image creator was in the business of exactly that, he was not in the business of producing goods bearing the image, and no goodwill could hence be shown.

During the 1980s though, an argument became accepted before the Australian courts[201] the effect of which was put to the image creators in a much stronger position. The reasoning was that, against the background that consumers expect to buy "officially" licensed or authorised merchandise and that the image creator is in the business of image licensing, the necessary implied representation made by defendant was that he had been licensed to use the image for merchandising purposes. Notwithstanding the previous authority, the fact that consumers are aware that such licensing of images by their creators takes place was finally accepted in English law in *Mirage Studios* v. *Counter-Feat Clothing* (*NINJA TURTLES*).[202] However, in order for the misrepresentation to be actionable, it must be shown that consumers may rely on it, that is to say, they would want to buy "official" merchandise licensed by the creator. In *NINJA TURTLES* it was thought that once the misrepresentation had been made out, no evidence of reliance on the misrepresentation need be adduced, and moreover the court

198 Ch.1, text accompanying notes 148–151, *supra*.

199 E.g. *Tavener Rutledge* v. *Trexapalm* [1977] RPC 275.

200 E.g. *Lyngstad* v. *Anabas* [1977] FSR 62.

201 See *Children's Television Workshop Inc.* v. *Woolworths (NSW) Ltd.* [1981] RPC 187; *Hogan* v. *Koala Dundee Pty. Ltd.* (1988) 83 ALR 187; and *Pacific Dunlop Ltd.* v. *Hogan* (1989) 87 ALR 14.

202 [1991] FSR 145. This decision may well have put paid to the alleged requirement of a "common field of activity". Clearly in these circumstances the image creator and pirate merchandiser are two completely different fields, but the pirate is damaging the creator by affecting his second line of business: the licensing of the use of his creations.

would be prepared to infer that consumers would not purchase the goods if they were not "the genuine article".[203] It was therefore thought that the courts had thereby recognised the right of image creators and their licensees to object to those attempting to take advantage of the success of their creation.

In fact, later cases preferred a more orthodox interpretation of passing-off. In *ELVIS PRESLEY Trade Marks* Laddie J. stated that he did not see *NINJA TURTLES* as:

> "laying down a finding of fact of universal application that the products of plaintiffs in similar circumstances [to those in *NINJA TURTLES*] are viewed by the public as 'genuine' and that traders in competing goods are making a misrepresentation."[204]

and that:

> "When people buy a toy of a well known character, I have no reason to believe that they care one way or the other who made, sold or licensed it."[205]

Whilst not necessarily rejecting the reasoning in *NINJA TURTLES*, the evidential burden has certainly been raised, and it seems that very persuasive evidence would need to be adduced of the public's desire to purchase "official" merchandise. A similar view can be taken of *Halliwell* v. *Panini SpA*[206] in which Lightman J. thought that passing-off would only be found if "the public would believe on seeing such a [product] that it was published by the plaintiffs or that its quality was authorised by them"—the classic 1970s approach—and the judge went on to say "whether [the product] is official or not is not a factor of any relevance to the purchaser".[207] It is significant that all of the recent judicial statements have either been made obiter or during interlocutory hearings. It remains to be seen what would be decided in a case which turns on the issue.

[203] Note that Browne-Wilkinson V.-C. also made the requirement that licensing must take place in images subject to copyright in order to establish the goodwill which passing-off will protect. Thus it was argued that this does not really seem to improve the position of image marketers since there will still not be any protection for names or simple logos, although they seem better off where copyright does subsist in the images, but where infringement cannot be shown. Elmslie and Lewis, for example, argued that the requirement is in fact artificial, since passing-off protects the goodwill attaching to a product (in this case a merchandisable image) not any particular intellectual property right, and so their presence or otherwise is irrelevant; what matters is the demand for the image built up by its creator in the course of his primary field of business (M. Elmslie and M. Lewis, "Passing-off and Image Marketing in the UK" [1992] *EIPR* 270, 273; they rely on Lord Parker's reasoning in *Spalding* v. *Gamage* (1915) 32 RPC 273).

[204] [1997] RPC 543, 553. The case in fact concerned trade mark rights, so Laddie J's observations are strictly obiter. Note that he did not discount the possibility of there being circumstances where such finding could be made.

[205] *Ibid.*, 554.

[206] LEXIS Transcript, 6 June 1997, Ch.D. Most recently, an application for summary judgment for passing-off was refused in respect of T-shirts bearing images of the Teletubbies, Laddie J. considering that it was quite possible that consumers who saw the products might well view them as merely illustrating the television characters without contemplating that the product may have been made under the plaintiff's control (*BBC Worldwide Ltd.* v. *Pally Screen Printing Ltd.*, unreported, 26 Jan. 1998, Ch.D.).

[207] Apparently the plaintiffs (the Spice Girls) had adopted the practice of requiring their licensees to mark their products with the designation "official" with the effect of negating any misrepresentation to consumers, to whom it was therefore quite clear whether any particular had in fact been licensed by the plaintiffs.

It is obvious from this brief survey that any willingness within trade mark law to protect creators of merchandising objects from those who seek to compete by taking advantage of consumers' supposed desire to purchase goods bearing an image authorised by its creator is rather tentative and possibly misconceived[208] in its formulation. An "official" merchandiser in a passing-off action is faced with a particular heavy evidential burden to discharage, assuming also that the misrepresentation as to licensing principle is accepted. If he is successful in obtaining a trade mark registration—an apparently difficult undertaking in itself—it is not clear whether the registration would be any use if the type of conduct which he seeks to prevent is not considered to be infringing.

Is Merchandising a Legitimate Concern of Trade Mark Law?

Merchandising as a marketing phenomenon is a lucrative business and is without doubt set to continue for the foreseeable future. However, as a legal issue, it still raises normative questions which we must briefly identify, although it is beyond the scope of this book to address them fully.[209] The immediate problem concerns the place of merchandising within trade mark law since English law's response to merchandising has been essentially pragmatic. Existing intellectual property rights have been put to the task of protecting merchandising objects on the assumption that there is someone, namely the object's creator, with a greater claim to exploit the consumer demand for goods bearing the object than others. Indeed on the face of it, merchandising falls quite logically within trade mark law. It is possible to rationalise both brand names and merchandising properties as symbols that may influence consumer purchasing decisions. Moreover, they share the characteristic of being symbols of commercial significance: the meaning for purchasers derives in both cases from how they have been used previously. This is true to the extent that sometimes it is difficult to differentiate between the two. It is in any event clear that there is at least the potential to protect merchandising properties as trade marks (both expressly by registration and implicitly through passing-off).

However, attempting to "shoe-horn" merchandising use of a symbol into formulæ more suited to analysing use as a brand name distorts the law of trade mark registration by attempting to procure a broader scope of the trade mark

[208] As Peter Jaffey has suggested to me, the reasoning adopted in *NINJA TURTLES* does seem a rather contrived method of creating a merchandising right and that it is bizarre to allow the issue to depend on consumers' opinion whether a licence is necessary for the use of the merchandising object or to treat this opinion as material to the purchasing decision.

[209] See Denicola, n. 172 above; Mostert, n. 137 above; Winner, n. 136 above; Kozinski, n. 182 above; P. E. Mims, "Promotional Goods and the Functionality Doctrine: An Economic Model of Trade Marks" (1984) 63 *Texas LR* 639 who put forward solutions to the broader question of whether owners of merchandising properties have any right to regulate their use, as well as H. E. Ruijsenaars, "Legal Aspects of Merchandising: the AIPPI Resolution" [1996] *EIPR* 330 and "The WIPO Report on Character Merchandising" [1994] *IIC* 532.

right than may be legitimate, and disguises the truth of the matter that it *seems* that the law is being used to protect the decorative value of symbols *in their own right*. This in itself is not as objectionable as might first be thought, since although it would appear that using trade mark law to protect merchandising properties effectively grants trade mark rights "in gross", in fact we are still not protecting symbols *per se*, but merely their meaning. The real objection is that this meaning is of a wholly different nature from that of a brand name and, without pre-empting the discussion in Chapter 4, it would appear that the trade mark right is being used for a purpose other than that for which it was intended. The technical problems mentioned above are symptomatic of the law's ambivalence in its attitude towards the broader issue of protecting merchandising rights. It is true enough that the trafficking prohibition, which was effectively a prohibition on treating trade marks as commodities in their own right, and the restrictive licensing provisions are now gone, and so by implication the White Paper now seems to be encouraging merchandising use of trade marks.[210] It also seems true that, barring some catastrophic judicial intervention re-affirming the principles from and effect of *HOLLIE HOBBIE* and *KODIAK*,[211] the use of registered trade marks to protect merchandising properties is increasingly entrenched, and that dogmatic assertions of the primacy of trade marks' branding function will not dissuade image creators from seeking protection in trade mark law.[212] Nevertheless, such protection is patchy, often arbitrary in its availability (witness the effect of applying the distinctiveness requirement for trade mark registration or the criteria for subsistence of copyright) and incoherent, in that there is no clearly articulated policy on whether and how merchandising properties should be protected. The White Paper "washed its hands" of the matter; the Whitford Committee was of the opinion that the most suitable form of protection was through the law of unfair competition, even though the nature of merchandising properties seems to weigh in favour of copyright protection.[213]

Of course, achieving theoretical coherence of the law is not a reason in itself to alter the law, but asking whether it is right that the law governing trade marks should protect symbols which are manifestly of commercial significance, but which may well be detached from the significance which trade mark law was originally concerned with, is a starting point in establishing a more practically satisfactory regime. Ultimately it is a normative judgment which be must be made. In favour of granting an exclusive right to exploit any particular merchandising object is the view that the exclusivity will give the necessary incentive to secure the image's optimal exploitation. The contrary argument maintains that anyone should be allowed to meet the demand for merchandise,

[210] N. 75 above, paras.4.40–43, although cf. n. 213 below.

[211] Which, given Laddie J.'s restrictionist attitude exemplified by *ELVIS PRESLEY Trade Marks*, does not seem so far fetched.

[212] Adams, n. 168 above, p.xxix.

[213] *Report on Copyright and Designs Law* (Whitford Committee), Cmnd. 6732 (London, 1977), para.909. In fact the White Paper, n. 75 above, expressly favours copyright or design law protection in para.4.42.

since otherwise consumers are being penalised for making the merchandising object popular in the first place, and the image creator is being allowed to extract monopoly rents. If we are not going to protect symbols because of the meaning surrounding their image, is it still a form of (proscribable) unfair competition for all-comers to benefit from the popularity of a particular merchandising object? If it is decided that this is the case, then the *NINJA TURTLES* principle must be broadened to cover the lacunæ in the utility of copyright in this context, given the potential for the tort of passing-off to develop in the direction of a general principle of unfair competition.[214]

CONCLUSION

Trade marks are a essential means by which consumers are induced into buying a particular product available on the market. By linking a consumer's knowledge of a product gained, in the main, through possible past experience and brand advertising with the product the consumer encounters in the "market place" (in the sense of a modern retail outlet), the consumer is able to identify various characteristics of the product that are likely to influence his purchasing decision. The separation of producer and consumer evident in the modern chain of distribution is thus overcome. Two points have become clear. First, the practice of selling products under a trade mark originated almost spontaneously in the market place and subsequently became assimilated as a legal institution as the trade mark became an increasingly fundamental aspect of late nineteenth and twentieth century commerce. For this reason it is possible to say that the relationship between modern consumer society and the trade mark as a legal institution is symbiotic, because legally protected trade marks are essential to how products are now marketed, and moreover providing legal protection for trade symbols would be meaningless in the absence of the purpose provided by modern commerce. Secondly, the potential range of meaning conveyed by trade marks has broadened enormously, mainly through the wide extent of brand advertising. As a result, it is no longer possible to base trade mark law on an outdated model of trade mark function founded on the historical preconception that modern trade marks, like their pre-industrial predecessors, indicate solely a product's origin. It is submitted instead that the only means by which the whole range of trade mark function may be taken into account is through the commercial significance rationale outlined above. However, this is still only a

[214] The alternative, of course, is legislative intervention introducing some new form of statutory merchandising right. It is believed that this is the more satisfactory route, since the creation of a new intellectual property right involves not only settling a dispute between two competing traders—such is the case in a passing-off action, for example—but also issues of public interest. See J. Mutimear, "Is There a Need for a Personality Right in the United Kingdom" Apr. 1998, *TW* 12 and more generally the comments in R. Jacob, "Industrial Property—Industry's Enemy" [1997] *International Patents Quarterly* 3.

theoretical rationale and, in practice, it is the *ability to differentiate* products that must now be seen as the distinguishing characteristic of a trade mark.

Merchandising, the practice whereby goods are sold bearing an image of some description which has gained popularity and hence marketability in an otherwise unrelated context, is a second phenomenon that has impinged upon trade mark law because of the basic need of those selling merchandise to gain exclusivity in order to make their undertaking worthwhile. Given the similarities between brand names and merchandised symbols, it is understandable that trade mark law has been used to secure protection, and so exclusivity. Nevertheless trade mark registration is being used for a purpose other than that for which it was originally intended, with certain ensuing practical difficulties. On the one hand it should be remembered that it is expressly stated in the White Paper that the law of trade mark registration is a legitimate means by which to protect merchandising objects; on the other there are valid reasons to suggest that merchandising objects are not worthy of protection, and their creators of the ensuing exclusivity of exploitation. Either way, the law must abandon its ambivalence to the practice.

Proponents of product branding as a key aspect of modern marketing tend to advance the twin arguments that the branding process (centred on legally protected trade marks) promotes a stable purchasing environment and facilitates competition. In favour of the former it may be suggested, for example, that the consumer feels comfortable with a stable range of identifiable products and the producer is assured a stable flow of custom; in favour of the latter we may cite Link:

> "there is a more active competitive democracy in our trade mark system than in our political democracy. People vote for or against trade marked articles not once a year, but every day. . . . The American people do not have to wait until election day to turn a bad trade mark out of office. They do not have wait for a government anti-trust action to put a trade mark out of business."[215]

By way of a brief economic analysis of trade mark law, the validity of these presumed advantages will now be considered.

[215] H. C. Link, "The Social Significance of Trade Marks" (1948) 38 *TMR* 622, 624.

3

Trade Marks in the Market Economy

INTRODUCTION

It is self-evident that trade marks have a prominent role in the allocation of resources in our society—witness the proliferation of brand names that confronts our every purchasing decision however large or small.[1] Indeed it may be said that the use of trade marks to facilitate such variety is an important distinguishing feature of a modern consumer society based upon the principles of the free market. Since the protection of trade marks is said to be "a piece of legal underpinning to an essential economic process"[2]—the distribution of goods and services from producers to consumers—any discussion of their rationale cannot take place in a legal vacuum. An economic analysis of the effects of trade marks in the market[3] will therefore enable us to address two central issues concerning the public interest in trade mark protection, namely what economically beneficial functions do trade marks perform that justify their protection and whether the protection of trade marks creates monopolies or at the very least promotes monopolistic behaviour.

Although these are two ostensibly separate areas of enquiry, from an economic point of view they are fairly closely intertwined since they both lead eventually to the same two market phenomena, product differentiation and consequent brand loyalty.[4] We shall begin by briefly looking at a crucial feature of the market economy, the preference of competition over monopoly and the consumer choice that this provides. The allegation that protecting trade marks promotes conduct which tends to distort the free market will then be examined.

[1] See Preface, text accompanying n. 2 above.

[2] W. R. Cornish and J. Phillips, "The Economic Function of Trade Marks: an Analysis with Special Reference to Developing Countries" [1982] *IIC* 41, 58.

[3] T. Martino, *Trade Mark Dilution* (Oxford, 1996), 70–2 provides a robust defence, if defence be needed, of applying an economic analysis to legal doctrine.

[4] Moreover the answers, as we shall see, correspond, to a certain extent, to the two broad strands of 20th century economic thought on the subject of trade marks. McClure in his comprehensive survey observed that one was in fact a reaction to the other and that it was therefore necessary to bear their historical background in mind (see also n. 31 below). Having said that, neither approach has been truly vindicated, and both remain useful for the purposes of our discussion. Indeed whilst they can be seen as two sides of the same coin of trade mark protection, they are not diametrically opposed, but rather address the problem from differing positions (a good analogy is one with the contrast between the positivist and natural law approaches to the identification of a valid law. See the famous "Hart–Fuller debate" in the pages of the *Harvard Law Review*: (1958) 71 *Harv. LR* 593, 630). The content of the two schools of thought will become clear in due course, below. See D. M. McClure, "Trade Marks and Unfair Competition: A Critical History of Legal Thought" (1979) 69 *TMR* 305, 309–10, 346, 353.

After all, given that the legal protection of trade marks does allow exclusive rights of a quasi-proprietary nature, it is understandable that an intuitive response to such protection is that it may encourage or indeed facilitate monopolistic behaviour. In contrast it is also argued that such exclusive rights in trade marks are justified by the information symbolised through their use. We must therefore examine the extent of these perceived benefits. Finally, the chapter will attempt in conclusion to reconcile the two conflicting views which emerge.

SOME PRINCIPLES OF THE MARKET ECONOMY: THE IMPORTANCE OF COMPETITION AND INFORMED CONSUMER CHOICE

Competition of one form or another is a cornerstone of the modern consumer society; it is seen every day in the market place struggle for our custom as consumers of goods and services, but why has it become such an entrenched and almost revered feature of our economic landscape? The answer lies with neo-classical economic theory which holds that social welfare will be maximised in the presence of perfect competition.[5] This basically means that resources will be allocated efficiently between different goods and services in the precise quantities consumers wish (as expressed through the price they are prepared to pay in the market), and that the goods and services will be produced at the lowest possible cost so that as little of society's wealth as is necessary is expended in their production.[6] Perfect competition is thought to require a large number of fully informed buyers dealing with a large number of sellers in interchangeable commodities in a market to which there are no barriers to entry or exit. However the existence of such a market in practice is unlikely, if not impossible,[7] and so represents an unattainable, theoretical ideal[8]: a standard against which the tendency towards economic efficiency of any conduct may be assessed.[9] On the other hand where one seller has control over the entire supply of a particular product, monopoly is said to exist. He gains a degree of market power and is able to influence price adversely and cause other undesirable effects, such as the sub-optimal allocation of resources, a reduction in consumer satisfaction, a

[5] R. Whish, *Competition Law* (3rd edn., London, 1993), 1. This account is, of course, only a bare outline of how markets are perceived to function, but will suffice to provide a context for our discussion with specific respect to trade marks. See also generally R. G. Lipsey, *An Introduction to Positive Economics* (7th edn., London, 1989), R. A. Posner, *Economic Analysis of Law* (4th edn., Boston, Mass., 1992); and F. M. Scherer and D. Ross, *Industrial Market Structure and Economic Performance* (3rd edn., Boston, Mass., 1990).

[6] *Ibid.*, 1–2.

[7] See also S. A. Diamond, "The Public Interest and the Trade Mark System" (1980) 62 *J Patent Office Society* 528, 536.

[8] Whish, n. 5 above, 2–3.

[9] It may however be legitimately asked whether perfect competition itself is manifestly beneficial, and indeed examples are cited of the useful effects of insulation from competition: collaboration in the pursuit of technological advance, economies of scale reaped by larger producers, ability to internalise social costs such as those of preventing pollution and incentives in the law of intellectual property to create and innovate (*ibid.*, 6–9).

lowered incentive to innovate and an unfair and discriminatory distribution of wealth.[10] Consequently the power of monopoly, although it is equally unlikely in its perfect state, is generally seen as socially reprehensible whereas the benefits which flow from a competitive market, productive efficiency and consumer choice make it worthy of preservation.[11] Moreover it is thought to be superior in its ability to achieve these ends to purely monopolistic and even governmentally regimented economies.[12] Indeed the observation made by the American federal judge and Legal Realist writer Jerome Frank that

> "There is a basic public policy, deep-rooted in our economy and respected by the courts, resting on the assumption that social welfare is best advanced by free competition."[13]

arguably applies with equal force to our own economy.[14] This conclusion is sufficient then to explain for our purposes why tendencies towards competition in the market ought to be encouraged and any towards monopoly be suppressed; the debate over what represents a satisfactory compromise must be left to the economists.[15]

Trade marks are interesting from an economic perspective because they exemplify, and are even partially responsible for, the clash between economic theory and commercial reality, a reality which can be seen to lie midway between the two extremes of perfect competition and perfect monopoly.[16] As we have already observed, perfect competition is thought to require trade in fungible commodities, where consumers' decisions are based solely on price. If this is so, then trade marks, for example, would be superfluous, since any indications that they make relating to factors such as source and quality would be irrelevant to the consumer's decision.[17] However trading conditions since the last century, which, as discussed in Chapter 2, witnessed the advent of branding and the acceptance of trade marks as legally protectable assets, have determined otherwise. Products therefore cease to be perfect substitutes, and such a process could be seen as effectively manipulating a product's value in differing ways to both consumers and producers.[18] We shall turn shortly to its implications.

Finally, another significant feature of modern consumer society is the variety of products available both (by definition) as a resulting benefit of competition

[10] *Ibid.*, 3–4.

[11] *Ibid.*, 10–11.

[12] L. H. Johnston, "Drifting Towards Trade Mark Rights in Gross" (1995) 85 *TMR* 19.

[13] *Eastern Wine Corp.* v. *Winslow-Warren Ltd.* (1943) 57 *USPQ* 433, 435–6.

[14] It is probably most accurate to describe our economy as a regulated free market economy since a true free market involves no state intervention at all, and consequently no protection for intellectual property such as trade marks; it is mid-way between true *laissez-faire* and complete state regulation (Johnston, n. 12 above, 20).

[15] See discussion of the theories of "workable competition" and "contestable markets" in Whish, n. 5 above, 10–12.

[16] *Ibid.*, 4.

[17] Diamond, n. 7 above, 535. A market for any given product may see one producer with a "natural" monopoly, oligopoly or indeed wide-scale competition approaching the classical model.

[18] *The Economist*, "The Year of the Brand", 24 Dec. 1988, 101.

and because this variety is demanded by consumers. Whilst economic theory is premised on such variety and the exercise of consumer choice, in that model, choice is affected by one factor only, price. Consumers are presumed to be immediately aware of any variations in this factor and to react accordingly.[19] In contrast contemporary consumers are concerned with a far greater range of additional factors, namely the geographical availability of the product, its physical attributes, the quality of the service offered by the manufacturer and its distributors and even the subjective image of the product which consumers have in their minds.[20] However, given the organisation of the modern market place with its centralised manufacturing structure and complex chain of distribution, they do not necessarily have either the time or the means to establish a full body of information upon which to base their jealously guarded choice. Trade marks must arguably play a role in this context by facilitating easier recognition of the multitude of product differences upon which competition is based. The paradox[21] is that in spite of facilitating this evidently useful dimension of consumer choice, some people seek to demonstrate that the legal protection of trade marks does quite the opposite by suppressing consumer freedom.

IS IT ANTI-COMPETITIVE LEGALLY TO PROTECT TRADE MARKS?

A charge which is frequently levelled at trade marks is that they create unfair monopolies, or at the very least promote monopolistic behaviour. The very fact that they confer exclusive rights, it is said, must be bad for competition. Given the undesirable effects of monopoly power and the opprobrium that it attracts, care must be taken in using such emotive language, and it is important to establish what is meant by a "monopoly".[22] In the legal sense, it generally means the *right to exclude* others from the use of a particular resource, for example an area of land, an invention that forms the subject-matter of a patent or, in this case, the ability to use a particular symbol as a trade mark.[23] Frequently it is in this

[19] See Posner, n. 5 above, 4–5.

[20] Scherer and Ross, n. 5 above, 571.

[21] Posner, n. 5 above, 370.

[22] University of Chicago Law Review, Comment, "The Anti-Competitive Aspects of Trade Name Protection and the Policy Against Consumer Deception" (1962) 29 *U Chicago LR* 371, 376.

[23] See W. M. Landes and R. A. Posner, "Trade Mark Law: An Economic Perspective" [1987] *J Law & Econ.* 265, 266–8, and P. A. Gorringe, "Trade Marks: An Economic Perspective", Oct. 1988 *Trade Mark World* 28, 28–9, for analyses of the costs surrounding the grant of property rights (which in an economic context are tantamount to monopolies), and in particular trade mark rights, for example the cost of defining the right through registration and litigation. Notice also measures taken in the law of trade marks to minimise rent-seeking by not protecting common descriptive terms and imposing a use requirement to prevent warehousing of marks. Such behaviour would otherwise increase the cost to others of naming products. It is possible to undertake a strict cost-benefit analysis of the law of trade marks by balancing such costs of state intervention to protect trade marks in the market against the benefits this would bring (see Gorringe, "Trade Marks: An Economic Perspective", Oct. 1988, *Trade Mark World* 28, 28–9), but we are presently more concerned with the market *effects* of trade marks, whilst taking the efficiency of protection for

way used to refer to the fact that the law will recognise exclusive rights to regulate the use of a trade mark under certain circumstances. However the term would seem often to be used in a somewhat indiscriminate manner by English judges[24] who appear to think, it is submitted, that recognition of trade mark rights will restrict the use of the *word* itself (rather than its use as a trade mark) in all circumstances.[25] Moreover there is a danger of what has been termed "monopoly phobia",[26] a fundamental misunderstanding[27] of the trade mark right which gives rise to the belief that, because trade marks can be said to be a limited monopoly in the legal sense, protection will lead naturally and inevitably to monopoly in the economic sense of market condition already mentioned above.[28]

In this case, it is alleged that trade marks, when legally protected, could be used as *instruments* of monopoly so as to give the proprietor an element of

granted. Finally, note that trade marks are unusual compared to other resources to which rights of proprietary nature attach, in that there is an almost infinite number of possible marks and the costs of devising them are low. Consequently protection involves attributing an artificial scarcity to them (see W P Kratzke, "Normative Economic Analysis of Trade Mark Law" (1991) 21 *Memphis State ULR* 199, 203) but again this is unimportant for our purposes since we are more interested in trade marks as an instrument of resource allocation than as a resource in its own right.

24 The law reports are replete with *dicta* which groundlessly denounce trade marks as monopolies, for example: "it should not be right to allow the respondents to *monopolise* . . . the name of an important city"; "traders could not obtain a *monopoly* in the use of such words"" YORK *Trade Mark* [1982] 1 WLR 195, 197, 199; "this is another attempt to expand on the boundaries of intellectual property and to convert a protective law into a source of *monopoly*"; "[t]his raises the spectre of a total and perpetual *monopoly* in containers and articles"; "[a] colour combination may tend to an undesirable *monopoly* in colours": *Re* COCA-COLA *Trade Marks* [1986] 2 All ER 274, 275–7, final quotation referring to *Smith Kline and French Laboratories Ltd.* v. *Sterling-Winthrop Group Ltd.* [1976] RPC 511; "our Act would be creating a new type of *monopoly* . . . in the trade mark itself. Such a *monopoly* could be likened to a quasi-copyright in the mark": *Wagamama Ltd.* v. *City Centre Restaurants plc* [1995] FSR 713, 731. Are judges certain what they mean when they invoke such an epithet? The fact is that no English intellectual property judge has ever formally addressed the economic implications of protecting trade marks.

25 This could not be further from the truth: see Diamond, n. 7 above, 534.

26 See B. W. Pattishall, "Trade Marks and the Monopoly Phobia" (1952) 50 *Michigan LR* 967.

27 Pattishall, a stout defender of trade mark rights, puts forward several reasons why this should be so. He cites the all-embracing "rush to destroy monopolies and promote free competition, [in which] the means and basis for competition [are] destroyed too", that is to say, anything that bore the mark of exclusivity was suppressed as anathema to business morality (970, 972. See also McClure's comments at n. 31 below). He also draws attention to the fact that the rationales of trade marks and other, intentionally monopolistic intellectual property rights became confused (970, 983): trade marks do not exist to provide any form of incentive to create new words (See Landes and Posner, n. 23 above, 271–3, who address the economics of language in this context) but instead are entirely creatures of commerce, arising through necessity, and are protected as such. He gives the analogy (drawing on his thesis that trade marks exist to facilitate a system of identity) with a person's name and signature, arguing that personal identity is protected against forgery and defamation, yet this does not draw allegations of monopoly nor does it restrict anyone's use of language (984–5). See also discussion of the problems resulting from the imprecise use of the idea of monopoly in University of Chicago Law Review, Comment, n. 22 above, as well as discussion of the rationale of the trade mark right in Ch. 4 below.

28 Compare this with patents which are universally acknowledged to be legal monopolies conferred with the intent of creating economic monopolies of finite duration for their owner. Trade marks can therefore be seen to be suffering from "guilt by association" with the other forms of intellectual property (Diamond, n. 7 above, 532).

market power of the type described above[29] through simply using and defending the trade mark. What we must now address is whether this is in fact true, and furthermore whether all trade marks are *inherently* conducive to monopoly, so leading to the conclusion that all trade mark doctrine must be condemned as anti-competitive; or whether only certain trade marks can engender *factual* monopoly, in the sense of brand strength, through their interaction with extraneous factors, in which case it is arguable that it is a matter for competition law and not a defect of legal trade mark protection at all.[30]

The Attack Outlined

Superficially there would not seem to be any objection at all to the protection of trade marks in a competitive economy.[31] The only aspect of a product that another producer cannot copy in order to compete is the trade mark. Otherwise he is free, subject to any other intellectual property protection, to replicate any, and indeed all, remaining aspects of the original and as a result the products would be, with the exception of their trade marks, perfect substitutes.[32] This restriction seems to be a negligible impediment to competition, and indeed because the mark will highlight the fact that two separate organisations were responsible for the products, it could arguably be said to enhance competition.[33] Furthermore advertising of the two brands will alert consumers to the availability of the products in the market and so facilitate the consumers' informed choice. However, if the trade mark was caused to have some significance to the consumer beyond purely indicating the product's source, then matters may be different.

In his attempt to establish a synthesis between the theories of competition and monopoly, neither of which realistically describe economic life, E. H.

[29] Text accompanying n. 10 above.

[30] See University of Chicago Law Review, Comment, n. 22 above, 380 and references cited therein.

[31] The hostile view of the economic consequences flowing from the legal protection of trade marks stems mainly from E. H. Chamberlin's work, *The Theory of Monopolistic Competition* (8th edn., Cambridge, Mass., 1962) and is generally referred to as the Harvard School. See also R. S. Brown, "Advertising and the Public Interest: Legal Protection of Trade Symbols" (1948) 57 *Yale LJ* 1165; A. G. Papandreou, "The Economic Effects of Trade Marks" (1956) 44 *California LR* 503; and S. Timberg, "Trade Marks, Monopoly and the Restraint of Competition" (1949) 14 *Law & Contemporary Problems* 323. This view was particularly prevalent during the middle of the century in America. It has been suggested that this was in keeping with a general mobilisation (in reaction to a previous permissiveness which initially accompanied the rise of modern industry) at that time against any concentration of economic power (McClure, n. 4 above, 316).

[32] See McClure, n. 4 above, 307; N. S. Economides, "The Economics of Trade Marks" (1988) 78 *TMR* 523, 532. This principle was recently re-affirmed in *Hodgkinson & Corby Ltd.* v. *Wards Mobility Services Ltd.* [1995] FSR 169. See in particular the comments of Jacob J. at 174–7.

[33] As Chamberlin and Brown, two of the main adherents of the Harvard School, are both forced to admit. Brown however is emphatic that such competition has no economic utility; it is not of a type contemplated by the classical model of perfect competition (Chamberlin, n. 31 above. ch.4; Brown n. 31 above, 1173).

Chamberlin[34] identified two market phenomena which he saw as tending to depart from the classical model of perfect competition. One of these was product differentiation,[35] the inevitable result of branding. He saw such a process as having a tendency towards monopoly, because any factor which distinguishes a product from competitive substitutes in the market removes the product from the rigours of direct competition (although it is still subject to the indirect competition of "more or less imperfect substitutes").[36] Put another way, if the product becomes in some way unique, then the producer, by definition, controls the entire supply, allowing him (rather than the action of the market) to determine price. Trade marks are a prime mover in the process of product differentiation because legal protection prevents the exact imitation of a particular product, so immediately conferring an element of uniqueness.[37] He apparently seeks to argue that by simply attaching without more the trade marks to their products, producers gain such market power that it justifies removing all trade mark protection:

> "The protection of trade marks from infringement and of businessmen generally from the imitation of their products . . . is the production of monopoly. . . . To permit such infringements would be to purify competition by eliminating monopoly elements. . . . For if the goods were perfectly standardised, buyers would have no basis for discrimination; one producer could secure no larger volume of sales than another and hence no larger profits. They are due to the dissimilarity, not the similarity of the goods, hence to the monopolistic, not to the competitive elements."[38]

Chamberlin therefore concludes that all trade marks are inherently conducive to economic monopoly.[39]

In spite of the extreme character of Chamberlin's thesis, it nevertheless played on fears of an exclusive legal right which had previously been viewed fairly benignly and spawned a school of thought arguing that successful differentiation of a product (which of course cannot be guaranteed[40]), especially through promotion of its trade mark by advertising, could have anti-competitive consequences. These consequences were that producers gain the ability to insulate their market shares from price competition, demand a premium for the differentiated products and cause barriers to entry into the market for the products in question.[41]

[34] See in particular Chamberlin, n. 31 above, chs.1 and 4 as well as Appendix E.

[35] The other being the fact that markets tend to have far fewer sellers than buyers (Chamberlin, n. 31 above, 8–9).

[36] *Ibid.*, 59, 62.

[37] McClure, n. 4 above, 330–1.

[38] See Chamberlin, n. 31 above, Appendix E, 270–1.

[39] He then proceeds to seek a policy-based justification for this monopoly, presuming that trade mark protection has the same economic effect as that of patents, that is to say trade marks are intended to create a justifiable economic monopoly (*ibid.*, 272–4).

[40] See Brown, n. 31 above, 1174, where it is observed that where demand for a product is in decline, no amount of advertising may remedy this. Note also the varying propensities of products towards differentiation.

[41] McClure, n. 4 above, 345.

Trade Marks and Advertising

Naturally attention focused on the relationship between trade marks and brand advertising, the primary context in which they can achieve economic significance. The connection between the two is quite clear: if advertising is to be effective, there must be a convenient link between the advertising and the product which it is promoting. This is provided by the product's trade mark. It is interesting, and indeed significant, that when unfairly competitive practices are alleged, it is generally the trade mark which is simply infringed rather than the related advertising being copied.[42] Indeed it can even be said that trade marks are a species of advertising in that they "both share three fundamental characteristics: brevity, continuity of use and control".[43]

The question still remains as to what is anti-competitive about the promotion of legally-protected trade marks in the mass media. Obviously advertising, in a commercial context, exists to sell the product being advertised[44]; this seems a quite legitimate aim in a society where producers and consumers are separated through a complex chain of distribution—there seem to be few other ways in which the existence of products could be effectively communicated. However, an important distinction,[45] generally accepted by economists, is made between advertising that provides information on the prices, quality and availability of products[46]—objective facts needed to perfect competition by ensuring that consumers are fully informed and advertising that merely seeks to create or re-enforce consumers' preferences towards particular brands[47]—preferences which consumers should arguably be free to form independently through their experience of the products concerned. A case may be made that such persuasive advertising is wasteful in itself of resources which could be better employed, for example in improving product quality, because "it does not increase total demand; it only increases wants. Effective demand arises, not from what we would like to have, but from the purchasing power of the community created by its productive power. We consume what we produce and no more."[48] More importantly, it is condemned for being the means by which consumers are persuaded that there are differences about the product in question that make it worthy of their preference. This is usually by associating the trade mark with spurious images or purely perceived advantages; influential factors which are presumed not to be conducive to economic efficiency because they encourage

[42] Brown, n. 31 above, 1185. However, compare this with the facts in *Cadbury-Schweppes Pty. Ltd.* v. *Pub Squash Co. Pty. Ltd.* [1981] RPC 429 where the defendant allegedly did just this.

[43] T. Martino and W. Ullah, "The Quality Guarantee Function of Trade Marks: An Economic Viewpoint" [1989] *EIPR* 267 (footnotes omitted).

[44] In a wider sense, advertising arguably exists to attempt to influence people's behaviour (*ibid.*).

[45] Brown, n. 31 above, 1168.

[46] N. Parr and M. Hughes, "The Relevance of Consumer Brands and Advertising in Competition Enquiries" [1993] *European Competition LR* 157, 158.

[47] *Ibid.*

[48] Brown, n. 31 above, 1169.

purchasing decisions to be made on irrational grounds. Rational grounds are presumed to be those supplied by informative advertising.

Brown gives the example of cigarettes,[49] and although the data are drawn from 1940s America, it is still useful for illustrative purposes. During this period, the (so-called) "Big Three" cigarette manufacturers were able to command a three cent premium over unadvertised competitors whose products cost on average ten cents. Their advertising was said to cost one cent per pack, and the higher quality tobacco used another half a cent, with the result that an extra one and a half cents in cost brought in three cents in revenues. Furthermore, blindfold tests demonstrated that smokers had difficulty in distinguishing brands, even as between the standard and premium brands. On this basis, Brown argues that even though the product differences are apparently spurious, if consumers believe that there is a difference and are willing to pay to satisfy the preference for the product advertised, then the producers have established their degree of market control. The trade mark is implicated in all this because it is the conduit for the advertising's persuasive powers. It identifies the body of images with the product and so serves as the instrument by which monopoly power is gained.[50]

In being persuaded that their loyalty must lie with one particular brand, consumers are bombarded with untested, and possibly untestable, information from rival undertakings. This is thought to inhibit rational purchasing decisions because the consumer is not provided with the information he needs to assess effectively the value to him of the product in question.[51] Instead, he is confronted by "appeals to sex, fear, emulation and patriotism regardless of the relevance of those drives to the transaction at hand", by the "endless reiteration of the advertisers' imperative" and by the "bewildering manipulation of comparatives and superlatives".[52] Furthermore, it may be argued that there is no choice at all between products, since choice is founded on an adequate presentation of alternatives; a choice between one illusion and another is by no means adequate.[53]

Aggressive promotion of a trade mark in order to increase or maintain market share not only affects the relationship between producers and consumers. As we have already observed, the only restriction on another producer wishing to market a competitive substitute for a trade marked product is his inability to copy the original trade mark and any features covered by any other intellectual property rights; moreover, he is quite entitled to use his own trade mark, thereby mitigating any unfair advantage that may have accrued to the senior user. Such a restriction, however, is greatly exacerbated by the presence of a body of perceived values created through advertising and attaching to a product through its trade mark, and this can potentially form a barrier to entry into the

[49] *Ibid.*, 1172.
[50] *Ibid.*, 1187.
[51] *Ibid.*, 1182–3.
[52] *Ibid.*, 1182.
[53] *Ibid.*, 1183.

market against another producer wishing to compete.[54] This barrier is a pecuniary one due to the advertising outlay which the competitor must incur to overcome the image of the first producer and alert consumers to the availability of a substitute. Its actual size depends first on whether the scale of the operation is so high that capital is difficult to raise in order to support it, and secondly on whether promotional expense over and above that of competitors is necessary. Even if such a barrier could be overcome consumer welfare would be reduced, in that high costs would be passed on to consumers with no accompanying benefit other than the substitution of one set of ephemeral values with another.[55]

On reflection, it seems natural that producers should want to gain a degree of market advantage that allows them to set their own pricing policy, to take control of their own destiny, rather than be thrown at the mercy of the whims of an impersonal market.[56] After all, the corporations which produce the bulk of goods on the market exist to maximise profits for shareholders, not to satisfy sterile economic theory. Profits will be maximised when all consumers choose to satisfy their needs with the particular producer's goods or services, and this is arguably the goal of free enterprise. However it is clear that the Harvard School's contention is that the quest to attain this goal by promotion of a product's trade mark will tend to distort the resource allocation process in an unacceptable manner. In order to assess the legitimacy of this profit maximisation tactic, we must examine the substance of the attack on trade marks. Commercial success should only be penalised if it has been achieved by illegitimate means.

To What Extent Are These Real Fears?

At a very simple level, trade marks are condemned as instruments of monopoly because, by their very nature, they render a product unique and so place its producer in a position to control the entire supply of the product. However, as Chamberlin himself observes, "[a] monopoly of LUCKY STRIKES does not constitute a monopoly of cigarettes"[57]; the producer may have a monopoly of the trade marked product but certainly does not have one of competitive substitutes. Even though a monopoly in a narrow, technical sense is present, it is difficult to envisage how the responsible trade mark could be economically damaging on its own when it merely distinguishes the product from competitive

[54] See Cornish and Phillips, n. 2 above, 53–4.

[55] *Ibid.*, 54.

[56] Brown, n. 31 above, 1171. The discussion in the first section of Prof. Brown's article centres around whether persuasive advertising is economically effective enough, notwithstanding any monopolistic aspects, to justify it as an incentive to investment for producers. He concludes that with limited exceptions it is merely "a luxurious exercise in talking ourselves into spending our incomes" (*ibid.*, 1183) and so seeks to attack any form of trade mark protection that may encourage or facilitate persuasive advertising: the dilution doctrine.

[57] Chamberlin, n. 31 above, 65.

substitutes. If is not possible to show that this monopolistic aspect of trade marks has any tendency to cause disruption to the resource allocation process, there is no basis to this case for attacking trade marks.

More credible are the attacks on the promotion by brand advertising of trade marks since they do not seek to remove the protection given to all trade marks. It is quite possible to imagine, although it is unlikely, that trade marked products may be sold without any supporting advertising. If this were the case, the only and rather unreal basis for condemning the protection of such trade marks is that they render the products concerned unique. What if advertising were to be used, but merely to indicate the availability and cost of the products? The answer would arguably be the same. If anything is objectionable, it is the use of trade marks in advertising to differentiate the products on bases other than those which are objectively verifiable. The essence of the complaint is therefore the way in which trade marks are used. Before further examining the claims made about the promotional advertising of trade marks, it is clear that it is impossible to condemn the whole of trade mark doctrine on this basis because the factors involved are peculiar to each brand. Even if the claims made are true, an analysis of the market conditions surrounding each brand concerned must be conducted in order to demonstrate that the trade mark is being used in an anti-competitive manner.[58] In other words, it is for competition law rather than trade mark law itself[59] to resolve any specific anti-competitive consequences of protecting trade marks since such protection cannot not said to be inherently defective.

The problem for trade marks is that they are the most convenient way of referring to a product, and as a result are inextricably linked with the "evils" of persuasive advertising. As far as those who seek to attack this form of advertising as anti-competitive are concerned, trade marks are the instrument of persuasion, the consequence of which is that any attack on the propriety of brand advertising will inevitably involve trade marks; in identifying the product in question, they are caught between the informative and persuasive functions of advertising. Supposing that trade marks and the advertising context in which they are used cannot be separated, the principal defence of trade marks is to question the assumptions underlying the criticisms, especially those directed at brand advertising.

The Questionable Reality of the Harvard School's Assumptions

The theme underlying the arguments of almost all those who criticise trade marks for being anti-competitive is that, were it not for the presence of differentiated brands facilitated by trade marks, all markets would consist of a number of firms competing to produce identical products at impersonally

[58] See McClure, n. 4 above, 330–1.
[59] Landes and Posner, n. 23 above, 275.

determined, low prices: a situation approaching the classical model of perfect competition.[60] It is submitted that this is simply untrue, assuming that traders will always seek to gain some form of competitive advantage regardless of the available means with which to do so.[61]

The central objection to trade mark protection is that it facilitates product differentiation. The assumption which appears to be made in this context is that product differentiation has an inherent tendency to distort competition since it departs from the classical model of perfect competition. This ignores market place realities because differentiation between ostensible substitutes is not only (although it undoubtedly is) a manifestation of producers' desire to escape from direct competition by marketing a product slightly different from their competitors'; it is also a "natural and healthy response to consumer demands".[62] It is indisputable that consumers' preferences are less than homogenous and the value placed on the differing features of functionally identical products varies enormously. One must finally not forget the differing propensities of products towards differentiation: it would be difficult to differentiate fungible commodities such as basic foodstuffs on any objective bases whereas more technologically sophisticated products are self-evidently capable of differentiation in a number all of which could be said to be of considerable utility to consumers. Consequently, any attempts to condemn trade marks for *generally* facilitating this process must be seen as futile.[63]

The second implication behind the attack on persuasive advertising is that rational consumers are only interested in the price of the product to be purchased and that any additional factors will cloud the matter; consumers will be "bamboozled"[64] by the inadequate presentation of choice. It may be argued, albeit not conclusively in the absence of empirical proof, that consumers take a much wider range of factors into account when assessing the value to them of a particular product. The fact, for example, that a consumer believes that a product may make him appear more attractive in the eyes of his peers could be at least as important as the price of the product in question. As Brown admits, the consumer is sovereign and "the utility of a good . . . is measured exactly by what people will pay for it".[65] It is not clear why it is any less rational to be motivated by non-pecuniary considerations rather than pecuniary ones, other than to consider the thought that by purchasing something because of the image it conveys to others, a consumer returns "to the satisfaction level they would have maintained without the persuasive assault on their preference structures".[66] In any event, purchasing decisions solely on the ground of price

[60] Cornish and Phillips, n. 2 above, 53.

[61] See Brown, n. 31 above, 1171.

[62] Scherer and Ross, n. 5 above, 571.

[63] And indeed, as we shall see below, the function trade marks perform in identifying the differing features of product is seen as the main *benefit* of trade mark protection.

[64] Landes and Posner, n. 23 above, 274.

[65] Brown, n. 31 above, 1180–1. See also Kratzke, n. 23 above, 212–3.

[66] Scherer and Ross, n. 5 above, 580.

seem as unlikely in reality as the random pairing of large numbers of sellers with buyers.[67]

Those who seek to attack advertising of trade marked products appear to aspire to the classical model of perfect competition and the perceived benefits of such a state even though it is entirely divorced from reality. For this reason their arguments warning of the anti-competitive nature of protecting trade marks are less than convincing. However, it is not possible to dismiss entirely their arguments because of the uncertainty behind the motives for consumer purchasing decisions and the close inter-relationship between informative and persuasive advertising.

Remaining Doubts: Brand Loyalty and Barriers to Entry

Since the advertising of a (trade marked) product may simultaneously be informative and persuasive in varying proportions, it may equally well perfect competition by enhancing consumers' objective knowledge about a product but also increase monopoly power by encouraging consumer preferences, rational or otherwise.[68] There is no consensus yet as to how these two aspects act against each other,[69] and in particular doubts still remain as to the legitimacy of image differentiation so, to this extent, objections to the role of trade marks could remain valid.

The problem here is not that a product is differentiated or that there is a risk that the consumer's purchasing decision may occur with respect to a factor other than price, but rather that the producer is actually able to command a premium for the trade marked product. Classic examples from the American market include CLOROX bleach, BAYER ASPIRIN and REALEMON lemon juice.[70] These are apparently standard products whose retail prices, it has been shown,[71] are consistently higher than the unbranded, generic substitute; they are also extreme examples of the branding process. The difficulty, when one seeks to condemn persuasive advertising, is in showing the link between brand advertising and a premium price; for example, Scherer and Ross comment that "it is questionable whether a superior image can be created simply by advertising vigorously".[72] The point is that even if the strength of a brand did confer a degree of market power, this may be the result of perfectly legitimate factors such as market-leading quality or convenient availability. Critics of branding see the premium price as simply producers extracting monopoly rents, but it is also possible to

[67] Brown, n. 31 above, 1180, n. 63.

[68] See generally Scherer and Ross, n.5 above, ch.16; Economides, n. 32 above, 532–7; Cornish and Phillips, n. 2 above, 53–4; Parr and Hughes, n. 46 above.

[69] Scherer and Ross, n. 5 above, 581.

[70] In America, ASPIRIN is a trade mark rather than a generic name and, unbelievably, "REALEMON" is also a registered trade mark.

[71] See Scherer and Ross, n. 5 above, 581–2, who also give an interesting discussion (582–4) of the mechanics of how a premium brand image arises.

[72] *Ibid.*, 584.

characterise it as a willingness on the part of consumers to pay for the *assurance* of consistent quality and return on the producer's investment in ensuring a high quality product,[73] indeed Landes and Posner go so far as to state that "the hostile view of brand advertising has been largely . . . rejected by economists".[74] Although the widely differing nature of products and potential grounds for differentiation make it impossible to generalise, here is at least a risk of the brand being used in an anti-competitive manner. The remaining objection to legally protected trade marks is that they create barriers to entry into the market for the product concerned. This is linked to the previous situation, in that it is brand loyalty stimulated *through* advertising of the trade mark which is alleged to cause the entry barrier.[75] Again, it is impossible to draw any unambiguous conclusions because of the widely varying grounds upon which products may be differentiated in the first place. The matter will depend on factors governing the context of how the trade mark is used.[76]

In spite of these dire warnings, we may conclude upon the fact that there has never been an English[77] or successful American[78] competition enquiry into the market strength of a trade mark in itself. Rather, any investigation into brand strength and consequent anti-competitiveness has centred around such factors as brand awareness, demand, quality differences, consumer willingness to switch brands and launch costs[79]; factors not directly connected with the promotion of a trade mark or brand name.[80] All this seems to support the initial assertion that trade marks are somewhat "caught in the crossfire" of the controversy surrounding producers' product and promotional policies; they have suffered from the manner in which they have been used, and it is therefore right that arguments condemning the role of trade marks in the market place "have gained no foothold at all in trade mark law, *as distinct from (competition) law*".[81]

[73] J. B. Swann and T. H. Davis, "Dilution, an Idea Whose Time has Gone; Brand Equity as Protectable Property, the New/Old Paradigm" (1994) 84 *TMR* 267, 272 citing C. Shapiro, "Premiums for High Quality Products as Returns to Reputations" (1983) 98 *QJE* 659.

[74] N. 23 above, 275.

[75] See Economides, n. 32 above, 535–7.

[76] See Scherer and Ross, n. 4 above, 598–600 in particular with respect to image differentiation.

[77] R. E. Annand and H. E. Norman, *Blackstone's Guide to the Trade Marks Act 1994* (London, 1994), 12.

[78] McClure, n. 4 above, 348. Notice however the examples given by Diamond (n. 7 above, 537–40) where there was "evidence of the use of the trade mark *as part* of a monopolistic scheme" (emphasis added). The real concern for a time in U.S. competition law was that compulsory licensing of trade marks would be ordered which would, of course, strike to the heart of the purpose of trade mark protection (see the *Re Borden Inc (REALEMON)* case (1978) 92 FTC 669).

[79] Parr and Hughes, n. 46 above, 160–2.

[80] This point seems to be supported by European competition cases such as *Warner Lambert & BIC SA* v. *Gillette & Eemland* [1993] 5 CMLR 559.

[81] Landes and Posner, n. 23 above, 274–5 (emphasis supplied). Compare this with the *Magill* case (Case T–69/89 *RTE* v. *Commission, Magill intervening* [1995] FSR 530) where the anti-competitive use of copyright subsisting in television listings was remedied by the actual removal of the intellectual property protection.

THE ECONOMIC BENEFITS OF TRADE MARK PROTECTION

Even if one accepts as unavoidable the fact that almost all competing products available in our society are differentiated to some degree,[82] and indeed that such differentiation is a healthy feature of a regulated free market economy,[83] the utility of legally protecting trade marks must still be addressed. As Posner points out, "a theory [in this case, that trade mark protection encourages anti-competitive behaviour] . . . is overturned not by pointing out its defects or limitations but by proposing a more inclusive, more powerful, above all more useful theory".[84] With this in mind, we turn to a second school of thought that sees the protection of trade marks, and the role that this enables them to perform between producers and consumers, as essentially beneficial to the functioning of the free market economy.[85]

Trade Marks as a Source of Information

It is undisputed that for any market to function properly, with the result that resources are allocated optimally within society, consumers must be fully informed so that they may make purchasing decisions in accordance with their preferences. That is to say, they must be aware of all the products (be they goods or services) available to fulfil their needs, and they must further be aware of the various qualities of the competing products so that they may decide which one best satisfies a particular need (after all, only the consumer himself can decide the utility of a particular product and so the price he is willing to pay). Given also the extent of product differentiation and the varying dimensions in which it inevitably occurs, the choice may well be between competing products that differ in the degree to which they may be substitutes for one another. It is further undisputed that, because the organisation of modern commerce is so complex, it can be difficult to obtain the requisite information firsthand and

[82] Whish, n. 5 above, 4–5.

[83] Scherer and Ross, n. 5 above, 571.

[84] Posner, n. 5 above, 26.

[85] This body of opinion has been characterised as the Chicago school of economic analysis in contradistinction to the restrictionist Harvard school (McClure, n. 4 above, 346). The most prominent contemporary proponents of this view are William Landes and Richard Posner. See generally Landes and Posner, n. 23 above, as well as L. Akazaki, "Source Theory and Guarantee Theory in Anglo-American Trade Mark Policy: A Critical Legal Study" (1990) 72 *J Patent & Trademark Office Society* 255; Cornish and Phillips, n. 2 above, Economides, n.32 above; Gorringe, n. 23 above; Martino and Ullah, n. 43 above; and Scherer and Ross, n. 5 above. Some of the more influential works in the economic literature concerning advertising and the economics of information include the following: Akerlof, "A Market for Lemons" (1970) 85 *Quarterly J Econ.* 448; Nelson, "The Economic Value of Advertising" in Brozen (ed.), *Advertising and Society* (1974); Coase, "Advertising and Free Speech" (1977) 6 *J Law & Society* 1; Nelson, "Advertising as Information" (1979) 82 *J Political Econ.* 729; Klein and Leffler, "The Role of Market Forces in Assuring Contractual Performance" (1981) 89 *J Political Econ.* 615; Shapiro, n. 73 above.

moreover that such difficulty will depend on the nature of the product in question.

The economic significance of trade marks is alleged to derive from the fact that a trade mark identifies the product to which it is attached with a whole body of information concerning the product,[86] in particular the actual description of the product[87] and also the fact that two competing products may be different in some way, although they are ostensibly identical.[88] In order to understand how this takes place, we must first consider how it is possible to categorise goods according to the ease with which their characteristics may be discovered. If the information can be discovered relatively cheaply, for example by physical inspection of the goods, then the goods are termed search goods. Examples of these are furniture or clothing. On the other hand, where the necessary information is only available at high cost, the term credence characteristics is used, for example in the case of the chemical composition of a fragrance. In between these two extremes are found experience goods, so-called because their characteristics are generally discovered through the experience of the consumer, but only in contrast to search goods, after the purchase has been made. These include mechanical goods or pre-packaged food.[89] In any event, it is clear that to a greater or lesser extent, a product will have characteristics which are unobservable by consumers until after the sale and use of the product, but which may nevertheless be crucial in determining the value of the product, so affecting consumers' purchasing decisions. Furthermore the producer will generally have better knowledge of these features than consumers giving rise to a phenomenon known as "information asymmetry".[90]

However, most products will have one especial observable feature: a trade mark.[91] This is thought to encapsulate a body of information concerning the product that is known to the consumer. The information may well have been obtained from a number of sources, in particular through use made of the product by the consumer, word-of-mouth, consumer organisations or through advertising featuring the product.[92] How the trade mark will function depends mainly on the frequency of purchase, the nature of the product's characteristics and the recall ability of consumers. Where the type of product in question is frequently purchased and its characteristics are generally unobservable, the functioning of the trade mark is directly linked to the consumers' previous experience.[93] Economides cites the example of a bottle of COKE.[94] Although the

[86] See Martino and Ullah, n. 43 above, 267.

[87] Landes and Posner, n. 23 above, 268–9; the trade mark is therefore a convenient shorthand for describing the product to which it refers.

[88] Economides, n. 32 above, 526.

[89] Martino and Ullah, n. 43 above, 268.

[90] Economides, n. 32 above, 526; Martino and Ullah, n. 43 above, 268; Cornish and Phillips, n. 2 above, 46–9.

[91] Economides, n. 32 above, 526–7; Martino and Ullah, n. 43 above, 268.

[92] Martino and Ullah, n. 43 above, 267–8.

[93] Economides, n. 32 above, 528.

[94] *Ibid.*

trade mark and information concerning its ingredients are apparent from the label, the determining factor, taste, can only be identified after consumption. However, once it has been sampled, for instance from a free introductory bottle, then the consumer is well placed to make future purchasing decisions based on his experience and with reference to the trade mark. On the other hand, if the product is infrequently purchased, for example an electrical item, then the trade mark assists the purchasing decision more indirectly.[95] The consumer may not have any personal experience of the product under consideration upon which to draw, and so must rely on other sources of information, although these might not be aimed at examining the consumer's exact preferences no matter how objective they be. However, the consumer may have experience of a brand of electrical product so that it will still be possible for the consumer to judge, albeit less exactly, the quality level of the product under consideration by reference to his previous experience. Martino and Ullah give this illustration:

> "[S]uppose that you have . . . owned a BOSCH oven in the past. . . . Instead of investigating the attributes of several ovens, you need only identify that bearing the . . . mark (which satisfied in the past). . . . Simply put, longevity, reliability, cooking speed . . . have been compressed into a word: BOSCH. . . . the mark will [therefore]—though to a lesser extent—signal a certain level of quality drawing from [one's] direct previous experience."[96]

Two conclusions can be drawn from this. First, the trade mark functions as a source of information in *summary* and is not a complete substitute for information in a more analytic form, but rather complements such information.[97] Secondly, for the trade mark to function in this way, it is not essential that consumers are aware of the identity of the producer of the particular brand[98]; far more influential for the purchasing decision are thought to be the actual product characteristics indicated by the trade mark.

In any event, for trade marks to function as a source of information in this way, three factors are presupposed: that consumers are able to recall information from whatever source to a reasonably effective extent; that the law will protect trade marks, such that there is no risk that a certain trade mark will only be perceived as relating to anything other than one particular product or group of connected products; and that features of a certain product will remain consistent between purchases.[99] Only if these conditions are satisfied will the perceived benefits of trade marks accrue to the economy in general.

[95] Economides, n. 32 above, 531.

[96] Martino and Ullah, n. 43 above, 270. However, as Economides points out, since the quality signalled is one step removed from the original experience, there may not be a clear correlation between the two; it all depends on the external factors governing the producer's decision as to what level of quality to apply in the case of the product in question. Having said that, "this is a significant improvement over a situation of no trade marks (and no signals)," (n. 32 above, 531).

[97] Economides, n. 32 above, 527.

[98] Landes and Posner, n. 23 above, 269, n. 9, quoting J. F. Coverdale, "Trade Marks and Generic Words: An Effect on Competition Test" (1984) 51 *U Chicago LR* 868.

[99] Economides, n. 32 above, 528–9.

The Resultant Economic Benefits

If a product did not have a trade mark which associated it with the body of information familiar to consumers concerning the product, then such information would have to be acquired some other way; consumers would generally be unable to identify the product which had previously fulfilled their needs or of which they have become aware, for example by advertising or word of mouth. Rather, given the apparent information asymmetry and complex organisation of trade, the information would have to be acquired by far more expensive and inconvenient methods, such as repeated enquiries in shops and the purchase of unsatisfactory goods. Consequently, the economic benefit of trade marks is said to lie with the fact that they tend to reduce the cost (in both time and resources) to the consumer of obtaining information about product characteristics, especially unobservable ones, and thereby alleviate information asymmetry.[100] In addition, the time taken by retailers dealing with customers' enquiries as to the availability and quality of products is minimised, with the further result that transaction costs are reduced and self-service retailing becomes a possibility. This in turn reduces the wasted opportunity cost of consumers' time.[101]

Of the three factors upon which this perceived benefit is thought to rely, we may safely presume that the average consumer is endowed with a reasonable memory so that he may easily make the association between trade marked goods and the information embodied in the mark. Equally essential is that the trade mark owner must ensure that the qualities of the product bearing the mark remain consistent over the course of time and for all consumers, because if it is to be effective, the trade mark must represent the same information as the consumer expects it to represent; otherwise the consumer must re-incur search costs in establishing which product is most suitable for his needs. Landes and Posner express it thus:

> "[A] trade mark conveys information that allows the consumer to say to himself, 'I need not investigate the attributes of the brand I am about to purchase because the trade mark is a shorthand way of telling me that the attributes are the same as that of the brand I enjoyed earlier'."[102]

This is the so-called self-enforcing feature of trade marks: a trade mark derives its economic as well as capital value from the fact that it denotes consistent quality; the mark will lose its value if variations in quality render the mark deceptive, because consumers will not be able to relate the trade marked product to past experience.[103] It is possible to see the total cost or "full price" of a trade

[100] Landes and Posner, n. 23 above, 269; McClure, n. 4 above, 346–7; Martino and Ullah, n. 43 above, 270; Cornish and Phillips, n. 2 above, 46; Scherer and Ross, n. 5 above, 578; Economides, n. 32 above, 526–7.

[101] Scherer and Ross, n. 5 above, 578.

[102] Landes and Posner, n. 23 above, 269.

[103] *Ibid.*, 270. This is the market incentive for trade mark owners to maintain product quality; the legal incentive is contained in s.46(1)(d) Trade Marks Act 1994 which provides for the revocation of

marked product incurred by the consumer in obtaining the product as consisting of the nominal price actually charged by the producer and the cost to the consumer of gaining information about the product.[104] One may then argue that even if the nominal price of the product is higher because of the producer's investment in maintaining the necessary product quality as well as in promoting and enforcing the trade mark, the full price to the consumer will still be lower because of the reduced search costs.[105] Posner observes that "the investment that a producer makes in his trade mark is like a hostage: it increases the cost to the producer of surreptitiously reducing the quality of the product or otherwise trying to deceive consumers, because when they catch on, the producer may lose his entire investment".[106]

The legal protection of a producer's trade mark is vital to this process, since the cost to a competitor of duplicating a trade mark is minimal compared with the cost of establishing a new brand and the associated trade mark with the reputation that it conveys.[107] If consumers found that the product did not correspond to the expectations engendered by the original trade mark, because another's use of the mark confused them or caused them to lose confidence in the original brand, the legitimate user's investment in such matters as service, quality of materials used and brand advertising would be undermined.[108] Protection is therefore justified because otherwise "free riding [would] eventually destroy the information capital embodied in a trade mark, and the prospect of free riding [could] therefore eliminate the incentive to develop a valuable trade mark in the first place".[109] In addition to enhancing consumer purchasing decisions, and hence reducing search costs, a second economic benefit of legally protecting trade marks becomes apparent; it creates incentives to invest resources in developing strong brands based on the assurance of consistent and desirable quality.[110]

a deceptive trade mark. However, this is arguably less effective than the market mechanism because it requires someone to initiate legal action. Realistically, this is only likely to happen by way of a counter-claim in defence to an infringement action. It is also unclear whether variations as to quality fall within the ambit of this section (see Annand and Norman, n. 77 above, 130–4). Compare this with the situation with respect to assignment and licensing where the law has abdicated all responsibility in this respect: see Ch.2, above: "Dealings in the Trade Mark—Assignment and Licensing".

[104] Landes and Posner have constructed a formal model to illustrate this point. See n.23 above, 275–80.

[105] Posner, n. 5 above, 43–4.

[106] *Ibid.*, 370.

[107] Landes and Posner, n. 23 above, 270.

[108] That is to say the trade mark is infringed both on the bases of confusion and dilution: see Economides, n. 32 above, 528–9.

[109] Landes and Posner, n. 23 above, 270.

[110] See *ibid.* and Economides, n. 32 above, 526. Landes and Posner consider but ultimately dismiss a further potential incentive deriving from the protection of trade marks; the incentive to ensure that there are enough words in the language with which to identify products in the same way that patents perform this role with respect to inventions. The incentive to create distinctive names for products in fact (they conclude) derives from within the market, because of traders' need to distinguish their product from those of competitors, although Landes and Posner do also conclude that a necessary precondition for protection of trade marks is a high availability of alternative descriptive words to those appropriated for trade mark use: see n. 23 above, 271–3.

The Anticipated Consequences of Not Protecting Trade Marks

If, however, no such incentive exists, dire consequences are predicted to result from the continuing information asymmetry. In the absence of any information provided by a trade mark, consumers would be forced to make a choice based only on observable features of a product. As a result they would only by chance pick the product with the desired unobservable features, the features which may otherwise be decisive in establishing the product's value to consumers.[111] This element of chance would greatly reduce the likelihood of the producer gaining a return for his investment in product quality superior to that of his competitors (because there is no means by which consumers may recognise this superior quality[112]), so in turn increasing the temptation to simply conform to the lowest common denominator.[113]

If trade marks were not protected in order that they may signal information about the unobservable features of a product and producers had no incentive to maintain quality, some other form of assurance of product standards would be necessary.[114] Briefly, the following are ways in which this could take place. Consumers, for example, could be empowered to take a more active role in the enforcement of product standards when deceived by producers' presentation of goods by offering them a greater range of private legal remedies.[115] However the problem of unsatisfactory product standards would be community-wide and arguably not an issue for the sole action of individuals. Greater state intervention in the market may therefore be advocated. Consumer protection law has played an increasingly important role in the market place over the course of this century and traditionally has used criminal sanctions against false and misleading trade descriptions.[116] Such methods have tended to complement the trade marking of products, but if the latter was discouraged by the removal of legal protection, a much more generalised intervention would be necessary to lay down standards in almost all conceivable areas of trade. It is doubted that such measures would be as efficient as the current mechanism. Regulatory bodies would have to be established along with the running costs these would entail; these costs are simply not present when a trade mark serves to indicate the standard of a product. Laying down standards would be a "static and reactionary"

[111] Economides, n. 32 above, 526. See also Martino and Ullah, n. 43 above, 269–70.

[112] See Scherer and Ross, n. 5 above, 577–8 for evidence of how this may occur.

[113] An illustration of this is Akerlof's "Market for Lemons" syndrome which is discussed in Economides, n. 32 above, 526, n. 10.

[114] Cornish illustrates the need with the example of Pakistan where, in an effort to combat spurious image differentiation and high prices of pharmaceuticals, trade mark protection was removed without any state control over product quality. The result was grave public distrust of the efficacy and genuineness of the products concerned (W. R. Cornish, *Intellectual Property: Patents, Copyright, Trade Marks and Allied Rights* (3rd edn., London, 1996), para.15–25).

[115] See Posner, n. 5 above, 370 and also generally D. Shanahan, "The Trade Mark Right: Consumer Protection or Monopoly" (1982) 72 *TMR* 233.

[116] Cornish, n. 114 above, para.15–26; University of Chicago Law Review, Comment, n. 22 above, 381.

process, whereas trade marked brands "are subject to rapid change and progress" because of the virtually instantaneous manner in which the effects of consumer purchasing decisions are communicated through the market.[117] Another problem manifests itself when one considers the distinction between variety features of products, characteristics such as appearance or taste which may be the subject of consumer preference and consequent disagreement, as opposed to quality features upon which objective agreement may be reached.[118] Whilst standards may be laid down, for example for the performance of a car, it would be very difficult to establish unanimity with respect to the flavour of a soft drink. This leads us back to the undeniable efficiency of the use legally protected trade marks to facilitate the expression of consumer desires for quality and variety.[119]

Have these Economic Benefits Been Proved?

The supporters of the role that trade marks perform in the economy and the corresponding benefits make a highly sophisticated case based on the flow of information which trade marks are thought to promote. However, two flaws are evident which may prevent it from being completely plausible. First, much is made of the ability of trade marks to reduce consumer search costs with respect to the unobservable features of experience goods; it is difficult to dispute this aspect. It may, though, be asked whether there is any scope for this to occur with respect to search goods. After all, it may be argued, the characteristics of search goods are already, by definition, quite obvious; "they flaunt their differences so self-evidently"[120] that any assistance branding could provide would be quite unnecessary.[121] That is to say, the reduction in search costs would be minimal since merely by inspection, it would be possible to identify the suitability of the product. The reply to this would be that even though there is little actual information to be gained from identifying the trade mark, the consumer is still assured that the trade mark denotes consistent quality. Take for example the product NUROFEN. This is essentially ibuprofen, the properties of which are commonly known, sold under a brand name, yet from my experience, consumers are

[117] H. C. Link, "The Social Significance of Trade Marks" (1948) 38 TMR 622, 626.

[118] Economides, n. 32 above, 525.

[119] The problem is particularly double-edged because as well as being economically inefficient, as will be seen in ch. 4 below, it is also damaging to the private interests of consumers as a discrete social group. The University of Chicago Law Review, Comment, n. 22 above, 381 also outlines the detriment to the consumer interest of schemes which allegedly benefit the economic interest through attacking trade mark protection.

[120] Brown, n. 31 above, 1174. Consequently Kratzke (n. 23 above, 205) argues that encouraging trade mark use (through the grant of protection) in this context is economically wasteful.

[121] This did not deter Safeway from launching their own brand of bananas insisting that "the move would give customers a greater guarantee of quality" (*Daily Telegraph*, "Yes, we have our own bananas", 21 Aug. 1996).

prepared to pay more for it than the generic drug available with equal ease from the same pharmacist. Why is this? Landes and Posner assert that:

> "[The] consumer will not be interested in the formula but in the manufactured product and may therefore be willing to pay a premium for greater assurance that good will actually be manufactured to the specification of the formula."[122]

Unfortunately, this approach falls into the same trap as those who seek to attack the use of trade marks in ostensibly persuasive advertising: presuming the reasons why consumers make purchasing decisions.

The arguments extolling the benefits of the use of legally protected trade marks thus also attempt to predict the workings of the consumer mind, and moreover do so in a further way that is more fundamentally unsatisfactory. It is a keystone of the Chicago school's case that trade marks facilitate recognition of products, the characteristics of which have previously satisfied a particular need of the consumer, thus enabling him to economise on the cost of finding the same product again. Arguably though, all this does is to encourage an automatic or even subconscious action[123]; how is it possible to show that a consumer actually assimilates the information which the trade mark purports to represent? The following quotation from McCarthy is illuminating:

> "Humans have a psychological momentum to continue doing the same thing in the same way as it was done in the past. Buying habits are no exception. There is a comforting security in returning to a product . . . with which one is familiar. Such a purchasing habit depends upon the tenacity of the past's hold upon the future."[124]

Akazaki therefore argues that this product loyalty, such as it is, results in consumer decision making not being "enhanced but abbreviated" because the consumer cannot be seen to make such a reasoned evaluation of factors than he otherwise would have done. Moreover, since effective brand loyalty has been achieved, the incentive to maintain product quality can in fact be *reduced*.[125] Again, without expressing a concluded view, we can at least question the assumptions concerning consumer decision-making which underlie the Chicago hypothesis. A final observation that may be made concerning the Chicago view of legally protected trade marking is that, although it arose as a reaction to those who saw the practice as conducive to market distortions, it never completely

[122] Landes and Posner, n. 23 above, 274–5. Consider also in light of this Safeway's actions with respect to their bananas.

[123] Akazaki, n. 85 above, 260.

[124] J. T. McCarthy, *Trade Marks and Unfair Competition* (2nd edn., Rochester, 1984), quoted in Akazaki, n. 85 above, 260. See also the point made in T. D. Drescher, "The Transformation and Evolution of Trade Marks: from Signals to Symbols to Myths" (1992) 82 *TMR* 301, 325–6, that advertising featuring trade marks has gradually been transformed from "explanation" to "suggestion", that is to say the information associated with the mark has shifted from being "reasoned persuasion", logical, objective facts in favour of its purchase, to consisting of "primarily visual, sensual appeals", presumably to the subconscious of the consumer with the hope of instilling the habit of repeated purchase.

[125] Akazaki, n. 85 above, 260.

refutes the attacks made[126] (and so fails to some extent in its undertaking[127]). Instead the two schools simply "disagree about whether product differentiation is caused by advertising"[128] and rely on differing characterisations of similar phenomenon.

CONCLUSION: THE CONFLICT RE-ASSESSED?

That trade marks play a role in the market economy is beyond question.[129] The subject of debate is an accurate description of the economic effect of this role. Having considered the two issues of whether the protection of trade marks distorts the competitive process and whether such protection in fact produces tangible benefits for the economy as a whole, it can be seen that, although they seek to portray the operation of trade marks in the market place from greatly differing perspectives, and so present two conflicting view points, they are intimately related to the extent that they are both forced to confront the phenomena of product differentiation and brand loyalty. Consequently, it may be possible to reach a partial synthesis that represents the utility of modern trade mark use.

The attack on product differentiation, either through trade mark use or otherwise, is now insupportable. Differentiating products so as to provide a product that consumers are more likely to buy because it has a particular combination of quality and variety features is an inevitable and arguably desirable aspect of modern commerce. Moreover, the presence on the market of a range of products fighting for similar business can tend only to promote competition. Trade marks contribute in two ways to this process: they first can be the basis in themselves by which differentiation takes place; they also bring to the consumer's attention other bases upon which the particular product is differentiated from similar products.[130] For example, a consumer who is contemplating buying a vacuum cleaner may consider models made by HOOVER and ELECTROLUX. The legally protected brand names not only distinguishes the two models, it also highlights any variation in features between the two, thus enabling the consumer to identify the most suitable choice. After all, consumers need information to distinguish between competing alternatives, and anything which enhances the information flow must be beneficial. Consumers do care

[126] See McClure, n. 4 above, 346–7.

[127] See Posner, n. 84 above.

[128] McClure, n. 4 above, 346.

[129] Note that the discussion in this chapter has been restricted to the economic analysis in general terms of trade marks used as brand names. However, economic analysis is also useful in the more specific contexts of dilution doctrine (Brown, n. 31 above, 1187–1200 applying some of the arguments outlined above), protection of a trade mark owner's investment (Kratzke, n. 23 above, 210) as well as trade marks used in a merchandising context (Landes and Posner, n. 23 above, 307–8; P. E. Mims, "Promotional Goods and the Functionality Doctrine: an Economic Model of Trade Marks" (1984) 63 *Texas LR* 639).

[130] Doubts do admittedly remain as to the efficiency of certain bases of differentiation, in particular by reference to image as discussed in Scherer and Ross, n. 5 above, ch.16.

where their products come from and wish to avoid possibly inferior substitutes; trade marks facilitate precisely this. Round one, then, to Chicago and continued trade mark protection; the central premise of the Chicago hypothesis sits far more comfortably with what is observable in the market place than does that of the Harvard school.

The real problem for the theory of trade mark law and market place phenomenon that has so far eluded consensus is the fact that a producer is often able to command a premium for a branded product (where the brand name is protected in its capacity as a trade mark) over the price for an equivalent "generic" product. In essence, adherents to the Harvard school characterise this as nothing less than unwarranted market power gained by duping consumers into buying the product through spurious images established in advertisements; the product is therefore differentiated on a wholly ephemeral basis. On the other hand, the Chicago school will argue that this premium is quite legitimate since consumers are quite content to pay for assurance of consistent quality that the brand name brings.[131] On the face of it, both views appear plausible, but who is right? First of all, the propensity of a product to be differentiated through branding, and so be sold at a premium, depends on the nature of the product itself. It is difficult to imagine a fungible commodity, such as apples or potatoes for example, ever being sold at a price higher than that determined by the market simply because of a brand name.[132] Compare this with the example given above of pharmaceuticals sold "over the counter" as well as sophisticated electronic equipment where a great variation in price may be encountered depending on manufacturer, intended application or whatever. More important, though, is an enigma of the modern consumer society, how consumers actually make purchasing decisions. Since it is accepted in economic theory that the consumer is sovereign, it follows that consumers are the best judges of a particular product's utility to them and, if they are willing to pay the price asked, then so be it regardless of what it is that creates this utility. Another important principle, that of freedom of contract, has meant that consumers are never forced into buying a particular product. However, it may be argued, if consumers do not have an adequate information base upon which to found their purchasing decisions (because of spurious advertised images), freedom of contract counts for nothing. Consider the following examples. The product NUROFEN, as mentioned above, is merely a branded version of the drug ibuprofen, but in spite of this, it retails at a far higher price than the generic equivalent. Is this because of heavy advertising or is it, as users have said to the writer, because they can be confident that NUROFEN will always have the desired, possibly placebo effect? ROLEX watches are known

[131] Therefore a trade mark is a "guarantee" in very loose legal terms of a product's quality as per Schechter's thesis outlined in the previous chapter, but in economic terms, it is cost that consumers must be willing to incur: there's no such thing as a free lunch!

[132] Note however the (possibly anomalous) decision of Case 27/76 *United Brands* v. *Commission* [1978] ECR 207, in particular paras.91–4 where the trade mark CHIQUITA which had been the subject of heavy advertising campaign was consequently held to be a factor leading to a dominant position.

for their hefty price tags, but the motives for paying this price are many: it may be the image associated with owning a ROLEX, it may be for the peerless Swiss craftsmanship or it may even be a family tradition of owning ROLEX watches. Such variations in motive are repeated across the whole market for consumer goods and services. This variety means that, in the absence of generally valid and wide-ranging empirical evidence, it is impossible to determine whether products differentiated by the advertising of trade marked products are detrimental to consumer decision-making. Brand loyalty, such as this is, must therefore be seen as a neutral concept, since there are perfectly innocent reasons why consumers may remain loyal to a particular product. Even presuming that the premium paid for a branded product is an illegitimate profit or monopoly rent unavailable in the absence of product branding, it is worth bearing in mind that "no product market has ever been defined as narrowly as a single brand"[133] and no market power can ever be said to be endless.[134]

It would appear to be the case that "there is a love-hate relationship between trade marks and competition"[135] and moreover between trade marks and some economists' perceptions of economic efficiency. It is clear that a legally protected trade mark cannot realistically be described as a monopoly in the economic sense, but it is possible for a trade mark to be used as an aspect of broader anti-competitive conduct, in particular to create barriers to entry into markets. This, however, will depend on surrounding circumstances rather than anything intrinsic in the nature of a trade mark, and is hence not a true concern within trade mark law. Equally, it is possible to see trade marks as performing an important positive role which could arguably not be successfully reproduced by other means. With this in mind, the best conclusion that can be drawn is that, regardless of the result of any necessarily hypothetical deliberations, there is an acceptance, implicit in the fact producers continue to sell and consumers continue *for whatever motive* to buy branded goods, that the proven advantages reasonably outweigh the disadvantages of legally protected trade marking. Moreover, this conclusion is forced upon us by market place reality: twentieth century commerce has not developed entirely along the classical lines contemplated, for example, by Adam Smith but instead has become essentially characterised by practices such as the use of trade marks and brand advertising. As a result, anyone who seeks to attack trade mark protection must overcome what may be termed the "institutional inertia" inherent in trade marking. By this is meant the facts that, first, trade mark use has long been entrenched in consumers' expectation; secondly, satisfactorily replicating the economic advantages of trade mark use would be difficult, if not impossible; and thirdly, the trade mark has taken on a peculiar nature as a primarily private good—an asset of the producer—but with public functions. For these reasons alone, it is justifiable that we continue to accord legal protection to trade marks; but on what basis?

[133] Swann and Davis, n. 73 above, 272.
[134] Whish, n. 5 above, 5.
[135] Annand and Norman, n. 77 above, 12.

4

The Basis of Protection

INTRODUCTION

The central issue in this chapter is quite uncomplicated: what motivates the legal protection of trade marks and to what extent? So far it has been seen that the law relating to trade symbols is willing to protect trade marks because of the commercial significance which they acquire in relation to particular goods or services, generally through functioning as a brand name (which indicates a product's source, consistent quality or whatever) but sometimes also as a decorative merchandising property. Whether the use of legally protected trade marks in the resource allocation process advances the public interest and benefits society as a whole is uncertain, but institutional inertia seems to shift the benefit of the doubt in favour of accepting that trade mark protection is sufficiently beneficial economically to justify its retention in some form. The *extent* to which this is the case is intimately connected with the interests trade mark protection serves and its perceived purposes. The problem which confronts us is that there is currently no expressly articulated policy guiding English trade mark law. Nowhere in the White Paper[1] which preceded the Trade Marks Act 1994 is there any statement of the purpose of rights conferred by the Act; there seems to exist a blind acceptance of the obligations imposed by the EC Directive and of the belief that trade mark protection must somehow be necessary. Similarly, the development of the passing-off action would appear to be hampered by judges failing to reach any consensus on why exactly they are granting relief.[2] We must therefore turn to the basis of complaint when unauthorised interference is alleged in order to identify specific interests contemplated by contemporary

[1] *Reform of Trade Marks Law*, Cm 1203 (London, 1990). Compare this state of affairs with the express Congressional intent behind the US Lanham Act:

> "The purpose underlying any trade mark statute is two-fold. One is to protect the public so that it may be confident that, in purchasing a product bearing a particular trade mark which it favourably knows, it will get the product which it asks for and wants to get. Secondly, where the owner of a trade mark has spent time, energy and money in presenting to the public the product, he is protected in his investment from misappropriation by pirates and cheats."

Senate Report no. 1333, 79th Congress, 2nd session cited in E. C. Bannon, "Revisiting 'The Rational Basis of Trade Mark Protection': Control of Quality and Dilution—Estranged Bedfellows?" (1990) 24 *John Marshall LR* 65.

[2] Contrast the progressive approach of Peter Gibson L.J. in *Taittinger* v. *Allbev* [1993] FSR 641 and Laddie J. in *Chocosuisse Union des Fabricants Suisses de Chocolat* v. *Cadbury Ltd.* [1998] RPC 117 with the rather restrictive attitude of Millett L.J. in *Harrods Ltd.* v. *Harrodian School* [1996] RPC 697 and of Jacob J. in *Hodgkinson and Corby Ltd.* v. *Wards Mobility Services Ltd.* [1995] FSR 169.

trade mark law, as well as how these affect the protection given and so attempt to redress the lack of normative clarity evident in the law.

Before coming to this question though, we must first discount two possible but in fact irrelevant reasons explaining trade mark protection. It is obvious that they are not protected for their own intrinsic worth. Compare this with, for example, human physical integrity, to which such worth is attached that we have laws criminalising any form of offence against the person, and providing civil remedies for any violation regardless of the presence of injury. It is not realistically possible to argue that a producer in using a trade mark creates a symbol of such novelty, charged with such meaning that it must without derogation be defended against unauthorised interference. Even in the case of decorative trade marks used in merchandising ventures, the protection is arguably given because their commercial significance to consumers is gained through how the mark or whatever has been used in another context by the producer rather than anything inherently desirable in the mark; the trade mark owner is not being rewarded in the same way as the author of a copyright work. It is also true that protection is not given in order to encourage people to invent new symbols or create attractive brand names and designs for products. Any incentive to this end must be found in the market; trade marks are invented because of the desire to be recognised amongst one's competitors, not because of the availability of a legal right in the brand name.[3] The number of products which are in fact marketed under brand names that are, perhaps initially, not legally protectable demonstrates this point. In other words, the rationale of the trade mark right is different from those of patents and copyright which manifestly are for the purpose of reward or incentive.[4] Rather, the trade marking of goods is protected as an emergent social phenomenon dating in its modern form from the time of industrial revolution; the rights granted may be seen as protecting the interests of those *affected by trade mark use* for fear of the consequences were these interests not protected.

There may broadly be said to be four groups of interests that are at least *contemplated* by the law of trade symbols: those of the producer who adopts a trade mark to be used in connection with his product; those of his competitors who understandably wish to minimise the "monopolisation" of effective and desirable information-conveying symbols; those of consumers confronted by a huge variety of products all identified solely by their trade marks; and the general public interest[5] in ensuring that society's resources are allocated efficiently

[3] If anything, the trade mark right *protects* the incentive rather than *providing* it (S. A. Diamond, "The Public Interest and the Trade Mark System" (1980) 62 *J Patent & Trademark Office Society* 528, 544).

[4] B. W. Pattishall, "Trade Marks and the Monopoly Phobia" (1952) 50 *Michigan LR* 967, 971; Diamond, n. 3 above, 531.

[5] Note that it is possible to distinguish between the interests of consumers, those who are economically active within the market place, and the general public interest, since everyone is affected in some way by the functioning of the economy even if they are not directly influential in it due, for example, to extreme youth or old age.

through the operation of the free market without distortion.[6] We have already examined this last, economic interest in the previous chapter and seen that it may be tentatively suggested that trade mark protection serves the public interest by helping to preserve the integrity of the free market. The competitors' interests will be touched upon in the next chapter when we come to what could be referred to as the descriptive use of trade marks by third parties and the special case of comparative advertising. Note of course that the restrictive effect of trade mark protection on third parties is mitigated in several ways, for example by the existence of an almost infinite variety of signs available for use by producers as trade marks and upon the availability of which legally protecting trade marks is premised.[7] There is also the requirement in the Trade Marks Act that a word which another producer may have a legitimate interest in using, namely a descriptive or generic term, must be shown to function as a trade mark before it will be protected (the sign must have secondary meaning).[8] However, it is proposed at this stage to concentrate first of all on the interests directly *served* by the legal protection of trade marks by the law of registration and whether these have been affected by the new bases of protection introduced by the 1994 Trade Marks Act. Of course registration is not the only method of protecting a trade mark, and indeed its use is not obligatory; an owner of a used trade mark may always seek to prevent its unauthorised use by way of an action in passing-off. However, passing-off, although it has the same historical roots as straightforward trade mark protection, is now of a significantly different basis and not merely common law trade mark infringement. For this reason, this chapter will concentrate on trade marks falling within the ambit of the current statutory registration scheme.

THE INTERESTS SERVED BY TRADE MARK PROTECTION

The trade mark right has been said to have a "Janus-like quality"[9] since each time a trade mark owner is enabled to prevent unauthorised third parties from using his mark, it is commonly thought that at least two things are achieved, namely "the *consumer* is assured of getting the product he wants" and "the *merchant* is assured of . . . the benefits of his goodwill . . . and the ability to compete with others in terms of his own reputation".[10] It is clear, then, that there is a

[6] The distortions are of a type which affect mainly private interests and which we will now address.

[7] W. M. Landes, and R. A. Posner, "Trade Mark Law: an Economic Perspective" [1987] *J Law & Econ.* 265, 273.

[8] See s.3(1)(c)(d) and proviso thereto Trade Marks Act 1994, as well as s.46(1)(c) which provides for the revocation of a mark which becomes generic.

[9] G. R. Stewart, "The Source Theory and Trade Mark Law Reform: A Functional Analysis" (1982) 20 *U Western Ontario LR* 337.

[10] Pattishall, n. 4 above, 971 (emphasis added). He therefore asserts that the objective of trade mark law is to maintain individual identity in trade which reconciles nicely any conflict between consumer and producer claims, but also limits the scope of protection to that which is necessary to

dichotomy in trade mark law because there are two groups of people who are directly affected by trade marks and so have an interest in their protection. In fact it is useful to see the law governing trade mark protection as part of the wider framework of legal rules pertaining to the conduct of commerce. It represents an intersection between two bodies of concern to which the interests of each group may be roughly said to correspond. These may be generally referred to as the protection of consumers against deception and the prevention of unfair competition,[11] although the latter concern is one with respect to which the law has traditionally only made a marginal intervention.[12] We must nevertheless attempt to identify the extent to which these intertwined interests are allowed to influence modern trade mark law, and even whether they are at all conflicting.

Conferring Protection With Reference to the Interests of Consumers

The influence of the interests of consumers on the law of trade marks is undoubted. One may argue that, since producers for the last 100 years at least have chosen to market goods in such a way as to cause consumers to rely upon trade marks as a source of information of one form or another, consumers have become accustomed to identifying through the trade marks the products best suited to their needs. The reason consumers choose a particular product is unimportant in this context; it may be "only a matter of whim, or style, or taste"[13] and it may relate to the product's quality or to its variety features. Consumers may even use the trade mark to identify a product which they wish to avoid. The fact is that they do, and so have a legitimate expectation that a particular trade mark will continue to signify the product with which they have been conditioned to associate it. Indeed the view is quite tenable that consumers have a general right to be able to make a rational, informed choice when purchasing goods and services without being deceived or having anyone else in the chain of distribution take advantage of them. In support of this we may cite the principle of consumer sovereignty in the market. As Judge Jerome Frank said,

facilitate the indication of product source; this is something beyond which Pattishall was in fact later keen to extend protection (see "The Dilution Rationale for Trade Marks and Trade Identity Protection: its Progress and Prospects" (1977) 71 *North Western ULR* 618). See also D. Shanahan, "The Trade Mark Right: Consumer Protection or Monopoly" (1982) 72 *TMR* 233, 234.

[11] The phrase "unfair competition" has at least three different technical meanings (see C. Wadlow, *The Law of Passing Off* (2nd edn., London, 1995), 31–2), but at this stage it is used more loosely to mean conduct (in this case the use in some way of a trade mark) on the part of a trader in the market place which injures the interests of another trader such that the law may be expected to intervene in some way.

[12] See most recently A. Robertson and A. Horton, "Does the UK or EC Need an Unfair Competition Law?" [1995] *EIPR* 568 who note that "English law has . . . refused to deal in concepts such as fairness or good faith in business, leaving the market place to determine its own morality without the force of legal sanction". Contrast this with continental courts which proceed on the basis that they must "enforce the 'honest usages' of the market place" (*ibid.*, 569).

[13] Diamond, n. 3 above, 528.

> "The magna carta of competition, Adam Smith's *The Wealth of Nations* made it clear that the consumers' interests were to be the dominant aim of the competitive system: 'Consumption,' wrote Adam Smith, 'is the sole end and purpose of all production; and the interest of the producer ought to be attended to, only so far as may be necessary for promoting that of the consumer. . . .' "[14]

Furthermore, the complex nature of the modern chain of distribution justifies empowering consumers in this way:

> "The advent of mass consumption has resulted in consumers facing an information gap when they enter transactions involving the purchase of products or the provision of services. Products are now being marketed in such number and in such a manner that it is more difficult for consumers to judge their qualities adequately."[15]

Otherwise consumers would be open to abuse by unscrupulous traders through the exploitation of this information gap. Finally, the presence of a large body of consumer protection law must surely militate in favour of recognising that consumers have a putative right to candour on the part of those with whom they deal in the market place.

Ever since the inception of trade mark protection, concepts such as misrepresentation, fraud and deception have been invoked in support of granting relief through the finding of unlawful interference with a trade mark. Although it was the producer and trade mark owner who had been indirectly defrauded of custom that would have otherwise have come his way, it was the consumer who was the direct victim of the defendant's conduct in interfering with the producer's trade mark. The statutory infringement action, which was first introduced by the 1905 Trade Marks Act, consolidated in the 1938 Act and expanded in the 1994 Act, likewise judges infringement by reference to the "likelihood of confusion on the part of the public"[16]; in other words, "the law defines the infringement of a trade mark in terms of its impact on the public" since "trade mark infringement is a tort [that] interferes with the marketing process in which the consumer chooses goods by their trade marks".[17] Since they have a right not to be deceived in the exercise of their free choice, they deserve not be confused

[14] *Eastern Wine Corp.* v. *Winslow-Warren Ltd.* (1943) 57 USPQ 433. He actually went on to argue that trade mark protection is anti-competitive for the reasons (that are not relevant here and have to a certain extent been discredited) which we have already discussed in Ch.3, above. Whilst consumption is self-evidently the *raison d'être* of production; perfect competition in the late 20th century has not shown itself necessarily to be the be-all and end-all of market economics.

[15] R. Cranston, *Consumers and the Law* (2nd edn., London, 1984), 1.

[16] S.10(2) Trade Marks Act 1994; the importance of this basis was re-affirmed in *Wagamama Ltd.* v. *City Centre Restaurants plc* [1995] FSR 713. Its predecessors (s.39 Trade Marks Act 1905, as interpreted in *Irving's Yeast-Vite Ltd.* v. *Horsenail* (1934) 51 RPC 110, and ss.4 and 5 Trade Marks Act 1938) contained substantially similar provisions. Note that the current provision is actually wider in that an identical or similar mark used on goods or services of *a similar as well as* the same description will infringe in the presence of a likelihood of consumer confusion. As seen in Ch.2 above, this is a recognition of the phenomenon (of which consumers are unquestionably aware) of brand extension, whereby a producer of an established product markets a new, possibly unrelated product under the same brand name or trade mark.

[17] Diamond, n. 3 above, 529.

about the nature of a particular product through third party interference with a familiar trade mark.[18] However, the influence of the consumers' interest does not cease to manifest itself with infringement. When considering the registrability of a particular symbol as a trade mark which, for example, is descriptive and so apparently prohibited under section 3(1)(c) of the Trade Marks Act 1994, the court must address the question whether the symbol has still acquired a distinctive character in accordance with the proviso to the section. Surely the most compelling and perhaps only evidence that this is the case is evidence that consumers recognise it as a trade mark?[19] To state, then, that "consumer psychology . . . is the foundation for the entire law of trade marks"[20] may be to put the case too strongly, but it is certainly true that "what is believed to be going on in the mind of the consumer is the basis for deciding both registrability and infringement issues".[21] The consumers' interests may be injured by a third party's conduct in relation to the trade mark; they are deceived or put at risk of being deceived into dealing with someone other than with whom they intended, but even in dealing with the trade mark owner, there is still the possibility of consumer deception.

Conflicting Interests: Do Trade Marks Confer Power Without Responsibility?

It is apparent that, broadly speaking, the law of trade marks has always given the trade mark owner the right to prevent the use of his mark by other traders when it is likely that, in doing so, the third party will confuse consumers. So in exercising his negative right, the trade mark owner also protects the interests of consumers. They may, for whatever reason, decide that the product bearing a particular trade mark is suitable for their needs, and so continue to purchase it by reference to the trade mark. Viewed from a different perspective, it may be said that the producer has conditioned consumers to expect certain qualities of the product denoted by his trade mark. There is, however, the temptation to exploit this in the short term and increase profits by marketing a product under the same trade mark, but which has been produced at a lower cost through sacrificing quality in some way.[22] For example, the

[18] Contrast this with the view cited in A. Kamperman Sanders and S. Maniatis, "A Consumer Trade Mark: Protection Based on Quality and Origin" [1993] *EIPR* 406, n. 28, that "the protection of consumers . . . was merely the device for applying the misrepresentation test and ensuring the purity of the trader's rights . . .".

[19] This was Jacob J.'s view in *British Sugar plc* v. *James Robertson and Sons* [1996] RPC 281, 304. In this case, the judge considered, but dismissed as inadequate, evidence of use of the mark concerned and of how the producer regarded such use of the mark. The interest of consumers therefore acts as a check on the acquisitive ambitions of producers since they would otherwise be free to appropriate any sign that they wished simply by making use of it or even by merely stating that they considered it to be their trade mark.

[20] Diamond, n. 3 above, 528.

[21] *Ibid.* See also Kamperman Sanders and Maniatis, n. 18 above, 409–10.

[22] W. R. Cornish, *Intellectual Property: Patents, Copyrights, Trade Marks and Allied Rights* (3rd edn., London, 1996) para.15–26; A. Michaels, "The Function of Trade Marks: the Law and the Reality" [1980] *EIPR* 13, 15–6.

manufacturers of HÄAGEN-DAZS ice cream have established it as a premium-priced product because of their use of only high quality ingredients in its manufacture. If they then substituted cheaper vegetable fat for the dairy cream to which consumers have become accustomed, so rendering the quality more like that of a supermarket's own-brand product but without informing consumers, a greater profit could be available.[23] Therefore a measure of the aptness of the modern trade mark law as a consumer protection device is the result of this conflict between the interests of consumers and those of producers in a situation of this type.

One answer to the situation just described is that consumers will soon realise that the trade marked product does not conform to their expectations, and cease buying it, as was the case with COCA-COLA in the early 1980s,[24] with the result that the value of the brand (to its producer) will decrease. This is the will of the consumer manifesting itself through the operation of the market in the classical sense. The question is "whether such economic sanctions have legal equivalents"[25] such that the trade mark owner is himself, in the name of consumer protection, restrained from this form of deception. We saw in Chapter 3 that one way in which trade mark function is rationalised is by seeing it as an indicator of consistent quality. If it is to enjoy continuing legal protection, it must fulfil this function. Section 46(1)(d) of the Trade Marks Act 1994 provides that "the registration of a trade mark may be revoked . . . [if] it is liable to mislead the public, particularly as to the nature, quality or geographical origin [of the goods or services in respect of which it is registered]". Clearly then at a theoretical, and indeed prescriptive, level[26] at least, the consumers' interest extends to preventing conduct that is likely to deceive even on the part of the trade mark owner who would seem to be obliged to ensure that, once he has caused consumers to have a legitimate expectation of the nature of the product sold under his trade mark, this expectation is satisfied. However, although anyone is entitled[27] to enforce this obligation through applying for the revocation of the mark in question, realistically speaking, it is of no practical use to the aggrieved consumer in the face of the huge cost and evidential burden to be overcome; the only party with any incentive to bring such an action would be another trader by way of counter-claim to infringement proceedings.

Given this practical weakness, several writers have fastened upon the idea that, since trade marks indicate to consumers a continual level of quality, producers should be under a much stronger obligation to ensure product consis-

[23] As Shanahan points out, a producer will not always have dubious motives for changing a product's formulation and, with an eye to retaining customer loyalty, will continually be seeking to *improve* product quality. Consequently, a change in the quality associated with a trade mark will not always be a necessarily bad thing (Shanahan, n. 10 above, 236).

[24] See N. S. Economides, "The Economics of Trade Marks" (1988) 78 *TMR* 523, 530.

[25] Michaels, n. 22 above, 16.

[26] In the sense conceived by the Legal Positivists that any law will have both a prescriptive element, the underlying norm, and a remedial element, the sanction or remedy for breaching this norm.

[27] S.46(4) Trade Marks Act 1994.

tency and thereby obviate the risk of consumers being misled.[28] The problem is that it is all very well saying that no one forces consumers to buy a particular trade marked product,[29] but in order to find out that a formerly satisfactory product has ceased to be so, consumers must incur expense which may be both damaging to themselves and economically wasteful.[30] One suggested solution is "to isolate a trade mark's function of conveying consumer information from the goodwill function to the extent of introducing a product mark"[31] whereby the trade mark owner, to ensure the continued protection of his mark, would be forced to adhere to a quality standard which he had himself originally specified. Consumers would consequently be protected without a shadow of doubt from relying to their detriment on trade marks whilst making purchasing decisions. Even more draconian measures are available to further the consumers' interest. One could introduce compulsory licensing of particular trade marks to the trade mark owner's competitors if they were able exactly to replicate the original product.[32] Whilst the benefit to consumers is plain, it would seem to be at the expense of producers using the trade marks. Since, by definition, a product mark indicates the characteristics of the product in question, it seem likely that any mark will, sooner rather than later, become the generic name for any product with those characteristics, with the result that the mark's capacity to preserve goodwill evaporates, and with it any motivation to use trade marks in the first place.[33] In addition, product marks would face the practical difficulty of there being no incentive for producers to use them, since the rigidity of the product mark regime would stifle the impetus to improve the product or, if producers did use them, the temptation would be to file vague standards allowing room for manœuvre; finally there would be a danger that consumers would not be aware of the standards, but rather rely on state bodies to enforce them.[34]

Alternatively, of course, the consumer could be given a far more active role through being encouraged within the framework of the trade mark system to take action both in the face of third party interference with trade marks and producers abusing their privilege.[35] Empowering consumers in this way "might well remove any doubt as to the complementary nature of these objectives of fair competition and consumer protection"[36]; however it would seem that trade

[28] E. W. Hanak, "The Quality Assurance Function of Trade Marks" (1975) 65 *TMR* 318; Michaels, n. 22 above; Shanahan, n. 10 above; Stewart, n. 9 above; Kamperman Sanders and Maniatis, n. 18 above.

[29] Diamond, n. 3 above, 544.

[30] Stewart, n. 9 above, 350.

[31] *Ibid.*, 350–1.

[32] It has even been suggested that consumers would benefit from the removal of protection from trade marks altogether so that they may benefit from the enhanced competition (See E. H. Chamberlin, *The Theory of Monopolistic Competition* (8th edn., Cambridge, Mass., 1962), Appendix E). We have already seen the fallacy of this argument in Ch.3 above.

[33] Stewart, n. 9 above, 351–2.

[34] *Ibid.*, 351.

[35] See Shanahan, n. 10 above, 236–7 who discusses the Australian experience of doing just this.

[36] *Ibid.*, 236.

mark law has a limited utility for the private vindication of consumers' rights. Cranston, writing in the context of general consumer protection formulates the problem in this way:

> "[T]here is an imbalance of power when consumers confront a business with a grievance. . . . Consumers are typically in a weak bargaining position because of the disparity in knowledge and resources between the parties, which narrows the consumer's access to a remedy. . . . Legal remedies may be available . . ., but the evidence demonstrates that many consumers are ignorant of their legal rights and/or either unwilling or unable to pursue them. For this and other reasons . . . the view is advanced . . . that *public control* is frequently the only way that consumers will be protected by law."[37]

What we must in fact acknowledge is that, although the interests of consumers have had an undoubted influence on the protection of trade marks through being conditioned to perceive them at the very least as indicators of information concerning product origin and quality, such influence has not been of such a degree that it has justified the re-formulation of trade mark law in the manner described above by means of the recent Trade Marks Act, nor should it have been so re-formulated. It is arguable that the level to which the consumers' interest was elevated at the inception of trade mark protection is also its "high-water mark" at which it has remained since then. After all, the consumer is thought to be guarded in two other ways that are *external* to trade mark law, one highly interventionist, the other emphatically not. First, the general importance of protecting the consumers' interest in the market place is acknowledged by the presence of a substantial core of specialist consumer protection law which has been "customarily the way of providing against"[38] conduct likely to deceive or take advantage of consumers; it takes the form of "a complex matrix of specialised laws and regulations, which have developed piecemeal to deal with particular forms of misconduct".[39] Moreover, it is a body of law enforced, often by means of criminal sanctions, by public agencies such as Trading Standards Offices established solely for that purpose. Secondly, it almost goes without saying that consumers are generally perceived to be the prime beneficiaries of competition in the market place and if one accepts that trade marks facilitate competition, then we see consumers protected as a by-product of trade mark protection. In any event, by facilitating product identification and ensuring that only the produce connected with a single trader may bears his unique trade symbol, the law of trade marks is protecting the consumers' interest to the greatest extent feasible without impinging on the other face of the trade mark right, the producers' interest.

[37] Cranston, n. 15 above, 3 (emphasis added and footnotes omitted).
[38] Cornish, n. 22 above, para.15–26.
[39] Shanahan, n. 10 above, 237.

The Shift in Favour of Protecting Producers' Interests

It must be recognised that trade mark law is so apparently producer-centred that it is unreal to suggest that consumer influence is anything greater than a secondary consideration. For example, evidence can be found of how the consumers' interest within trade mark law is in fact being weakened if we look at trade mark licensing. Until the Trade Marks Act 1938, trade mark licensing was strictly prohibited, and any attempts to license the mark were greeted with a loss of rights for the proprietor, as was the case in *Bowden Wire Co. Ltd.* v. *Bowden Brake Co. Ltd.*[40] Ironically (in the light of what was to come), the reason for this was consumer protection "since consumers relied on a trade mark as a symbol of the single, physical source of the product to which it was affixed, 'licensed' goods would not emanate from that single source and would therefore confuse and deceive the public".[41] The 1938 Act changed this situation by providing for "registered users" of trade marks beside the proprietor. In order to acquire this status, the intending registered user was required to satisfy the registrar that the licensing agreement contained adequate quality control provisions in order to minimise the risk of the new user causing consumer deception. It was later suggested that these provisions—which admittedly were rather maligned, if not abused, since of course it is unrealistic to believe that the registrar would be able to examine as well as monitor quality control provisions—be strengthened so that they may play an enhanced consumer protection role.[42] In fact the opposite occurred, such that under the Trade Marks Act 1994 trade mark licensing is now possible without any substantive restriction. In justifying this, the preceding White Paper had the following to say:

> "Whatever may have been the position in 1938, the public is now accustomed to goods or services being supplied under licence from the trade mark owner. . . . The potential for deception is therefore less. Moreover the strongest guarantee that a proprietor will maintain control over the way in which a trade mark is used is that it is in his interest to do so. A trade mark is a valuable piece of property. . . . Its value is however ultimately dependent on its reputation with the public. If the proprietor tolerates uncontrolled use of his trade mark the value of this property will be diminished. In an extreme case the registration may become liable to be revoked if it has become deceptive or generic through such use. It is however the responsibility of the proprietor, not the registrar, to prevent the devaluation of his own property."[43]

Notice the complete lack of concern with consumer protection in this passage; the only expressly perceived consequence of indiscriminate licensing of a registered trade mark is a depreciation in the value of the producer's mark. Not only is the trade mark owner largely free to do as he pleases as far as allowing others

[40] (1914) 31 RPC 385.

[41] K. Parks, " 'Naked' is not a Four Letter Word: Debunking the Myth of the 'Quality Control Requirement' in Trade Mark Licensing" (1992) 82 *TMR* 531, 533.

[42] Michaels, n. 22 above, 16.

[43] *Reform of Trade Marks Law*, Cm. 1203 (London, 1990), para.4.36.

to produce goods under his mark or set up franchised services is concerned, he is also (subject to the rights of any licensees) the owner of the rights in the trade mark and the one who regulates their enforcement. It seems to be, to put it charitably, a very altruistic conception of the law to say that when an action is brought for infringement, the owner is fighting for the interest of consuming public as the "vicarious champion"[44] of the consumers' rights. Admittedly this is the *effect* of the enforcement of trade mark rights, but a radical re-modelling of the law of the type rejected above would be necessary to facilitate this as a substantial objective of trade mark protection in order to give consumers active rights rather than a merely passive interest in the outcome of an infringement action.

The explanation for this state of affairs is, it is submitted, straightforward; whilst protecting consumers against deception is a legitimate concern for trade mark law, it is no longer a guiding principle. Parks expresses the situation well:

> "[T]he primary purpose of trade mark law is to protect trade marks and the interests of trade mark owners. . . . Of course, consumers who suffer physical injury caused by truly defective, unreasonably dangerous products should and do have recourse against manufacturers and sellers . . . pursuant to theories of product liability and warranty. But trade marks are not warranties and the [Trade Marks Act 1994] is not a 'consumer protection' statute. Rather, as has always been the case, the 'public protection' afforded by trade mark protection is indirect, flowing from successful infringement suits, thereby eliminating public confusion as to the true source of marked goods."[45]

This is not to say by any means that the interests of consumers are irrelevant to the concerns of modern trade mark law. By securing the integrity of the mechanism by which consumers identify products, it is ensured that they will always receive the produce of the manufacturer that they expect; this is complemented by the specialist body of consumer protection law which exist primarily for the consumers' benefit. The policy is implicit in trade mark law, though, that the prime concern is protecting to a greater or lesser extent traders against each other.

Having preliminarily determined that this is the case, it is still necessary to turn to the precise nature of the producers' interest and how it can be said to have come to dominate trade mark law. In the same way that consumers have become accustomed to recognising products in an impersonal market place by reference to their trade marks, producers have equally long regarded them as nothing less than the visible manifestation of their products' identity, the foundation of their reputation and the means by which responsibility for their prod-

[44] *Per* Learned Hand J., *Ely-Norris Safe Co.* v. *Mosler Safe Co.* (1925) 7 F 2d 603.

[45] Parks, n. 41 above, 560–1 writing in the context of the Lanham Act (footnotes omitted). This is echoed by the comment that "the interest of mark holders remains the driving force for enhanced trade mark protection in the General Agreement on Tariffs and Trade (GATT) Trade Related Aspects of Intellectual Property Rights (TRIPS) Draft Convention" (Kamperman Sanders and Maniatis, n. 18 above, n. 28).

ucts attaches.[46] The peculiarly dichotomous character of the trade mark has always demonstrated itself in the fact that whenever a producer is allowed to prevent another from using his trade mark, as well as assisting consumers he is serving his own interest because he is, for example, saving himself from the loss of trade or damage to his own reputation that may ensue from the mark being used on another's goods or services. What he is doing is no more than protecting his identity and that of his products in a similar fashion to how a person's signature is protected by the law of forgery.[47] Yet given that

> "Trade mark pirates are growing more subtle and refined. They proceed more circumspectly, by suggestion and approximation, rather than by direct and exact duplication of their victims and marks",[48] and

> "There seem always to be those whose inclinations are to reap where they have not sown and to ride as long as possible on the coat-tails of the diligent and successful; and . . . the ingenuity of the 'free-rider' has developed in proportion to the value of the ride",[49]

it could moreover be said that protecting the trade mark plays a role in enforcing what might be termed commercial morality. After all, producers in the market place are entitled to use any means available to gain an advantage over their competitors so long as these means are "fair".[50] Insinuating that goods are the product of someone else by imitating his trade mark and so reaping the benefit of any public predisposition towards the latter's goods may reasonably be said to be unfairly competitive. If it is accepted that trade mark law is primarily concerned with protecting the interests of producers, then it may be concluded that another influential factor is the need to prevent unfair competition rather than just the arguably narrower concern of securing a system of trade identity. As we have noted already, unfair competition is a multi-faceted concept, and in asserting that trade mark protection is influenced by the need to prevent unfair competition, it is not necessarily suggested that trade mark law is formally "but a part of the broader law of unfair competition".[51] Rather, it shares the motive of restricting conduct which may be harmful to the interests of a particular producer and which *ought* to be restricted. Although the traditional attitude of the law has been one of minimal intervention as between competitors in the market place[52] since "to draw a line between fair and unfair competition, between what

[46] Pattishall, n. 4 above, 984–5. In particular, see also E. S. Rogers, "The Social Value of Trade Marks and Brands" (1947) 37 *TMR* 249, 249–50, who develops the idea that a trade mark is to a product and its manufacturer what a signature is to a person and with the same moral effect: H. E. Pearson and C. G. Miller, *Commercial Exploitation of Intellectual Property* (London, 1990) 217.

[47] This is Pattishall's central argument to support trade mark protection (n. 4 above, 983–4).

[48] F. I. Schechter, "The Rational Basis of Trade Mark Protection" (1927) 40 *Harv. LR* 813, 825.

[49] Pattishall, n. 4 above, 971.

[50] And of course legal, although of course the likelihood is that unfair means will have been rendered unlawful. See Diamond, n. 3 above, 535.

[51] Pattishall, n. 4 above, 980.

[52] See n. 12 above; market forces are seen as the most appropriate means for resolving any such conflicts.

is reasonable and unreasonable, passes the power of the courts",[53] two developments in the law have emphatically shifted concern in favour of protecting producers against what may at least be generally termed unfair competition.

When the law first intervened to protect trade marks, the concern could be loosely described as lying with the prevention of fraud or deceit rather than protecting any intellectual property right that a producer may have in a trade mark.[54] Indeed it may be argued that the consumer interest was dominant at that time, given that protection was restricted to the imitation of marks on directly competitive goods.[55] As trade mark use developed and increased in the manner and in response to the factors described in Chapter 2, so did the form of the producers' interest in protecting their marks against the interference of others in the market place, since they began playing a far more active role in the marketing process almost as an integral part of the product. The meaning of the trade mark became much more than simply the name of the manufacturer to the extent that psychological models view the values surrounding the mark as whole "networks of associations that may be triggered by brand name merchandise".[56] Moskin gives the following illustration:

> "The stimulus 'NIKE running shoes', for example, may provoke associations with the 'swoosh' symbol used on the shoes, with the cost of the shoes, with a specific experience of the consumer . . . or with competitive brands."[57]

Trade marks could therefore be said to have developed a "wider integrity"[58] and so "simply cannot be viewed as mere abstract indications of source"[59]; it consequently became clear that a trade mark owner's interests may be injured by actions of another which are not actually directly competitive[60] or indeed motivated simply by a wish to divert custom. It is submitted that there is a second premise embodied in trade mark law. Not only is the dominant interest that of

[53] *Mogul Steamship Co.* v. *McGregor* (1889) 23 QBD 598, 626, *per* Fry L.J. Compare this *laissez-faire* attitude as well with the vast body of competition law which has arisen in recent times with the primary objective of securing the general public interest, but which undeniably also functions to protect producers against concentrations of market power.

[54] Schechter, n. 48 above, 820 and n. 33. Of course, as we saw in Ch.1 above, one stream of authority *was* in fact keen to recognise a proprietary interest in favour of the trade mark owner, but this did not prevail and was in any event overtaken by the advent of trade mark registration (Wadlow, n. 11 above, 18).

[55] University of Chicago Law Review, Comment, "The Anti-Competitive Aspects of Trade Name Protection and the Policy Against Consumer Deception" (1962) 29 *U Chicago LR* 371, 373.

[56] J. E. Moskin, "Dilution or Delusion: The Rational Limits of Trade Mark Protection" (1993) 83 *TMR* 122, 135.

[57] *Ibid.* (footnotes omitted).

[58] The phrase is taken from R. E. Annand and H. E. Norman, *Blackstone's Guide to the Trade Marks Act 1994* (London, 1994), 155.

[59] J. B. Swann and T. H. Davis, "Dilution, an Idea Whose Time has Gone; Brand Equity as Protectable Property, the New/Old Paradigm" (1994) 84 *TMR* 267, 297.

[60] Consequently, s.12(1) Trade Marks Act 1938 prohibited the registration of a mark which was identical or similar to a prior mark in respect of both identical *and similar* goods. However, it was only in the 1994 Act that this restriction was extended to the infringement action. See also n. 16 above.

producers, there is also an acceptance that the more successful the product underlying a trade mark is, the more heavily advertised it is and the more aware consumers are of it, the greater is the extent to which it is deemed worthy of protection, since the investment which the producer is trying to protect is correspondingly greater. The first development which recognised this and was intended "to compensate for the absence of a general unfair competition law"[61] was the now defunct provision in the Trade Marks Act 1938 for the "defensive" registration of well-known trade marks.[62] Secondly and more importantly, in the new grounds for finding a registered mark either capable of blocking the registration of a later mark or infringed, sections 5 and 10 of the Trade Marks Act 1994 display a distinct bias in favour of protecting producer interests and an acceptance that the strength of a mark is proportional to the protection of which it is worth.

THE IMPLICATIONS OF THE NEW GROUNDS FOR INFRINGEMENT

If there is one thing that is uncontroversial about the circumstances under the 1994 Trade Marks Act in which a trade mark owner may enforce his exclusive rights, it is that they represent an expansion upon those contemplated by the 1938 Act. Ignoring the provisions concerning comparative advertising, that Act defined infringement as being the use of a trade mark which was identical or deceptively similar to the registered trade mark in respect of goods for which the mark was registered[63] except, in the case of Part B marks, where the defendant could show that his particular use was not confusing, or alternatively would not imply a connection in the course of trade between the two parties' goods.[64]

Contrasting this with the position under the present Act, it is clear that at the very least all these circumstances are covered by the new infringement provisions.[65] However, as already outlined in Chapter 1, there are three areas in which the ambit of the old infringement provisions has been built upon. First, infringement can now be found where the defendant's product is merely similar to the one in respect of which the plaintiff's mark is registered.[66] This, it is suggested, is nothing more than an acknowledgement that consumers who have become accustomed to a particular trade-marked product will often expect a related product bearing an identical or similar trade mark to be an extension of the familiar brand. Secondly, in cases more complicated than straightforward "trade mark piracy" (where the marks and the underlying products are both

[61] Cornish, n. 22 above, para.15–11.

[62] See *ibid.*, and also the second edition of this work at paras.17–046–8 and White Paper, *Reform of Trade Marks Law*, Cm. 1203 (1990), paras.3.17–9.

[63] Ss.4(1)(a) and 5(1) Trade Marks Act 1938 read in conjunction with s.68(2B) Trade Marks Act 1938.

[64] S.5(2) Trade Marks Act 1938.

[65] S.10(1)(2) Trade Marks Act 1994 as interpreted in *WAGAMAMA*.

[66] S.10(2) Trade Marks Act 1994.

identical), the critical factor for the finding of infringement is evidence that consumers are confused or at least are likely to be confused, typically *but not necessarily*, as to the provenance of the two products. The rationale for this has been discussed at some length here and elsewhere, its essence being that consumers must not be deceived as to a product's source and producers must not have their business diverted away from them by means of such deception. However the actual wording of the statutory provision, that

> "a person infringes a registered trade mark if . . . [by reason of the fact that the sign and mark are identical or similar and the underlying goods are also either similar or identical] there exists a likelihood of confusion on the part of the public, which includes the likelihood of association with the trade mark",

has been commented upon[67] and is beginning to be interpreted[68] in a manner that suggests that infringement may be made out in circumstances where there is little evidence of source confusion but far greater evidence of other distinct factors such as the mere semantic association of the sign and the mark.[69] Thirdly, if the offending sign is used in respect of an unrelated or dissimilar product and the registered mark has a "reputation" in the United Kingdom, then infringement is likewise proved if the third party's conduct can be shown to "[take] unfair advantage of or [be] detrimental to the trade mark's distinctive character or repute".[70]

As we have already seen in Chapter 1, of these provisions the second is controversial (for reasons both of interpretation and effect) and the third not yet fully tested. If it is ultimately accepted by the courts that the scope of the likelihood of confusion concept in section 10(2) is wider than its equivalent measure under the old law and presuming that section 10(3) does not succumb to the same fate that befell defensive registration (it was marginalised by the courts),[71] the crucial fact for our purposes is that adoption of these new bases of protection will entail tacitly accepting certain premises and value judgements underlying them. They concern when a trade mark will be damaged and the consequent extent of the owner's interest.

[67] See, amongst others, Annand and Normand, n. 58 above, 154–6; P. A. Harris, "UK Trade Mark Law: Are You Confused?" [1995] *EIPR* 601; and C. Gielen, "Likelihood of Association: What Does it Mean?", Dec. 1995/Jan. 1996, *TW* 20.

[68] Case C–251/95 *Sabel BV* v. *Puma AG* [1998] RPC 199.

[69] In the *Puma* decision, the ECJ decided that in fact something more than a mere likelihood of association by itself is necessary to show that there is a likelihood of confusion on the part of the public (contrary to the argument put forward in WAGAMAMA concerning the infamous and now disclosed Council Minute indicating that intended effect of provisions deriving from Art.5(1)(b) of the Directive), although it is still difficult to say how much wider this is than the scope admitted by Laddie J. in WAGAMAMA.

[70] S.10(3) Trade Marks Act 1994.

[71] Unfortunately the (admittedly only interlocutory) decisions in *BASF plc* v. *CEP (UK) plc* LEXIS Transcript, 26 Oct. 1995, Ch. D. and *Baywatch* v. *Home Video Channel* [1997] FSR 22, 30–31 do not augur well in this respect.

The Likelihood of Confusion

In a majority of cases, it is fair to assume, the critical finding will be whether there is "a likelihood of confusion on the part of the public, which includes the likelihood of association with the trade mark". After all, we are told in the Directive that "the likelihood of confusion . . . constitutes the specific condition for . . . protection".[72] To be precise, the particular consequences flowing from the adoption of the likelihood of confusion as the primary touchstone of trade mark infringement will depend to a large extent on the preferred interpretation, of the concept. This issue is generally characterised in the literature as a conflict between the expansive Benelux interpretation which accepts that there will be infringement even where consumers see a mere resemblance between marks,[73] and the restrictionist English view, which finds infringement in nothing less than circumstances of confusion as to the commercial source of the products in question. It will be recalled that when the differing interpretations of section 10(2) first clashed in *Wagamama Ltd* v. *City Centre Restaurants plc*, the English view was overwhelmingly preferred by Laddie J. on the grounds that evidence indicating that the legislators intended the Benelux approach to prevail was inadmissible[74] and that in any event the English approach was consistent both with the wording on the face of the statute and the previous case law of the European Court of Justice (ECJ).[75] *Sabel* v. *Puma*, a reference from the German Federal Supreme Court, provided an opportunity for the ECJ to consider the Community provision[76] to which section 10(2) is related, and the Court, it is suggested, chose a middle course somewhere between the two approaches. It was clear to the Court that "the mere association which the public might make between two trade marks as a result of their analogous semantic content is not in itself a sufficient ground for concluding that there is a likelihood of confusion".[77] The Court then went on to make several telling points concerning the scope of the likelihood of confusion which are worth quoting in full:

> "[T]he appreciation of the likelihood of confusion 'depends on numerous elements and, in particular, on the recognition of the trade mark on the market, of the association which can be made with the used or registered sign, of the degree of similarity between the trade mark and the sign and between the goods or services identified'. The likelihood of confusion must therefore be appreciated globally, taking into account all factors relevant to the circumstances of the case."[78]

[72] 10th Recital of the Preamble.

[73] The main characteristics of the Benelux approach are summarised at paras.14–16 of *Sabel* v. *Puma*.

[74] [1995] FSR at 726–28.

[75] *Ibid.*, at 728–31.

[76] The case concerned Art.4(1)(b) of the Directive, but, as the court pointed out at para.13, is applicable to Art.5(1) by analogy. *Sabel* v. *Puma*.

[77] *Sabel* v. *Puma*, *ibid.*, para.26.

[78] Para.22.

> "In that perspective, the more distinctive the earlier mark, the greater will be the likelihood of confusion. It is not impossible that the conceptual similarity resulting from the fact that two marks use images with analogous semantic content may give rise to a likelihood of confusion where the earlier mark has a particularly distinctive character, either *per se* or because of the reputation it enjoys with the public."[79]

In spite of the rejection of the Benelux approach to the likelihood of association at its most expansive, the ECJ has in essence confirmed that the likelihood of confusion is nevertheless to be seen as a quite broad concept and that a court must regard as material a wide variety of factors surrounding a registered trade mark when assessing the likelihood of confusion. It is notable that the Court implicitly rejects two aspects of the English approach to the 1994 Trade Marks Act. The first is that trade mark infringement can only be made out on what Laddie J. termed "classic grounds",[80] that is in circumstances of consumer confusion only as to product source. The second is contained in the seemingly innocuous statement by Jacob J. in *Origins Natural Resources Inc.* v. *Origin Clothing Ltd.* that section 10(2) requires the court to "assess a likelihood of confusion in relation to the way in which the defendant uses its mark, *discounting external added matter or circumstances*. The comparison is mark for mark".[81] Such "external added matter or circumstances" are quite relevant.

Even more notable are the matters to which the ECJ has left the door open. Writers on both sides of the English Channel[82] have pointed out that the mark in question in *Sabel* v. *Puma* was not particularly well-known to the public and contained little imaginative content. This leads one to the question of what the Court would require to be shown in circumstances involving a stronger mark. The second passage cited above accepts the argument that "some trade marks are more equal than others".[83] In other words, although in order to secure registration a mark may only have to display distinctiveness which satisfies a minimal threshold, distinctiveness is in fact a matter of degree, with the result that the more distinctive it is, the easier it will be to show that it has been infringed. It is therefore conceivable that section 10(2) could allow the owner of a strong enough trade mark to object to the use of a sign when consumers are merely likely to associate the marks concerned and with only marginal evidence of confusion as to the actual origin of the underlying goods. That this can be so evidently implies that some interest is liable to be injured in the presence of such an association. Furthermore, if a trade mark can still be infringed with only a marginal number of consumers being left in doubt as to the trade origin that it signifies, then clearly there is some other significance conveyed to consumers by the

79 Para.24.

80 WAGAMAMA, at 731.

81 [1995] FSR 280, 284 (emphasis added).

82 A. Carboni, "Confusion Clarified: *SABEL* v. *Puma*" [1998] *EIPR* 107, 109, and C. Gielen, "*SABEL* v. *Puma*: A Benelux Perspective" [1998] *EIPR* 109, 110.

83 This view is also supported by para.32 in the Opinion of the A.G. in Case C–39/97 *Canon KK* v. *Pathe Communications Corp*, unreported, 2 Apr. 1998.

trade mark which is interfered with by the infringer's actions.[84] The nature of this significance was discussed at some length in Chapter 2 and, as mentioned above, may conveniently be referred to as the trade mark's "wider integrity". It is all those things conveyed by the mark other than the origin of the underlying product which have become associated with the mark through its use in the market place. It must not be forgotten, though, that the "wider integrity" of a mark will vary from case to case. Whilst it must be shown in order to secure a mark's continued protection that it is recognised as distinctive of a particular producer, it is always possible and demonstrable by evidence that a trade mark has acquired and conveys a meaning greater than just indicating a product's origin.

That the law will, in the appropriate circumstances, protect this "wider integrity" is apparent not only from inferences that may be drawn from a consideration of factors said to be relevant to a finding of a likelihood of confusion. The ECJ recently considered the question of the circumstances in which trade mark rights may legitimately be used to oppose the re-sale under the trade mark of parallel imports. It is a feature of European trade mark jurisprudence[85] that a producer's interest in his trade mark will not generally be injured where goods are re-sold in one area of the EEA having been purchased in another in order to exploit price differentials, because the consumer is getting the same product that he would have got had he purchased it directly from the authorised distributor of trade-marked goods. In Case C–337/95 *Parfums Christian Dior SA* v. *Evora BV* it was held that a legitimate reason[86] for opposing the re-sale of goods through the assertion of trade mark rights is where "the presentation of the . . . goods is liable to damage the *reputation of the trade mark*".[87] The court expressly conceives of damage being done to an element of how consumers are conditioned to perceive the trade mark. A week later in Case C–349/95 *Frits Loendersloot* v. *George Ballantine & Son Ltd.*,[88] the Court re-asserted that in its jurisprudence, the purpose of the exclusive right in the trade mark was "to protect [the trade mark owner] against competitors wishing to take unfair advantage of the status and reputation of the trade mark".[89] Furthermore, in a situation involving repackaging, the parallel importer must take care "not to damage the reputation of the trade mark and its owner"[90] and in assessing this, a national court must "take into account . . . the interest of [the trade mark owners] . . . in protecting the luxury image of their products and the considerable

[84] After all, according to 10th Recital of the Preamble to the Directive, indication of a product's origin is mentioned as a *particular* function of a trade mark, but it is *not the only* function (Gielen, n. 67 above, 21). Cf. the view of Jacob J. in *British Sugar plc* v. *James Robertson and Sons* [1996] RPC 281, 298 that said "[n]o other purpose is mentioned . . . this sole purpose permeates the whole Directive and hence our 1994 Act."

[85] Originally developed in the context of Arts. 30 and 36 of the Treaty of Rome and now contained in Art. 7 of the Trade Marks Directive and hence s.12 Trade Marks Act 1994. See Ch.1, text accompanying, 202–208.

[86] Within the meaning of Art.7(2) of the Directive and hence s.12(2) Trade Marks Act 1994.

[87] [1998] RPC 166, para.43 (emphasis added).

[88] [1998] FSR 544.

[89] Para.22.

[90] Para.29.

reputation they enjoy".[91] Finally, the Advocate General in Case C–63/97 *BMW AG* v. *Deenik*[92] continued this line of reasoning when he submitted that the saving which provides that it is not an infringement of a registered trade mark to use indications of various attributes of a product[93] is limited in its ambit to situations where the use of such indications does not "seriously damage the reputation of the mark".[94] These situations where the ECJ has protected the trade mark owner's interest in the "wider integrity" of his mark are all the more significant for the fact that there is simply no opportunity for source confusion, since the goods in which the defendant is dealing are those of the trade mark owner.

The clear assumption, then, is that if it is likely that consumers will associate the mark with the offending sign or parallel imports are re-sold "inappropriately" as the case may be, consumers' *perception* of the trade mark concerned will be affected as to a factor other than the source that it indicates. Nevertheless, the confusion or interference occurs with respect to a factor that is still germane to the consumer's purchasing decision. This is demonstrated by the first American case to recognise the doctrine, *Ortho Pharmaceutical Corp.* v. *American Cyanamid Co.*[95] The plaintiff's product was an innovative and highly successful pharmaceutical product marketed under the trade mark RHOGAM; the defendant later entered the market with the drug, but using the trade mark RHO-IMMUNE. It was found on the evidence that, given the nature of the product, it was unlikely that confusion as to source could arise; however, it was also found that where a hospital used both products, users would be likely, through a mental association of the trade marks, to attribute to the defendant's product the "qualities and reputation that has come to be associated with RHOGAM, thereby giving RHO-IMMUNE an advantage in the utilisation of its product by medical personnel that it would not have had if it had chosen a different trade mark".[96] It may therefore be concluded that:

> "The court was not protecting the brand differentiating role of the mark, but rather was preventing its exploitation as a symbol of quality and a carrier of positive associations; it was protecting the mark's advertising value and guarding against an unconscious attribution of quality and desirability, a displaced sense of confidence in the product, produced by the imitating mark."[97]

A similar conclusion was reached by the Court of Appeal in the passing-off case of *Taittinger* v. *Allbev*[98] where there was negligible evidence of consumer con-

[91] Para.33.

[92] Unreported, 2 Apr. 1998.

[93] Contained in UK law in s.11(2) Trade Marks Act 1994.

[94] Para.57.

[95] (1973) 179 USPQ 649. The doctrine is referred to as "subliminal confusion", but the effect is similar.

[96] S. H. Hartman, "Subliminal Confusion: The Misappropriation of Advertising Values" (1988) 78 *TMR* 506, 510–1.

[97] *Ibid.*, 512.

[98] [1993] FSR 641.

fusion as to source; consumers were unlikely to believe that ELDERFLOWER CHAMPAGNE originated in France. Instead, the prestigious image of quality that surrounds the product champagne was protected. An observation in another American case emphasises why the assumption underlying the likelihood of association doctrine is arguably well-founded:

> "[A]dvertising and trade marks rely on impressions. The consumer does not memorise the mark. He has a feeling about it from past exposure. That feeling may be vague, subliminal it is said, but it comes to consciousness when the article is seen with the trade mark affixed."[99]

Purchasing decisions do not take place clinically, with the benefit of hindsight in court rooms and, although consumers may not ultimately be deceived, their decision-making process is undoubtedly affected.[100]

The more serious consequence of the association of trade marks is the unfair advantage that may be gained from the connection made by consumers, since, in the absence of source confusion, the second user may keep his own identity intact whilst benefiting from the positive associations connected with the original user, "in effect, turning the mark against itself".[101] The main difference between this form of confusion and source confusion is that a product's source is an objectively determined feature which will remain constant regardless of the characteristics and merits of the product, whereas the desirability and consumer satisfaction of a product are attributes represented by the trade mark that only come about through manufacturer's investment in and management of the brand. They are therefore factors which must be tested on the evidence in each case.

There is however at least one practical objection that may be raised to trade mark protection which goes beyond mere source confusion.[102] In *WAGAMAMA*, Laddie J. commented that:

> "[I]f the broader scope were to be adopted [which, it is suggested, the ECJ is leaning towards], the Directive and our Act would be creating a new type of monopoly

[99] *Londontown Mfg. Co.* v. *Cable Raincoat Co.* (1974) 182 USPQ 20, 23.

[100] Indeed this consideration was not lost on pre-1994 English law. Cornish cites (n. 22 above, para.17–92) examples of situations where imperfect recollection of marks and the "the idea of a mark" were taken into account when assessing confusion.

[101] Hartman, n. 96 above, 508.

[102] A second is rather more fundamental in nature and difficult to address within our current analysis. In substance, it is suggested that in the absence of confusion as to a product's source, there is no real damage to any of the interests surrounding the trade mark. This complaint was articulated by Jacob J. (R. Jacob, "Industrial Property—Industry's Enemy" [1997] *International Patents Quarterly* 3, 13ff.). He asserted that "real trade marks" are "robust" enough to withstand the dangers of association and suggested that

> "one could investigate, for instance, what trade marks in the 'dark ages' [i.e. pre-1994] were damaged by the kind of association favoured by the wide school of thought. If none, or only a few can be found, that would militate against the extended view of 'association'."

The gauntlet has been well and truly thrown down!

> not related to the proprietor's trade but in the trade mark itself. Such a monopoly could be likened to a quasi-copyright in the mark."[103]

and to a certain extent, he was, with respect, quite correct to do so since the broader protection becomes, the nearer one gets to an absolute prohibition on reproducing the mark concerned. Moreover, protecting trade mark owners against other producers being able to associate their product with the values attaching to another's does seem like copyright protection; the investment that the producer has made in making his brand attractive to consumers is being protected. However, the analogy is by no means complete, since first the mark is not protected for its intrinsic worth, but rather the intangible values surrounding the product and attaching to the mark; and secondly a copyright work is protected, without reservation, from the time of its "fixing", whereas "trade marks require sustained investment and management in order to add value to the mark and to fend off both product and brand competition" since, after all, "registration is only the first step in the process, for if the mark is not distinctive or strong enough, the 'association' criterion . . . will not be of help to the plaintiff in obtaining relief".[104] Obviously, a trade mark owner must prove that association is likely as has always been the case with respect to likelihood of confusion.

Laddie J. in confirming to himself the correctness of the *narrowest* interpretation of section 10(2) (that the only actionable confusion is that as to product source) concluded that the likelihood of association as applied under Benelux law would constitute "a new millstone around the neck of traders"[105] and his supporters have clarified this as meaning "that widening the monopoly makes it more difficult for [the trader] to choose a safe mark to use in the first place".[106] However, given the huge investment that may go into a brand, the greater the significance of a brand to consumers, the less legitimate the claim of another trader becomes to use the trade mark or one similar. Surely it is fairer for an inconvenience to be overcome at the outset than to allow another to gain a free ride at the expense of an established product? Looking at the situation from an economic perspective, it seems that it is being presumed, without the aid of any formal economic analysis, that the greater the level of protection given to a mark becomes, the greater is the risk to free competition. We saw in Chapter 3 that there is no *direct* effect on competition which may result from

[103] [1995] FSR 713, 731.

[104] A. Kamperman Sanders, "The Wagamama Decision: Back to the Dark Ages of Trade Mark Law" [1996] *EIPR* 3, 4.

[105] N. 102 above. Similar views would appear to be shared by Jacob J.: speaking extra-judicially at the University of Bristol on 29 Feb. 1996, on being asked whether he believed that trade mark rights should be augmented to reflect the investment made in them by their owners, disagreed and stated that he was "very pro-competition". It is submitted that the implied belief behind this is that *any* increase in the scope of trade mark rights would endanger competition.

[106] P. Prescott, "Think Before You Waga Finger" [1996] *EIPR* 317, 318, and if "corporations do not spend too much time worrying about association without confusion" (*ibid.*), would Mr. Prescott care to explain why own-brand lookalikes (see Ch.5 and Appendix B, below)—an excellent example of where association may occur without any confusion as to source—trouble them so much?

trade mark protection. Rather, it may be said that the cost of finding an unobjectionable mark becomes greater as the scope of protection accorded to earlier marks increases. This, on the face of it, may be described as inefficient because of the barrier to entry into a market that this may create, and because of the apparent waste of money spent searching for a name. However, this must be balanced against the amount that producers undoubtedly spend on promoting their brand (and brand name) which may be jeopardised in the presence of consumer confusion in the market place. While this is difficult to quantify, it is no less a concern than the increased cost in finding a brand name in the first place resulting from a wider scope of trade mark right and is arguably greater. It is submitted, though, that even if a broader trade mark right leads to increased costs in creating new product or business names, corporations are quite capable of spending vast amounts on creating new names regardless of the cost of Trade Mark Act compliance.[107]

It is quite clear that in any event the interest protected by the emerging jurisprudence of the ECJ in relation to the likelihood of confusion is that of the trade mark owning producer and is moreover his interest in retaining the benefit in developing and promoting a trade-marked product. Such a conclusion is consistent with the premise that the overriding concern in trade mark law is to protect trade mark owners against unfairly competitive behaviour, although since "subliminal confusion results in the misappropriation of advertising value *through consumer deception*, it implicates both public and private injury".[108]

Third Party Use on Unrelated Products: The Dilution Doctrine

Assessing the likelihood of confusion and admitting a broad range of factors related to the circumstances in which consumers may encounter a trade mark may be seen as a development of the traditional source confusion basis of protection and contains at least a passing consideration of the consumers' interest.[109] Section 10(3), which in certain circumstances will allow a trade mark

[107] Consider the amount reputedly spent on dreaming up "Diageo" following the merger of Guinness and Grand Metropolitan. Another compliance cost which is alleged to increase in proportion to the scope of protection granted is that of the registration process. One argument advanced in *Canon* v. *Pathe*, n. 83 above (see para. 43 of the A.G.'s Opinion) against the consideration of the strength or reputation of a mark (which are obviously relevant when owners of existing marks are given a broad right to object) at the stage of registration was the cost and delay of such a consideration. The A.G. brushed aside this argument saying that:

> "The French Government stated . . . that, in its experience, such consideration did not unduly lengthen or complicate the procedure. Indeed, it may be in the interest of legal certainty to ensure that mark whose use may be challenged successfully are not registered in the first place" (*ibid.*).

[108] Hartman, n. 96 above, 510 (emphasis added).

[109] The literature on the dilution doctrine is vast as well as controversial, and a complete discussion is beyond the scope of this book. However the case law in several jurisdictions is reviewed in T. Martino, *Trade Mark Dilution* (Oxford, 1996) and the following articles have been useful:

owner to object to the use of an identical or similar mark on *unrelated* goods, is entirely new,[110] and it is aimed at a wholly private injury. The notion that a trade mark, and hence some interest in it, may be injured in the absence of consumer confusion as to the source of goods through use of this nature is customarily attributed to the article published by Schechter in the 1927 *Harvard Law Review*.[111] Although section 10(3) does not refer to it as such, the circumstances contemplated in the provision are of the type generally referred to as trade mark dilution.[112] It was seen in Chapter 2 that the thesis advanced by Schechter was instrumental in causing people to acknowledge the increasingly broad functions performed by the use of trade marks.[113] However, he went further in asserting that these functions required commensurate protection which the law did not confer at that time[114]; it seemed to him the case that,

> "The history of important trade mark litigation within recent years shows that the use of similar marks on *non*-competing goods is perhaps the *normal* rather than the exceptional case of infringement. . . . In each instance the defendant was not actually diverting custom from the plaintiff. . . . The real injury in all such cases can only be gauged in the light of what has been said concerning the function of a trade mark. It is the gradual whittling away or dispersion of the identity and hold upon the public mind of the mark . . . by its use upon non-competing goods. The more distinctive or unique the mark, the deeper is its impress upon the public consciousness, and the greater the need for protection against vitiation or dissociation from the particular product in connection with which it has been used."[115]

Schechter, "The Rational Basis of Trade Mark Protection", n. 48 above; G. E. Middleton, "Some Reflections on Dilution" (1952) 42 *TMR* 175 (hereinafter Middleton, "Some Reflections") and "Some Aspects of Trade Mark Dilution" (1957) 47 *TMR* 1023 (hereinafter Middleton, "Some Aspects"); Harvard Law Review, Note, "Dilution: Trade Mark Infringement or Will O' The Wisp" (1964) 77 *Harv. LR* 520; B. W. Pattishall, Dilution Rationale and "Dawning Acceptance of the Dilution Rationale for Trade Mark and Trade Identity Protection" (1984) 74 *TMR* 289; R. C. Denicola, "Trade Marks as Speech: Constitutional Implications of the Emerging Rationales for the Protection of Trade Symbols" [1982] *Wis. LR* 158; T. Martino, "Trade Mark Dilution: I hear you Knocking but You Can't Come In: *Mead Data Central* v. *Toyota*" [1990] *EIPR* 141; Bannon, n. 1 above; D. S. Welkowitz, "Re-examining Trade Mark Dilution" (1991) 44 *Vanderbilt LR* 531; Moskin, n. 56; K. L. Port, "The 'Unnatural' Expansion of Trade Mark Rights: Is a Federal Dilution Statute Necessary?" (1995) 85 *TMR* 525.

110 Although the principles underlying the right are similar to those underlying the former defensive registration scheme. See W. R. Cornish, *Intellectual Property: Patents, Copyrights, Trade Marks and Allied Rights* (2nd edn., London, 1989), paras.17–046–8.

111 Schechter, n. 48 above.

112 Several writers on English law have made this equation: Annand and Norman, n. 58 above, 156; R. Lewin, "The New Trade Marks Act: A Godsend for Trade Mark Owner or a Goldmine for their Lawyers?" [1994] *EIPR* 91; B. Mills, "Own Label Products and the Look-alike Phenomenon: A Lack of Trade Dress and Unfair Competition Protection?" [1995] *EIPR* 116; Robertson and Horton, n. 12 above; and see also Port, n. 108 above, n. 6. The word "dilution" is sometimes used to indicate the erosion of a trade mark's commercial significance regardless of the context (see e.g. Welkowitz, n. 108 above, 534.), but is used here simply to meaning such damage in the context of use on *unrelated* products.

113 Schechter, n. 48 above, 816–9.

114 *Ibid.*, 822.

115 *Ibid.*, 825. Interestingly, Port observes that in America between 1978 and 1995, there have only been *four* cases where dilution has been the sole ground for relief (n. 108 above, 537).

Although the terms of section 10(3) have yet to form the *ratio decidendi* of any final judgment in the Chancery Division,[116] it does seem that the language used mirrors the concerns of Schechter. The fact that reputation must be established for the relief under the section to be available implies that protection is not available to any old registered trade mark; beyond this it is difficult to predict which marks will fall into this category, although one may hazard a guess that it will be those that are recognised by a substantial proportion of the consuming population as a whole.[117] We are also told that relief is conditional on conduct that takes unfair advantage or is detrimental to the trade mark's distinctive character or repute. The phrase "distinctive character" is also used in section 3(1)(b) as a requirement for registrability,[118] and it was suggested in Chapter 1 that this meant that consumers must regard the sign seeking registration as having trade mark significance. Therefore, it would seem that section 10(3) is aimed at protecting the meaning that trade marks convey to consumers and, because the provision contemplates marks with a greater consumer recognition than otherwise, it would also seem that it is the aspect of the trade mark's meaning *other* than that which differentiates its underlying product from other products that is protected (since this is what all trade marks mean and do), namely its consistent quality, advertised attributes and so on. It is that aspect of the trade mark's meaning that arises from the experience of those who encounter the product[119] which in turn has arisen from the producer's investment in the product's development and marketing, or indeed from what consumers have been conditioned to relate to the mark through advertising.

It does seem that the actual subject-matter of protection is becoming increasingly intangible and nebulous, but this does not of itself make it any less worthy of protection. This trade mark significance does not sound very different from that recognised and protected under the likelihood of association rationale described above; indeed both are the values recognised in the product by consumers and symbolised by the trade mark. However the major difference[120] is that, whereas under the ECJ's conception of the likelihood of confusion the trade mark meaning is thought to be surreptitiously transferred through the consumer's sometimes "subliminal" confusion, here it is possible that the meaning, and hence value, of the trade mark which has been established through

[116] The decisions in *BASF plc* v. *CEP (UK) plc*, LEXIS Transcript, 26 October 1995, Chancery Division and *Baywatch* v. *Home Video Channel*, [1997] FSR 22 were only interlocutory and the ECJ's remarks in *Sabel* v. *Puma*, [1998] RPC 199 as well as those of Jonathan Sumption QC in *Marks & Spencer plc* v. *One In A Million*, [1998] FSR 265 were obiter.

[117] See Annand and Norman, n. 58 above, 157 who observe that American law has tended to protect more famous marks, whereas Benelux law (predictably) has been less discriminating in its recognition of "reputable" marks.

[118] Port points out that in America use of the traditional trade mark terminology to "capture the dilution rhetoric" has served to blur the distinction between the bases of protection and resulted in hindering the development of the dilution rationale (n. 108 above, 547).

[119] Pattishall, n. 10 above, 631.

[120] Another difference is that empirical proof, albeit somewhat imperfect, of the likelihood of confusion is much easier than dilution, as we shall see below, text accompanying nn. 114–19.

consumer recognition is nevertheless damaged independently of any effect on consumer perception of the product *in that particular instance*. Therefore, it is damage only to the value of the trade mark as a marketing tool that is contemplated and thus preventing it entails protecting only the producer's interest.[121]

Protecting, under either the dilution rationale or the broad likelihood of confusion, the value of a trade mark which derives from the meaning accumulated by the marketing of the underlying product is, it is submitted, unobjectionable. Moreover, it is arguably quite supportable by reference to the natural rights doctrine of John Locke.[122] Locke maintained that all things were initially held in common by all[123] and that all that a man could be said to own was labour of his body. Only by mixing his labour with an object of nature does it become his property,[124] such that it is now of some use and thus worthy of ownership.[125] Very crudely, in the context of trade marks, by adopting a trade mark and marketing a product under this trade mark, with the result that a brand is created that is desirable to consumers, the trade mark user has exerted his labour through product development, advertising and promotion upon the trade mark, thereby creating communicative values surrounding the mark in which the producer has a claim for protection.[126] This should not be interpreted as an incentive[127] to innovation since the incentive lies in the market place recognition of a product's merits and the ensuing profit potential; rather it is protecting the means by which the incentive arises: the continuing recognition by consumers through the medium of a trade mark of a meritorious product. In any event, it may be seen that the Lockean natural rights analysis is guiding the extension of trade mark protection beyond mere source confusion.[128] Having said that, it may be argued that "there is no inherent right to perpetual fame"[129] once the commercial significance of the mark is established, since "trade mark recognition requires at least periodic advertising to remind the consuming audience of the trade mark's presence"[130] as well as that of the underlying product, but although a trade mark owner may not claim perpetual fame, he may reasonably expect protection against others losing that fame for him. After all, the trade mark's reputation must be made out on each occasion protection is sought

121 Pattishall, n. 10 above, 626; Denicola, n. 108 above, 183.

122 This discussion is taken from Port, n. 108 above, 561–3 who in fact denies that Locke's theory is applicable in this context, but I would argue that there is more than one interpretation of Locke so that it can be seen to be the case that protecting the value of a trade mark is perfectly consonant with Locke's writings.

123 J. Locke, *Two Treatises of Government* (ed. M. Goldie, London, 1993), Second Treatise, para.25.

124 *Ibid.*, para.27.

125 *Ibid.*, para.28.

126 See Port, n. 108 above, 562.

127 Cf, *ibid.*, 562–3.

128 *Ibid.*, 572–3.

129 Welkowitz, n. 108 above, 586.

130 *Ibid.* See generally D. A. Aaker, *Managing Brand Equity: Capitalising on the Value of a Brand Name* (New York, 1991) concerning the continual management that a brand will require during its life.

under secton 10(3) and, if the brand has been neglected, the trade mark owner will experience difficulty.[131]

Some commentators[132] have objected to the acceptance of this aspect of a trade mark's significance by saying that to protect it creates copyright-like rights in a trade mark *as if this was somehow inherently reprehensible*, and so protects the mark itself rather than the underlying trade. We saw above that the analogy to copyright is valid to a certain degree, but it is definitely untrue to the extent that it implies that trade mark law will prevent all uses in all circumstances. No-one has ever suggested that this is or should be the case. It is also difficult to see how protecting the meaning of a trade mark beyond its indication of a product's source is "exalting the mark above the trade".[133] Admittedly, Schechter's original formulation that "arbitrary, coined or fanciful" marks were inherently more worthy of protection[134] probably is flawed in this respect, but if one adopts Pattishall's argument that the only meaning that may be diluted and so be worthy of extended protection in the first place was that significance which the mark gained through use in trade, then it is hard to sustain Middleton's (and indeed Laddie J.'s) objection.[135] As soon as the significance expires, so does any claim to extended protection. Finally, others object to the effect of dilution protection because of the way it interferes with traditional trade mark doctrine.[136] So what? Orthodox trade mark doctrine developed at a time when trade mark function was more limited, and so expanding protection is doing no more than recognise this fact.[137] As Prescott points out, introducing a new right and assessing the efficiency of doing so is the prerogative of Parliament,[138] but is this not exactly what it has done in enacting section 10(3) Trade Marks Act?

Recognising and Protecting the Trade Mark's Wider Integrity: Is Dilution Necessarily the Most Appropriate Means?

Despite the fact that rights have now been conferred on trade mark owners throughout most of the European Union as well as the whole of the United States,[139] enabling them to object to certain uses of signs identical or similar to their own on unrelated products, and which, in so far as it accepts a model of

[131] See Welkowitz, n. 108 above, 586 when he points out Schechter's assumption that "distinctive" (i.e. strong) marks are inherently and so will always remain so.

[132] Middleton, n. 108 above; Laddie J. in WAGAMAMA (n. 102 above); Port, n. 108 above, 573–4.

[133] Middleton, Some Reflections, n. 108 above. 177.

[134] Schechter, n. 48 above, 828.

[135] Port, n. 108 above, 573–4, also makes this objection but takes it a stage further and claims that dilution grants a copyright "in the idea of the trade mark in the mind of the consumer".

[136] See amongst others Port, n. 108 above, 529–30.

[137] This is one of the central themes in F. I. Schechter, *The Historical Foundations of the Law Relating to Trade Marks* (New York, 1925).

[138] N. 105 above, 318.

[139] Through Art.5(2) Trade Marks Directive (which, although optional, has been adopted in all 15 member states) and the 1995 Federal Trade Mark Dilution Act respectively, and note also Art.9(1)(c) Council Regulation of 20 Dec. 1993 on the Community Trade Mark (40/94/EEC, OJ [1994] L11/1).

the function of trade marks which is wider than mere source indication, is in principle unobjectionable,[140] it may still be argued that for practical reasons such protection is unjustified or unnecessary. A problem commonly faced in America is discerning what constitutes dilution such that courts and commentators alike have become entangled in various metaphors in an attempt to isolate the specific complaint[141] beyond merely believing that unauthorised use on unrelated goods is somehow wrongful.[142] In English law however, we have the advantage that we are in fact told by section 10(3) that the complaint is that the third party use either *takes unfair advantage* of or is *detrimental* to the mark's distinctive character. The real problem that both courts and the advisors of trade mark users face is how one or other of these conditions may be empirically proved. As Schechter himself points out[143] and as is generally accepted, trade marks are devices through which consumers are induced into purchasing products. Although this may sometimes be as a result of the decorative value of the mark on goods, it is generally because of the information that the trade mark imparts to consumers about the underlying product.[144] It would therefore seem that the only way in which the trade mark may be damaged is by the conduct of other traders which has the tendency to interfere with the significance of the trade mark to consumers. It would follow from this that the best measure of any interference is the consumers' resulting perception of the mark or at least how the mark may be seen to come over to consumer. Where the offending product is identical or similar to the first user's product, interference is of course judged by reference to the likelihood of consumer confusion, but if the products are dissimilar, it is not relevant in deciding whether the conduct complained of falls within section 10(3); it must be implicitly presumed that consumer confusion or even mere association is impossible, but also that damage to the significance of the trade mark to consumers is still nevertheless a possibility.

Whilst in the case of the likelihood of confusion between marks in respect of identical or similar products it may conceivably be demonstrated that, because of the similarity between the products, consumers identify qualities of the senior user's product with those of the junior user's through the association of marks,

[140] Another principled objection to the dilution doctrine is in fact put forward by Moskin (n. 56 above, 136–7) who argues that an allegation of dilution is only the "thin end of the wedge", as it were, in that the defendant's conduct is only an aspect of the gradual weakening of the mark; the real damage will only occur if other (hypothetical) defendants are allowed to do the same. Liability for dilution, so it is said, is therefore an unacceptable form of vicarious liability. However (as Helen Norman has suggested to me), is this not similar to the widely practised remedies of interlocutory relief and injunctions *quia timet* which are both regarded as perfectly acceptable and granted in the absence of existing damage?

[141] Moskin, n. 56 above, 130–3.

[142] *Ibid.*, 135.

[143] N. 48 above, 819 and 822.

[144] In parenthesis, it seems that where a famous brand name is used in an unauthorised merchandising venture, this may constitute taking unfair advantage. See Welkowitz, n. 108 above, 580–1, and more generally Denicola, n. 108 above. Having said this, it would appear that this form of damage was not quite the same as that originally envisaged by Schechter since, as seen in Ch.2 above, merchandising was not nearly as widely established when he wrote as it is now.

but Moskin submits that where the products are unrelated, not enough is understood about consumers' mental processes to demonstrate when a mark is being weakened[145] or even to presume so, such that certain categories of conduct may be deemed to be injurious; "argument by metaphor is no substitute for empirical study".[146] "Blurring" of a mark's distinctiveness, for example by selling KODAK pianos or ROLLS-ROYCE aspirin on the one hand or T-shirts in the trade dress of COCA-COLA stating "Enjoy Cocaine"[147] or a fake AMERICAN EXPRESS card containing a condom under the slogan NEVER LEAVE HOME WITHOUT IT[148] on the other may seem intuitively unfair and are examples of what the dilution doctrine and so section 10(3) are aimed at, but can they be *shown* to weaken the mark's advertising power or cause consumers to shun the product concerned?[149] It would seem that there is no other way of demonstrating this other than through evidence of consumer experience since the language of section 10(3), it is submitted, assumes that the "unfair advantage" or "detriment" affects the consumer perception and must be defined with reference to it because the distinctive character derives from consumer recognition in the first place; but "the difficulty of finding a witness able to detect in his or her own conscious or unconscious mind a gradual watering down of his or her loyalty to a branded product, or one concerned enough about the phenomenon to complain about it"[150] would appear to be practically insurmountable.

It is worth considering that when Schechter was writing, the "traditional" confusion rationale for trade mark protection was not nearly as highly developed as it is now. It was difficult to prove public confusion with respect to goods that were less than directly competitive and the only form of confusion that would suffice was confusion as to the products' origin. In contemporary trade mark law, we have the doctrine of non-origin confusion,[151] the much broadened scope of section 10(2) (acknowledging the marketing practice of brand extension and its acceptance by consumers) and the statement in the Directive that the "*recognition* [or strength] of the trade mark on the market"[152] is now relevant

[145] Moskin, n. 56 above, 134–5.

[146] *Ibid.*, 136.

[147] Swann and Davis, n. 59 above, 274.

[148] Annand and Norman, n. 58 above, 156.

[149] Although the Benelux Court of Justice (1 Mar. 1975, [1975] *Nederlandse Jurisprudentie* 472) may have famously supported the decision to enjoin KLAREIN (for detergent) because of the danger of diluting CLAERYN (for gin) by stating that "the consumer should not, for one moment, get the taste of soap in his mouth when drinking gin", the writer for one has never got the taste of JIF bathroom cleaner in his mouth when eating JIF lemon juice on his pancakes! More seriously, there have been years of concurrent user of the mark JIF without any allegations of mutual detriment.

[150] Moskin, n. 56 above, 138. He hypothesises that goodwill (in the sense of a positive disposition towards a particular product) does not exist in the mind, but rather is "detectable only from the conduct it precipitates" and so is only measurable by behavioural studies "of a kind realistically foreclosed to trade mark law".

[151] To use Laddie J.'s label in WAGAMAMA *Ltd.* v. *City Centre Restaurants plc* [1995] FSR 713, 721.

[152] See the 10th Recital of the Preamble to the Trade Marks Directive (emphasis added). This means that the greater the strength (or indeed distinctive character) of the mark, the greater the probability that likelihood of confusion will be made out; this is similar to Middleton's argument that a mark's strength is a question of degree or "penumbra" that will be cast ("Some Reflections",

to assessing the likelihood of confusion, such that many of the considerations envisaged by Schechter are today well-established.[153] In other words, Schechter's abstract concern, protecting the wider integrity of a trade mark, has been recognised by the development of "traditional" doctrine, and consequently the need for protection against dilution has been overtaken. This is not to say that allowing trade mark owners to object to the trade mark use of others on unrelated goods under section 10(3) is of no practical utility. Gross tarnishment is a case in point as illustrated by the ENJOY COCAINE case. Although logically, as described above, tarnishment does not seem to be possible in the absence of attribution by consumers of the tarnishing image to unrelated goods, psychological research has revealed that "the mind . . . may retain unfavourable associations with a product even in the face of direct evidence that the association is unjustified".[154] In so far as section 10(3) prevents this type of detrimental conduct, it must be surely be seen as necessary.

CONCLUSION

In spite of all this exaltation of the producers' interest, it must be stressed that it is not at the expense of the consumers' interests. On the contrary, as long as consumers are conditioned to select products by reference to trade marks and therefore place their reliance on them, consumers' interests will always be central to trade mark law; indeed without consumer reliance, trade mark law would be pointless, since in protecting them the law presumes both producers continuing to apply them to products and consumers continuing to recognise them in a retail environment. However, this factor has never provided a reason for restricting protection. As the trade mark has become ever more embroiled in the marketing process, it has amassed a significance, interference with which may damage the producer using the particular mark without necessarily causing any problems to the consumers encountering the mark in the market place. In other words, another trader's conduct may infringe a trade mark because of its unfairly competitive consequences. Taken with other evidence in trade mark law that protection of the interests of producers is the dominant policy, it is therefore no longer necessary to restrict trade mark protection by reference to concept of consumer confusion as to product source.[155] We can therefore see a

n. 10 above, 178; "Some Aspects", n. 108 above, 1033). Note however the seemingly innocuous statement by Jacob J. in *Origins Natural Resources Inc.* v. *Origin Clothing Ltd.* [1995] FSR 280, 284, that s.10(2) Trade Marks Act requires the court to "assess a likelihood of confusion in relation to the way in which the defendant uses its mark, *discounting external added matter or circumstances*. The comparison is mark for mark" (emphasis added). This seems implicitly to contradict the Preamble to the Directive. Doubt has since been cast on Jacob J.'s interpretation at para.22 in *Sabel* v. *Puma* [1998] RPC 199.

153 Moskin, n. 56 above, 145; Welkowitz, n. 108 above, 583.

154 Moskin, n. 56 above, 147.

155 This in itself provides the compelling interest felt necessary by two commentators (Pattishall, n. 10 above, 627; Denicola, n. 108 above, 183) to justify departure from the previous restraint seen in trade mark protection.

firm shift away from trade mark protection's historical basis in the prevention of the deceitful conduct in the market, and so another of Schechter's historical pre-conceptions is (thankfully) laid to rest.[156] As may be expected, there are some who view the extension of the exclusive rights in a trade mark as nothing more than a pernicious attempt to confer new monopolies to the detriment of all in the market place. What opponents of the broader (and, it seems, the true) interpretation of section 10(2)(3) do not seem to accept is that one cannot assume that simply because the law is *willing* to confer the right, it *will* confer the right in all cases. The requirements of the statutory provisions must be made out before infringement may be found, and this will depend on several factors including the "strength" of the mark. The likelihood of confusion between one highly descriptive, unadvertised mark and another will, without fear of contradiction, be far less than between, say, KODAK and a similar mark. Enough was said about the alleged monopolistic tendencies of trade marks in Chapter 3, it is submitted, to answer the fears of Laddie J. and Peter Prescott QC. However, the people who worry in emotive terms about the trade mark "monopoly" (as if it were a patent) seem to have difficulty in appreciating that a trade mark is more than simply an entry on a register or a document in court; it is something that is used daily in the market place, in which investment is made and to which goodwill attaches. Moreover, it is something that is recognised by consumers as representing something tangible, a particular product. Given the contemporary organisation of commerce, it is difficult to fathom why one producer would ever have a legitimate interest in using a particular sign as a trade mark when it is in use by another. Trade mark protection can, it seems, perhaps become too over-enthusiastic or, at least, protect against non-existent threats. The so-called dilution protection apparently envisaged by section 10(3) is based to a greater rather than lesser extent on premises that have been overtaken by events; a lot of the mischief at which such protection was originally aimed is now covered under the less radical confusion rationale and consequently "dilution laws . . . have been eclipsed in practice by [protection with reference to consumer confusion] as the [doctrine] has come to provide a remedy and means for preserving the advertising value and commercial magnetism of trade marks".[157] Hopefully in practice as well as theory.

156 Schechter, n. 136 above, 147.
157 Moskin, n. 56 above, 147.

5

Other Protection Issues: Comparative Advertising and Trade Dress

In this chapter, we come to two specific areas that find themselves at the periphery of trade mark protection, but which illustrate well the overlap between the law of trade marks and the more general concern with unfair competition, as well as being issues of contemporary importance. Comparative advertising is a concern of trade mark law because trade marks are the primary means by which a producer may identify his competitor's product in his advertisements. Whether this should be allowed involves an examination of some of the issues underlying trade mark protection which have already been addressed in previous chapters. A product's get-up or, to use a more self-explanatory term, trade dress is of interest due to the fact that it shares one vital function with trade marks, namely it can serve to identify the product. Although it is dictated to a certain extent by the nature of the product, aspects of its design are equally capable of becoming distinctive of a particular manufacturer or product. In spite of this, it is difficult, if not impossible, for manufacturers to object to its imitation.[1] Given especially the widespread occurrence of own-label goods that are often suspiciously similar to the original product in their trade dress,[2] the question must surely be asked whether this form of competition is sufficiently unfair to warrant limitation through trade dress protection.

THE USE OF A COMPETITOR'S TRADE MARK IN COMPARATIVE ADVERTISING

The objective of any brand advertising is to cause consumers to buy a product both by informing them of objective factors such as its availability or price and by persuading them, for example through appeals to the senses or their vanity, that they wish to own or make use of whatever is on offer.[3] One way in which a producer may seek to do this is by comparing his product with that of his com-

[1] See Ch.1 above.

[2] Some examples (which have mostly been the subject of litigation) are reproduced at Appendix B, figs. 1–4 and 7–9 below. A recent dispute, e.g., is that between Kellogg's and Tesco concerning the packaging of Tesco's breakfast cereal (*Daily Telegraph*, "Tesco corn flake packs get frosty response", 16 Aug. 1996, 3).

[3] As we saw in Ch.3 above the economic utility of this latter form of advertising has been questioned.

petitor, inevitably in order to portray his own in a superior light. There may be various reasons why he may choose to indulge in this form of advertising and we shall come to these presently, but regardless of this it is fair to say that his competitor will not be content with this state of affairs. A recent example to reach the courts is the ORANGE mobile phone company's campaign which claimed that "on average, ORANGE users save £20 per month" (in comparison with clients of VODAPHONE).[4] In order to undertake his comparative advertisement, the advertiser must somehow identify his competitor's product. He may do this by describing the competing product and naming its manufacturer without expressly naming the product. This method, though, carries the risk of ambiguity ("[t]he yeast extract spread produced for CPC (UK) Ltd." does not have the same immediacy of comprehension that permeates "MARMITE") and moreover defeats the object of advertising, one aim of which may be said to be brevity,[5] and hence ease of digestion. Also he may simply replicate his competitor's get-up in the advertisement so as merely to insinuate the product's identity. Such was the case in EVER READY's campaign comparing their batteries with those of DURACELL.[6] Again, this option is not always open because not all manufacturers' get-ups are as instantly recognisable as that of DURACELL.[7] The obvious choice, however, is to use one's competitor's trade mark in the comparative advertisement. Note that an advertisement can be comparative without actually naming the competition, for example consider CARLSBERG's slogan that it is "probably the best lager in the world" which by implication claims that all other lagers are inferior.[8] This is known as indirectly comparative advertising, but this is not of such immediate interest to us because it does not involve use of another's trade mark.

Given the outrage which a trader may feel at seeing his trade mark interfered with in this way, it is understandable that he may seek to prevent the advertisement, and one way that may be open to him is to assert his rights in the trade mark. We saw in Chapter 1 that the owner of a registered mark must rely on the proviso to section 10(6) of the Trade Marks Act 1994 to prevent the (*prima facie* legitimate) third party use of his mark in this context, although following Laddie J.'s interpretation of the provision in *Barclays Bank plc* v. *RBS Advanta*,[9] it would seem that the circumstances in which this is possible are fairly limited. In the case of an unregistered mark, the owner will only be able to prevent the

[4] *Vodaphone Group plc* v. *Orange Personal Communication Services Ltd.* [1997] FSR 34.

[5] T. Martino and W. Ullah, "The Quality Guarantee Function of Trade Marks: An Economic Perspective" [1989] *EIPR* 267.

[6] See C. J. Parkinson, "The Re-awakening of Comparative Advertising in the UK", Dec. 1990, *TW* 44–5. For further examples of comparative advertisement by "extrinsic allusion", see V. Pasek, "Are Comparisons Odious?", Aug. 1988, *TW* 44, 45.

[7] Referring to another trader's product by its get-up brings its own issues because, as we shall see below, text accompanying nn. 91–8, it currently falls outside of the trade mark registration scheme.

[8] B. Mills, "Comparative Advertising: Should It Be Allowed?" [1995] *EIPR* 417.

[9] [1996] RPC 307. Not to mention the subsequent approval of it in *Vodaphone Group plc* v. *Orange Personal Communication Services Ltd.* [1997] FSR 34 and *British Telecommunications plc* v. *AT&T Communications (UK) Ltd.* [1997] EIPR D–134.

comparative use of his mark if the advertisement is so confusingly worded as to cause a misrepresentation concerning the source of the goods (this is what occurred in *McDonald's Hamburgers Ltd* v. *Burger King (UK) Ltd.*[10]), so again the protection is limited. There are other means, though, for tackling the issue to which we shall later return. What we shall examine first are the merits of allowing comparative advertising to take place and whether it can correctly be said to affect the basis of the trade mark right, before returning to the question of the most appropriate means of regulating the phenomenon. It could be argued that such a discussion would be sterile and academic, given that the subject has so recently been legislated upon. In fact the contrary is true since the EC has recently adopted a Directive aimed at harmonising legal provisions governing comparative advertising within the Community[11] and the UK government will have to decide if and in what way the law in this country will have to be changed as a result. Consequently comparative advertising as both a legal and a political issue is by no means settled.

The Merits of Comparative Advertising

The case for allowing a producer to name his competitors' products in his advertising has been gaining favour in recent years. The notion came to legal prominence in *Irving's Yeast-Vite Ltd* v. *Horsenail*[12] when it was held that a trade mark owner was unable to prevent a rival from advertising his product as "a substitute for YEAST-VITE" which was the trade mark owner's product. At the time, during the 1930s, this was thought somehow to be an unfair invasion, plain and simple, of a trade mark owner's goodwill[13] and a practice which therefore ought to be curbed; so the infamous section 4(1)(b) of the Trade Marks Act 1938[14] was enacted, thereby allowing trade mark owners to object to virtually all comparative advertisements involving their trade marks. However, when the matter was reviewed by the Mathys Committee in 1974,[15] sympathy for trade mark owners had become rather more equivocal. It was felt by some who gave evidence that it was a legitimate competitive practice so long as the facts were accurate; others argued that "although the facts may be accurate, the method of presentation may be chosen to give the goods of a seller using another's registered trade mark a boost at the expense of the other in a wholly unacceptable

[10] [1986] FSR 45; see F. Clark, "*McDonalds Hamburgers Ltd.* v. *Burger King (UK) Ltd.*: '. . . a Nice Advertisement for Everybody . . .' " [1985] *EIPR* 264 (the copy read "It's not just Big, Mac").

[11] European Parliament and Council Directive amending Directive 84/450/EEC concerning misleading advertising so as to include comparative advertising (97/55/EC OJ [1997] L290/18).

[12] (1934) 51 RPC 110.

[13] *Report of the Departmental Committee on the Law and Practice Relating to Trade Marks* (Goschen Committee), Cmd. 4568 (London, 1934) paras.184–5.

[14] I will gladly resist quoting MacKinnon L.J.'s now hackneyed opinion of the provision delivered in *Bismag Ltd.* v. *Amblins (Chemists) Ltd.* (1940) 57 RPC 209!

[15] *British Trade Mark Law and Practice* (Mathys Committee), Cmnd. 5601 (London, 1974) paras.80–4.

manner"; it was even said that comparative advertising had become increasingly common and, although traders objected infrequently, it was "a moot point whether and to what extent most of these practices did any harm".[16] This feeling was shared across the Atlantic to the extent that the U.S. Federal Trade Commission (FTC) began to encourage the media to accept comparative advertisements in the conviction that they were beneficial to consumer decision making[17]; previously American advertisers had been wary of them because of a belief that they were possibly "not the done thing" or otherwise unlawful.[18]

There are broadly two reasons that support permitting comparative advertising. First, it is thought to enhance the information upon which consumers base their purchasing decisions thereby enabling a more rational and informed choice. If two or more products are compared, it seems self-evident that consumers will be able to differentiate between and evaluate them on meaningful and objective criteria rather than having to rely on possibly impressionistic recollections of competitors' publicity. However, although this sounds appealing and indeed manifestly beneficial, it is not clear whether such benefits have been conclusively proved. There is an assumption underlying the arguments of those who favour comparative advertising that it necessarily has much in common with the reports produced by consumers' organisations such as the Consumers' Association and will consequently contain factual and almost impartial observations aimed primarily at facilitating the consumer's decision, but not influencing it.[19] Although the growth of "consumerism" may have led to the need for more objective advertising, the overall assumption is unrealistic. Comparative advertisements are arguably no different from other (non-comparative) advertisements, in that they share the primary goal of selling the product that is being advertised; educating consumers must only be a secondary concern "in so far as it can act as a persuasive element in the advertisement".[20] The information is therefore not in reality framed with the consumers' interest in mind. It is of course possible to remedy this by requiring that comparative advertisements contain only objective information of a certain nature, but it would be theoretically inconsistent not to require this of advertising in general since this is a potential criticism of all advertising; consumers are aware of the presentation of advertisements and to attempt to influence their content in this way "runs contrary to the spirit of advertising"[21] whilst seeking to protect consumers unduly at the expense of advertisers' freedom. Nevertheless to the extent that

[16] *Ibid.*, para.83.

[17] S. B. Conlon, "Comparative Advertising: Whatever Happened to 'Brand X'" (1977) 67 *TMR* 407, 407–8; apparently now comparative advertisements account for approximately half of all advertisements in America (Mills, n. 8 above, 424).

[18] See L. D. Gaughen, "Adverts which Identify Brand 'X': A Trialogue on the Law and Policy" (1967) 57 *TMR* 309.

[19] Both the Mathys Committee (n. 15 above, para.83) and the FTC (Mills, n. 8 above, 424) seem to be of this belief.

[20] Report of the EC Committee on the Environment, Public Health and Consumer Protection (see COM(91)147 final) cited in Mills, n. 8 above, 418.

[21] *Ibid.*

consumers' ability to assess the relative merits of two products is concerned is facilitated, there must be some benefit. A more fundamental factor is that it has never been empirically shown that comparing an advertised product with its competitors will benefit consumers; its proponents are again proceeding on the basis of assumption.[22] Indeed Mills uses the example of Proctor and Gamble's campaign against Unilever's product PERSIL POWER to illustrate how consumers simply did not believe the claims made in their advertisements and so "are not always taken in by the claims of advertisers".[23] Equally, though, there is no evidence to disprove the assumption. In any event, these factors cannot be seen as reasons in themselves for prohibiting comparative advertising, but rather they call into question the self-evidence of the benefits that this variety of advertising brings to consumers.

The second advantage of comparative advertising is thought to be that it assists the entry of a product into the market, so furthering the interests of the advertiser and at the same time increasing competition, since some even perceive the inability to name one's competitor in an advertisement as being a distortion in the competitive market.[24] Notice at this stage that the actual comparison made in an advertisement can take several forms and it is possible that this may affect the legitimacy of a particular advertisement, and indeed its perception by consumers.[25] The vital distinction is between advertisements that seek to *associate* the products in question and those that *differentiate*. For example in the EVER READY case,[26] the defendant was attempting to differentiate itself from the other leading brand, DURACELL, that was of roughly equal status, whereas in *Chanel* v. *Triton Packing Ltd.*[27] a newcomer wanted to associate itself with the reputation surrounding the plaintiff's more famous brand of fragrance, a product where reputation is crucial. What is important is the exact brand positioning that this allows the advertiser to achieve. This perceived benefit *has* been established by research:

> "In the US, Pechmann and Ratneshwar conducted various experiments to assess the effectiveness of comparative advertisements in relation to brand positioning and found that by far the most effective use of (directly comparative) advertisements was in the area of associating new brands with established brands. In contrast, the use of (directly comparative) advertisements to promote established brands can tend to simply reinforce consumers' stereotypic beliefs that the advertised and comparison brands are much the same thus tending to associate them rather than differentiate them."[28]

[22] *Ibid.*, 419.

[23] *Ibid.*, 419–20. She mentions, however, that the lack of any clear picture of the situation may be due to the inadequacies of the market research techniques used.

[24] See Pasek, n. 6 above, 46.

[25] Mills, n. 8 above, 417–8.

[26] *Duracell International Ltd.* v. *Ever Ready Ltd.* [1989] FSR 87.

[27] [1993] RPC 32.

[28] Mills, n. 8 above, 419 (footnotes omitted), with the result that the volume of wasted, ineffective advertising would be raised (G. Dworkin, " 'Knocking Copy' Comparative Advertising: A Survey of UK Practice" [1979] *EIPR* 41).

Depending on one's viewpoint, the ability of comparative advertising to relate products to other brands with which consumers are already familiar and to which they may even be loyal has a further economic benefit.[29] As we saw in Chapter 3, adherents to the so-called Harvard school were of the opinion that by protecting a product's trade mark, undeserved market power is conferred on the trade mark owner because no-one else could manufacture a perfect substitute for a product, and that moreover, so Professor Brown argued,[30] non-informative advertising of the trade marked product "mesmerises" consumers into the "belief that [the product] has some differentiating virtues"[31] and so effectively raises a barrier to entry into the market for that product. Although many now dispute this view,[32] comparative advertising nevertheless offers a concession to those who are critical of the effects of product differentiation especially through brand advertising, in that the ability of a producer to relate his product in some way to his competitor will enable him to mitigate any market power secured by the competitor's trade mark right.[33] At the very least, the public is saved the cost of being presented with the same message twice.[34] Unfortunately, any economies made in avoiding the cost of informing consumers of a product's characteristics without reference to competitive substitutes are at the expense of justice between the two producers: the first main objection to comparative advertising.

The problem is that what to one producer may be legitimate brand positioning may to another be illegitimate free-riding. The manufacturer of a successful brand will generally have achieved the reputation of his product with the consuming public through diligent market research, investment in development and quality control, as well as advertising and distribution, to ensure that its intended purchasers have the opportunity of buying it. In other words, there has been no small commitment both financially and otherwise in order to establish brand equity. It has always been felt, to a greater or lesser extent, that to allow another to reap the benefit of this, "like the social climber who acquires the status of the people with whom he associates",[35] is unfairly competitive. A further complication arises if consumers do heed the message of the advertiser and are then disappointed; there is the risk that this will reflect back on the original producer.[36] Alternatively, the advertiser may seek deliberately but truthfully to disparage his rival, and whilst this may not in itself be said to be unfair, opponents argue that the opportunity to do this should not be given in the first place. Thus,

[29] See J. M. Livermore, "On Uses of a Competitor's Trade Mark" (1969) 59 *TMR* 30, 35.

[30] R. S. Brown, "Advertising and the Public Interest: Legal Protection of Trade Symbols" (1948) 57 *Yale LJ* 1165.

[31] Livermore, n. 29 above, 35.

[32] In particular, W. M. Landes and R. A. Posner, "Trade Mark Law: an Economic Perspective" [1987] *J Law & Econ.* 265, 275.

[33] S. Nye, "In Defence of Truthful Comparative Advertising" (1977) 67 *TMR* 353, 355–7.

[34] *Ibid.*, 356.

[35] A. Robin and H. B. Barnaby, "Comparative Advertising: A Sceptical View" (1977) 67 *TMR* 358, 361.

[36] *Ibid.*, 365.

the conflict underlying comparative advertising manifests itself in the tension between the advertiser and his competitor.

As well as harming the interests of the manufacturer of the object of comparison, opponents of comparative advertising also see the practice as *detrimental* to consumer decision-making. Since two or more necessarily similar products are named in an advertisement, there is, it is argued, a risk that consumers will once again be confused as to the nature of the products in question. At best, consumers will be none the wiser; at worst, they will purchase the wrong product.[37] We can, though, reject this line of argument immediately. Consumers, it may safely be said, are generally more intelligent than the hypothetical "moron in a hurry",[38] and in any event such an argument presupposes the incompetence of advertisers; surely the whole exercise has been self-defeating if the consumer has been left in any doubt about which product the advertiser wants him to buy? Alternatively and more realistically, there is a danger of confusing the consumer with "information overload"[39] through "presenting him with irreconcilable claims",[40] with the consequence that the efficacy of the decision making process is reduced. Again, this is a matter that is instrumental in the success of an advertisement in communicating its message, and so is a factor that must be considered by the advertiser rather than a reason in principle to oppose permitting comparative advertising. Finally, a factor essential to the validity of arguments supporting comparative advertising is that it must be *truthful*. Any advertisement that deliberately deceives consumers is obviously unacceptable, and this is even more so when the deceit also injures the reputation of a third party trader. There are a variety of sanctions dealing with such behaviour,[41] in particular the injured producer may bring an action in trade libel.[42] On the other hand, the practice of "trade puffery" is one of which advertisers, consumers and courts[43] alike take a robust view. In comparative advertising, of all forms of advertising, one must be careful that it does not convey "misleading information as a result of selective comparison"[44] and that one is aware of the potential unfairness to the compared product resulting from something that is not literally untrue; a balance must be struck, bearing in mind the motives of the advertiser. Nye argues that the ever vigilant producer will soon challenge any claims made against him such that eventually the truth will out,[45] although Mills is of the

[37] Robin and Barnaby, n. 35 above, 362.

[38] *Morning Star Co-operative Society Ltd.* v. *Express Newspapers Ltd.* [1979] FSR 113, 117.

[39] Mills, n. 8 above, 418.

[40] Dworkin, n. 28 above, 41.

[41] On which see *ibid.*

[42] See, e.g., *Compaq Computer Corp.* v. *Dell Computer Corp. Ltd.* [1992] FSR 93.

[43] It was first recognised in *White* v. *Mellin* [1895] AC 154 and recently re-affirmed in *Barclays Bank plc* v. *RBS Advanta* at p. 315.

[44] Dworkin, n. 28 above, 41.

[45] N. 33 above, 354–5. Nye gives an amusing account that bears repeating in full, of the exchanges which took place in 1976 concerning TWA's claim to having a superior punctuality record:

> "First of all the Wall St. Journal tells us that:

opinion that public bickering of this kind can only damage consumer perceptions of the producers concerned.[46]

The arguments for and against allowing comparative advertising appear finely balanced, although the only reason in principle that militates against it is the unfairly competitive consequences for the trader whose product is the object of the comparison. The consumer benefit, whilst attractive, is not as clear-cut as some would like to think, and in fact is arguably no greater than that of non-comparative advertising. The party that stands to gain most is apparently the advertiser. However, what can be perceived from the literature is a growing belief that there is certainly nothing unethical about naming one's competitors in advertising and that the trend is to do so if the party advertising considers that it would be beneficial to his success.[47] Furthermore, it is felt that the practical objections regarding the potential risk to the interests of consumers and the producers who are the object of comparison may be overcome if appropriate safeguards could be put in place, be it in the law of trade marks or elsewhere so allowing a balance to be struck:

> "Comparative advertising is a sales promotion device that compares products or services. It can be a useful source of information, provided that it is strictly regulated. However, it must be specified at the outset that the main aim of the proposal should extend beyond consumer protection; the rights of the manufacturer whose product is being compared must be respected in equal terms with those of the consumer. . . . Accordingly, comparative advertising should only be permitted insofar as it meets those two priority requirements."[48]

Does Comparative Advertising Affect the Producer's Interest in his Trade Mark?

Notice that there has never been a specific ban on comparative advertising in English law,[49] although any form of advertising that makes false claims has

> 'Officials of several other airlines have reacted angrily to the campaign. "TWA is losing whatever friends it had in this industry," one said yesterday.'

Now, that may be true, but since when is popularity with one's competitors the measure of success in our system?

Next we are told that American Airlines became so exercised about the TWA campaign that it considered retaliating with a comparative advertisement campaign of its own featuring its superior safety record.

Now that is one I am waiting for with baited breath. I can see the copy now. 'American may not always land on time, but it always lands at the airport.'"

46 Mills, *Comparative Advertising*, 417 giving the example of the PERSIL POWER incident.

47 Lest it be forgotten that "just because something is permitted doesn't necessarily mean it will oversaturate the market" since "any ad campaign requires a considerable expenditure of money, market research and repetition" and so is not something that will be undertaken lightly (Pasek, n. 6 above, 47).

48 Opinion of ECOSOC on the first draft of the Directive (OJ [1992] C49/10).

49 Compare this with the situation in other EC countries, e.g. Germany, Italy and the Benelux (S. M. Willimsky, "Comparative Advertising: An Overview" [1997] *EIPR* 649).

always been effectively prohibited through the criminal law, the voluntary codes of advertising practice and occasionally at the instance of the person injured; instead between 1938 and 1994 there was a prohibition merely on the use of registered trade marks in comparative advertisements. Even this was not absolute since there were a number of exceptions that are now only of historical interest.[50] Notwithstanding the fact that use of its trade mark is probably the most convenient manner in which a competing product may be identified in an advertisement, it may reasonably be asked why comparative advertising involving a trade mark is any different from comparative advertising involving another manifestation of the competitor's identity. Logically there seems to be no reason why the matter is any concern of the law protecting trade marks. The answer, of course, is that in terms of the advertising's purpose and effect, there is no difference. However as symbols of commercial significance to both producers and consumers in whose interests they are legally protected and which are an exception to the principle that, subject to any protection in patent or copyright, a competitor is free to replicate any aspect of a trader's product,[51] they arguably justify special consideration, at least in this context. Moreover and regardless of whether one sees a trade mark as a mere abstract indication of a product's source or as an integral part of the product and the focal point of its surrounding brand equity, it is undeniable that comparative advertising will affect the trade mark relating to the product that is the object of comparison. This is because use of the trade mark in a comparative advertisement will influence consumers' perception of the underlying goods and, potentially, their propensity to buy them, which in turn affects the value attaching to the trade mark. In this respect, the effect of comparative advertising is the same as that of non-comparative advertising, but with one crucial difference: consumers are in general likely to be *dissuaded* from purchasing the product in favour of the advertised brand. The "goodwill" attaching to, symbolised and protected by the trade mark can therefore be damaged.[52]

Although trade marks can in many ways be described as property and calls have been made to recognise a property right in a product's brand equity, trade marks have not (as yet!) been deemed to be inviolate; instead they are only

[50] See Dworkin, n. 28 above, 43.

[51] See most recently the comments of Jacob J. in *Hodgkinson and Corby Ltd.* v. *Wards Mobility Ltd.* [1995] FSR 169, 174–7.

[52] Robin and Barnaby, n. 35 above, 364–5. It has even been suggested that use of a trade mark in a comparative advertisement is in effect nothing less than dilution and should consequently be treated as such (N. S. Greiwe, "Anti-dilution Statutes: A New Attack on Comparative Advertising?" (1982) 72 *TMR* 178, 186–9). This is thought to be the case because first "the comparative use diverts the trade mark's images to the competitor's products" (*ibid.*, 187) and secondly it damages the trade mark by "encumbering the image the mark has previously gained through advertising" (*ibid.*, 188). Admittedly, this does rather give the impression of constituting the elements of dilution damage, but ignores the fact that the rationale of the dilution doctrine is aimed at the unauthorised use of trade marks on *unrelated* products; the very broad protection it confers also ignores the other legitimate interests in comparative advertising; and finally dilution is in any event notoriously difficult to prove.

infringed in the circumstances specified in the Trade Marks Act; that is to say there is nothing inherent in the nature of a trade mark that will render infringing its use in a comparative advertisement. This point is emphasised by *Irving's Yeast-Vite* itself where it was held that a trade mark (under the 1905 Act which applied at that time) was only protected against use by third parties *as a trade mark*, that is, actually attached to goods in order to indicate their origin. When the Goschen committee recommended that trade marks be protected against comparative advertising, it was effectively recognising that trade mark owners had a legitimate interest in their marks which may be injured by conduct other than simple passing-off. This, along with the introduction of "defensive" registration,[53] would represent the start of a shift whereby it became clear that the primary motivation of modern trade mark law is, on the whole, to protect the interests of the manufacturers of trade marked products against unfairly competitive practices. It is in this way that comparative advertising has *become* a concern of trade mark law through the recognition of trade marks' increasing significance and the growth of the extent of protection of the producers' interests accordingly.

The almost absolute bar that used to be imposed by the 1938 Act on the use of trade marks in comparative advertisements can be seen as analogous to equitable fiduciary duties[54], in that the necessity of examining the merits of each particular instance was avoided by simply not allowing the occasion to arise; the potential for harm was thought sufficient to justify conferring such protection on the trade mark without further investigation. Contrast this with the attitude taken by American courts, where the presumption has been that any comparative advertisement is legitimate and does not infringe the trade mark in question as long as, besides being truthful, it does not cause source confusion. That this was the effect of the Lanham Act was confirmed in *Smith* v. *Chanel Inc.*[55] at roughly the same time as the FTC's initiative to encourage greater utilisation of comparative advertising. In supporting this decision, the court relied heavily on the view that the public interest in free competition far outweighed any claim of the producer and, so it would seem, was influenced by the reasoning of the Harvard school[56] as to the economic consequences of trade mark protection:

> "The courts have generally confined legal protection to the trade mark's source identification function for reasons grounded in the public policy favouring a free, competitive economy. . . . Imitation is the lifeblood of competition. It is the unimpeded availability of substantially equivalent units that permits normal operation of supply and demand to yield the fair price society must pay for a given commodity. . . . A large expenditure of money does not in itself create legally protectable rights. [Trade mark owners] are not entitled to monopolise the public's desire for

[53] W. R. Cornish, *Intellectual Property: Patents, Copyrights, Trade Marks and Allied Rights* (3rd edn., London, 1996), para.15–11.

[54] See Ch.1, n. 66.

[55] (1968) 159 USPQ 338.

[56] See Ch.3 above.

> the unpatented product, even though they themselves created that desire at great expense."[57]

Assuming for the moment that they are correct, such arguments are admittedly easier to swallow in the context of comparative advertising because whereas they may be defeated with respect to preventing unauthorised use of a trade mark actually "affixed" to a product by the need to maintain product identity in trade inviolate, use purely to refer to a product in an advertisement is one step removed from this, and so does not challenge the trade mark's essential function. Otherwise, "the inability to refer to a trade mark in this way would be a bar to effective communication of equivalence claims, not to mention a barrier to new entrants into the market".[58] The problem with this analysis (which is in effect the exact opposite of the position under the 1938 Trade Marks Act) is that it presumes all descriptive uses of another's trade mark are legitimate in the interests of competition. It is not clear whether this is correct. Unfettered competition of the type contemplated in *Smith* v. *Chanel* is not the sole end of our economy given the undesirable consequences canvassed in Chapter 3. Furthermore, it is alien to the culture in this country, and even more so on the continent, both in that "there is a strong sentiment to protect the goodwill associated both with an established trade mark and the goods *per se*"[59] and given the apparent adoption of the "wider integrity" model of trade mark protection in EC trade mark jurisprudence.[60]

The most telling criticism, however, of both the American and 1938 Act approaches is that they do not acknowledge that a balance can and must be struck between the competing interests in comparative advertising. As Dworkin observes, "there are cases where it may be morally defensible to make truthful non-disparaging statements of a competitor, if his goods do not possess the qualities claimed for them. Equally, it may be morally indefensible to make truthful non-disparaging references to a competitor's goods."[61] Into this latter category seem to fall advertisements where the advertiser is merely seeking a "free ride" or "reaping without sowing". Mills illustrates this with the example of *haute couture* and fine fragrances.[62] In these cases:

> "the advertising and promotion used in conjunction with the original brands are as much about the emotional attributes of the brand . . . as the functional attributes. . . . Where the newcomer promotes his brand as a adapted from a design by CHRISTIAN DIOR or equivalent to a fragrance by CHANEL, he is not simply saying that

[57] Quoted in Mills, n. 8 above, 426–7.

[58] *Ibid.*, 426.

[59] *Ibid.*

[60] See in particular the recent decisions in Cases C–337/95 *Parfums Christian Dior SA* v. *Evora BV* [1998] RPC 166 and C–349/95 *Frits Loendersloot* v. *George Ballantine & Son Ltd.* [1998] FSR 544.

[61] Dworkin, n. 28 above, 45.

[62] Although see *Fine Fragrances: A Report on the Supply in the UK for Retail Sale of Fine Fragrances*, Cm. 2380 (London, 1993) concerning the allegedly anti-competitive manner in which the manufacturers market their products.

> the functional aspects are the same—for this could be achieved by simply describing [the product]. . . . On the contrary, the aim of the equivalency statement here is surely to seek to transfer/associate the emotional elements or the reputation of the established brand with which the consumer is familiar with the newcomer's own brand which is significantly cheaper."[63]

She continues by arguing that the likelihood of the products being exactly equivalent is extremely small, and hence the advertising claims are quite probably deceptive, then concludes that "to deny a manufacturer the opportunity to refer specifically to the trade mark of a competitor in these circumstances does not, in reality reduce competition, since it is still open to the newcomer to refer to his brand by some other, generic, means".[64] In addition, the advertiser's motive certainly causes his claim to lose sympathy as well as negating any appeal he may otherwise be able to make to the consumers' interest. On the other hand, to use Dworkin's description, an advert such as that in the EVER READY/DURACELL case is quite morally defensible given that both products have approximately equal reputations and that the motive of the advertisement in naming the competitor is to differentiate the two products on the basis of objectively verifiable performance[65] rather than take advantage of any accrued goodwill.

The scope of the trade mark owner's recognised interest is now such that comparative advertising is a concern of trade mark law, and it is clear that use of a trade mark in a comparative advertisement will harm the trade mark. What is also clear is that naming a competitor's product through his trade mark in a comparative advertisement may be more or less legitimate, so that there is the possibility of allowing the practice in the interests of greater consumer information without doing violence to the original producer's interest. "The question to address is where to draw the line."[66]

The Directive on comparative advertising has been constructed with great sensitivity towards the interests of all parties affected by comparative advertisements and how they may be safeguarded. It amends the Directive concerning misleading and unfair advertising[67] to allow both direct and indirect comparative advertising provided that certain positive requirements (that the advertisement must be objective, relevant and verifiable and must compare fairly chosen and representative features of products in question[68]) and negative requirements (that it must not mislead, create a risk of confusion, refer to the personality or personal situation of a competitor nor, most importantly, discredit or denigrate the trade marks or products of a competitor nor "principally capitalise" on the reputation of a trade mark of a competitor[69]) are complied with. It is interesting that, according to the eleventh Recital of the Preamble to the Directive, use of a

[63] Mills, n. 8 above, 426.
[64] *Ibid.*, 427.
[65] See Parkinson, n. 6 above, 44.
[66] Mills, n. 8 above, 427.
[67] 84/450/EEC (OJ [1984] L250/17).
[68] New Art.3a (Art.1 of the Directive).
[69] *Ibid.*

trade mark in a comparative advertisement is *not* trade mark infringement[70]; rather it is a form of trade mark use which may be prevented through the effect of the Directive. Before we consider this approach further, we must first consider current UK trade mark law.

It is widely believed that Parliament acted in a somewhat precipitate manner in enacting section 10(6) of the Trade Marks Act 1994, given the fact that the adoption of the Directive just mentioned was pending at the time.[71] Nevertheless, the provision was enacted and it removed the previous prohibition on use of trade marks in comparative advertisements subject to a proviso aimed at protecting the interests of the trade mark owner identified. It has been suggested that the provision would have had a similar effect to the comparative advertising Directive[72] and indeed that as a result no legislative action would be necessary once the Directive had been promulgated.[73] However, this was to count without the intervention of Laddie J. in *Barclays Bank plc* v. *RBS Advanta* whose opinion, subsequently confirmed by Jacob J. and Michael Crystal QC[74], was that for a trade mark owner to be able to rely on the proviso to section 10(6), the advertisement would have to be "substantially misleading" in the eyes of a reasonable member of the consuming public; various elaborate interpretations[75] of the proviso were thus discarded, and English trade mark law with respect to comparative advertising now seems to find itself effectively in a situation little better than that of U.S. law as represented by *Smith* v. *Chanel*.[76]

Other Means of Regulating Comparative Advertising

The decision of Laddie J. is, it is submitted, something of a blessing in disguise for those who feel that section 10(6) deserves a more expansive interpretation even though, and perhaps because, it seems to have left trade mark owners in a rather more precarious position than originally anticipated[77] and has therefore *possibly* subverted the legislative intent. The practice of comparative advertis-

[70] Mills, n. 8 above, 424.

[71] R. E. Annand and H. E. Norman, *Blackstone's Guide to the Trade Marks Act 1994* (London, 1994), 159.

[72] Mills, n. 8 above, 422–3.

[73] *Ibid.*, 424.

[74] In *Vodafone Group plc* v. *Orange Personal Communication Services Ltd.* [1997] FSR 34 and *British Telecommunications plc* v. *AT&T Communications (UK) Ltd.* [1997] EIPR D–134 respectively.

[75] See e.g. Annand and Norman, n. 71 above, 160; J. Holyoak and P. Torremans, *Intellectual Property Law* (London, 1995), 320; Mills, n. 8 above, 422–3.

[76] In fairness to the judge, the section seems to be, as the Protocol to Art.69 of the European Patent Convention was described, a "politician's sentence" (B. Sherman, "Patent Claim Interpretation: The Impact of the Protocol on Interpretation" (1991) 54 *MLR* 499, 503, n. 25 and accompanying text). In other words it seems to be a mass of ill-defined aspirations than a true, unambiguous statutory provision.

[77] See P. Walsh and J. Watts, "Honest Practices in Comparative Advertising in the UK", Mar. 1996, *TW* 26, 27–8.

ing is now at a cross-roads. With the promulgation of the comparative advertising Directive, there now exists the opportunity for the government to start again with a "clean sheet" by repealing section 10(6) and putting in place a far more coherent and effectual scheme to govern comparative advertising[78]; the incentive for this could be provided by the interpretation that was accorded to section 10(6), but which appears at odds with the intention expressed by paragraph 3.28 of the White Paper.

Although the interests underlying a trade mark are without doubt affected in some way whenever it is used in a comparative advertisement, it may well be asked whether the law of trade marks is necessarily the best forum for resolving the conflict of interests that any such advertisement entails. In *Barclays Bank plc* v. *RBS Advanta*,[79] Laddie J. observed that "the Act does not impose on the courts an obligation to try to enforce, through the back door of trade mark legislation, a more puritanical standard [of advertising copy]"; indeed the Trade Marks Act should not be a vehicle for regulating advertising standards, but in spite of Laddie J.'s protest to the contrary, is there a legislative attempt being made to use the Act for something for which it is not suited? Perhaps we should consider whether courts are that well qualified to judge on the merits of advertising copy. Making provision for the partial control of comparative advertising within the law of registered trade marks leaves the inconsistency that has been present in the law since 1938, that unregistered marks and other distinctive forms of product identification are treated differently. Although it was seen earlier that it is possible to argue for special treatment for trade marks, the subject of comparison is, after all, still the underlying product regardless of how it is identified, and this alone surely justifies greater consistency of treatment. The comparative advertising Directive, on the other hand, whilst aware of the communicative value of trade marks, applies to comparative advertising in general and does not seek to limit artificially its ambit. It is therefore able to respond to another criticism of the regulation of comparative advertising under English law that it requires a "clear, . . . rational code" rather than be derived from a number of sources.[80]

It must be recognised that comparative advertising represents an overlap in concern between trade mark law and other areas of commercial regulation, in particular of advertising itself. Whilst a trade mark infringement action confers a right directly on the trade mark owner, its effect, namely enabling the producer that is being subjected to comparison to prevent the offending advertisement, may be achieved in other ways, leaving the law to deal with more morally clear-cut situations such as when the advertisement is demonstrably false rather than simply unfair. The Mathys Committee, for example, believed

[78] Note however the government view that the current provisions of the Trade Marks Act 1994 adequately cover the provisions of the Directive such that no further implementing legislation is required (see J. McCormick, "The Future of Comparative Advertising" [1998] *EIPR* 41).

[79] [1996] RPC 307, 315.

[80] Dworkin, n. 28 above, 45.

that voluntary regulation through the British Code of Advertising Practice was "more likely to be effective than further attempts at statutory control [through the law of trade marks]".[81] This code is administered by the Advertising Standards Authority (ASA) which was established to avoid state intervention in the advertising industry. It is seen as more conducive to co-operation and speed of resolution[82] as well as being more flexible, so being able to respond to changes in acceptable public standards.[83] Given judicial discomfort at ruling on notions such as "fairness"[84] that are inherent in the comparative advertising Directive, the prevailing government preference for deregulation in administrative matters[85] and the feeling that has been expressed in some quarters that in matters of alleged unfairly competitive practices, attempts should be made at least initially not to resort to the courts,[86] it seems reasonable to assign the role of "first line of defence" to the ASA, but with resort to the judicial process as a form of long stop. After all, the comparative advertising Directive mandates some form of legislative action, if only to amend the provisions made in response to the misleading advertising Directive. These empower the Director General of Fair Trading in investigate complaints and to seek judicial remedies in the interest of protecting both consumers and producers.[87] Interestingly, he must first of all satisfy himself that other means, such as voluntary control, have been used to attempt to resolve the matter. Concentrating regulation in this way apart from trade mark law seems to the most appropriate means by which to safeguard the interests of those affected by comparative advertising, whilst securing more coherent guidance to those wishing to use it.

TRADE DRESS PROTECTION

A product's trade mark is a key element of how it is presented for sale in contemporary retailing. Without it consumers are unable to distinguish it from a similar product of another manufacturer, relate it to any possible past experience of the product or indeed identify it with any advertising which may initially have prompted the purchasing decision. However, it is not the only element,

[81] N. 19 above, para.84.

[82] Cornish, n. 53 above, para.2–25.

[83] Dworkin, n. 28 above, 44.

[84] A. Robertson and A. Horton, "Does the UK or EC Need an Unfair Competition Law?" [1995] *EIPR* 568 comment that "English law has traditionally refused to deal in concepts such as fairness or good faith in business" and give the example (at n. 7) of Lord Ackner who said in *Walford* v. *Miles* [1992] AC 128 at 138 that "a duty to negotiate in good faith is unworkable in practice".

[85] Best exemplified in trade mark law by the new licensing regime.

[86] The remarks were actually made in the context of own-brand look-alikes, but can apply with equal validity to comparative advertising. See *The Economist*, "Unreal", 14 May 1994, and *The Times*, "Brand of logic", 20 Apr. 1994 and "The £903 million story behind big names in daily cereal", 16 Aug. 1996.

[87] Under the Control of Misleading Advertisements Regulations 1988. See Cornish, n. 53 above, para.15–20.

since experience shows that products in supermarkets, for example, are not generally presented for sale in plain packaging with only a trade mark. The goods will in fact come in all sorts of elaborately designed packaging, may well be chosen from a shelf specially laid out to highlight the goods and may even be located in an area of the store created to portray the goods in their most flattering light and thus make consumers better disposed to buy them. All these aspects of presentation may fall under the rubric "trade dress" and most importantly for our purposes, they have the common feature that they could quite conceivably become distinctive (in the trade mark sense) of a particular trader. Although it has been suggested (perhaps somewhat ambitiously) that the next area to fall within the ambit of the law concerning trade symbols will be the "branded experience" or actual purchasing environment,[88] we are interested solely in the trade dress applied to products themselves, namely the design of the packaging, since this type is most closely associated with trade marks and consequently has the most in common in terms of function. After examining the extent to which trade dress of this nature may currently be protected, we shall turn to the reason why protection of a product's trade dress (or lack of it) is probably the most controversial area of trade mark law, and certainly the area that has received the most public attention[89]: retailers' own-brand look-alike goods. We shall then ask both in the light of this whether more protection for trade dress is necessary.

Protecting Trade Dress under the Current Law

Unsurprisingly given the broad nature of the concept, there is no definition of what constitutes protectable trade dress, and instead we must look in several places in the law of intellectual property to establish how a producer may object to imitation of his trade dress. Protection under the Registered Designs Act 1949 seems to be a possibility, albeit one of limited application, since the appearance of the article in question to which the design is applied (here, the packaging of goods) must be material to those acquiring it.[90] Generally people do not buy a

[88] T. D. Drescher, "The Transformation and Evolution of Trade Marks: from Signals to Symbols to Myths" (1992) 82 *TMR* 301, 332–8; G. McCormick, "Updating the Intellectual Property Wardrobe: Consider Trade Dress" [1995] *Trade Mark Yearbook* 9. Consider also *Re Dee Corporation plc* [1990] RPC 159 where attempts were made unsuccessfully to protect a particular style of trading by seeking trade mark registration in respect of services ancillary to the supply of goods and included "the provision of advice to customers, a particular selection of goods, a congenial atmosphere in which to shop, car-parking and checkout and credit facilities".

[89] Witness the huge newspaper coverage of what is an otherwise esoteric legal field surrounding the Sainsburys Classic Cola incident (*The Times*, "Brand of logic", 20 Apr., and "Cola war hits Coke", 11 May 1994, and *Independent on Sunday*, "Superstores stalk the superbrands", 20 Feb. 1994) and now Tesco's breakfast cereal (*The Times*, "The £903 million story behind big names in daily cereal" and *Daily Telegraph*, "Tesco corn flake packs get frosty response", 16 Aug. 1996). The topic has even been thought worthy of a mention on the BBC consumers' programme "Watchdog"!

[90] S.1(3) Registered Designs Act 1949.

product simply because it has æsthetically pleasing packaging, but an example that probably would be protected is the container of TOILET DUCK disinfectant. The other problem is the limited duration of the right which may prove to be inadequate in this context.[91] Infringement, however, is determined in a similar manner to that of a patent and so is not reliant on notions such as consumer confusion or derivation (in the copyright sense). The definition of what may be registered as a trade mark under the Trade Marks Act 1994 includes "designs . . . or the shape of goods or their packaging".[92] For highly distinctive packaging such as the COCA-COLA bottle or the JIF lemon juice container that clearly functions as a trade mark, protection is secure, but for others, it is thought that matters are not so certain.[93] Notice also the absolute ground of refusal of registration contained in section 3(2) (the relevant aspect of which is the exclusion of signs that result from the nature of the goods themselves) that is similar in effect to the U.S. doctrine of functionality which seeks, amongst other things, to prevent traders from attempting stifle product design under the guise of protecting trade mark rights.[94] Finally and for the reasons discussed in Chapter 1,[95] protection of aspects of packaging design that are any more complex than those just mentioned will tend not to fall within the criteria for registration.[96] Having portrayed a fairly uninspiring image of the potential for protecting trade dress within the framework of the Trade Marks Act, the Benelux decision of *The Proctor and Gamble Co* v. *NV Regina* (*ALWAYS/REGINA*)[97] offers some hope, in that ALWAYS was held to infringe REGINA for identical goods (sanitary towels). This was not because of any confusion between the marks (even with my limited knowledge of Dutch, this clearly was not possible on comparing the marks alone) but because of the likelihood of *association* between the brands due to the similarity of the packaging used![98] Following Laddie J.'s views on the likelihood of association in *WAGAMAMA*, though, such a revolutionary decision seems a long

[91] 25 years: s.8.

[92] S.1(1) Trade Marks Act 1994.

[93] Annand and Norman, n. 71 above, 61; White Paper paras.2.13 and 18. Fairly strong evidence of distinctive character would have to be adduced to the Trade Marks Registry otherwise it is likely that registration would be refused under s.3(1)(b) (devoid of any distinctive character), although notice Jacob J.'s recent complaint whilst speaking extra-judicially (at the 1996 Stephen Stewart Memorial Lecture) that the Trade Marks Registry is mistaking "unusual" for "distinctive" and too readily granting registrations in respect of the shape of containers that do not necessarily function as trade marks (R. Jacob, "Industrial Property—Industry's Enemy" [1997] *IPQ* 3).

[94] Annand and Norman, n. 71 above, 61–2; see also J. Lahore, "Product Simulation and Copying the Get-up of Goods" [1979] *EIPR* 146 and A. E. Dowell, "Trade Dress Protection of Product Design: Stifling Progress of Science and the Useful Arts for an Unlimited Time" (1994) 70 *Notre Dame LR* 137. A recent illustration of the question in passing-off is *Hodgkinson & Corby* [1995] FSR 169.

[95] See text accompanying nn. 51 and 52.

[96] Annand and Norman, n. 71 above, 62.

[97] 27 May 1993, [1993] Intellectuële Eigendom en Reclamerecht 112.

[98] B. Mills, "Own-label Products and the Look-alike Phenomenon: A Lack of Trade Dress and Unfair Competition Protection?" [1995] *EIPR* 116, 123.

way off in English law especially given the tradition in our system of comparing marks in a fairly abstract manner.[99]

The primary means of trade dress protection still currently lies with the tort of passing-off. The essence of this is a misrepresentation on the part of the defendant trader which confuses consumers and damages the "goodwill" of the plaintiff trader. In principle, there is no objection to preventing the unauthorised replication of a product's trade dress in this way, since consumers may well be confused as to the origin of goods on seeing two products with similar trade dress, one of which is distinctive of the plaintiff, and indeed this has been recognised as being possible as long ago as the turn of the century in the leading cases of *Payton and Co.* v. *Snelling, Lampard and Co.*[100] and *Williams (JB) Co.* v. *H Bronnley and Co. Ltd.*[101] However, a producer seeking to bring such an action has to overcome a huge (but not insurmountable) evidential burden and, as Wadlow observes, "[i]n practice, cases fought and won entirely on get-up have been very few".[102] Proving the first aspect of passing-off, that goodwill attaches to the product in question, is relatively straightforward since the product packaging will often be elaborate, and of course there will be a brand name present, although where the packaging is very simple, as was the case in *Reckitt and Coleman Products Ltd* v. *Borden Inc* (JIF lemon),[103] then particularly convincing evidence is necessary. In that case, the packaging consisted of a plastic container in the shape of a lemon and was therefore "descriptive", since it actually contained lemon juice. In spite of this, the plaintiff were able to demonstrate that distinctiveness had been acquired because it had had the advantage of virtually exclusive use of the trade dress over 30 years. Compare this with *Imperial Group plc* v. *Phillip Morris Ltd*[104] where, although the plaintiff had indulged in far heavier advertising involving its trade dress of a black cigarette packet with a gold JPS trade mark than its competitors, the others had still concurrently been marketing cigarettes in similar black packaging, and so there could be no finding of distinctiveness. The main problem, however, is the nature of the misrepresentation to which the defendant's conduct must be shown to amount. In the most recent decision on this aspect of passing-off, *Hodgkinson & Corby*,[105] it was reiterated that "in the absence of any patent or trade mark infringement, it is only unlawful for a trader to copy and market a rival's product if that rival could show that purchasers were being or would be deceived into buying the copy in mistake for the original".[106] This is a question of fact in each case and,

[99] Consider e.g. *Origins Natural Resources Inc.* v. *Origin Clothing Ltd.* [1995] FSR 280. The ECJ decision in Case C–251/95 *Sabel BV* v. *Puma AG* [1998] RPC 199 which mandates considering the likelihood of confusion in light of all the circumstances may bring this slightly nearer in English law.

[100] [1901] AC 308.

[101] (1909) 26 RPC 765.

[102] C. Wadlow, "Passing-off Enters the Supermarket Age" [1990] *EIPR* 104.

[103] [1990] 1 All ER 873.

[104] [1984] RPC 293.

[105] N. 93 above.

[106] Précis suggested by Mills, n. 97 above, 122.

as was emphasised in the *JIF Lemon* case, must be judged by reference to consumer perception of the products, and not one judge's impressions.[107] In any event, there is clearly potential to protect the immediate trade dress of goods, but is it adequate to deal with the specific trade dress conflicts now arising in the market place?

The Own-label Look-alike Phenomenon

The reason for the prominence of trade dress protection on the lobbyist's, if not the mainstream, political agenda is the recent trend in how retailers have chosen to market their own-brand products.[108] In order to appreciate the challenge that this presents to the current law, we must examine briefly the background to the practice of own-labelling, especially as found in the grocery trade. In Chapter 2, it was seen that an explanation for the huge increase in trade mark use at the end of the last century was that many consumer goods which had previously been bought in bulk from local retailers on the strength of the retailer's reputation, were now bought pre-packaged under the brand names (protected as trade marks) of the manufacturers or suppliers of the goods. This enabled the manufacturers amongst other things to charge a premium for the consistent quality that the brand guaranteed and which the retailers themselves were unable to deliver at that time.[109] Nevertheless, this did not stop retailers from obtaining similar products and selling them more cheaply under their own names; indeed the first time that this happened was as long ago as 1880.[110] What must be considered is that "power has ebbed and flowed in the grocery trade over the past century. Before the First World War it was food wholesalers that called the shots, using sheer size to screw down small suppliers on the one hand and get top prices from small retailers on the other. Between the wars, the manufacturers were on top. By developing strong, desirable brands, they persuaded customers to demand their products in what academics now term a 'pull through' strategy. The retailers were squeezed. In post war years, wholesalers withered away and retailers came to the fore, developing their own names as brands themselves—sufficiently convincing to make own-label acceptable."[111] Own-labels came of age in the early 1970s as a response to both the recession and

[107] Wadlow, n. 101 above, 105.

[108] The British Brands Group is using the passage of the Competition Bill to try to persuade Parliament to introduce greater protection in this regard. It is spurred on by market research which suggests that consumers "were almost twice as likely to think that [a heavily marketed brand and a 'look-alike'] were made by the same manufacturer if they were similarly rather than distinctively presented" (*Financial Times*, "'Lookalike' packaging leaves shoppers confused", 16 Apr. 1998).

[109] *The Economist*, "The Year of the Brand", 24 Dec. 1988.

[110] *The Economist*, "Knocking brands off the shelf", 24 Feb. 1990.

[111] *Independent on Sunday*, "Superstores stalk the superbrands", 20 Feb. 1994. See *The Economist*, "Shoot-out at the checkout", 5 June 1993, for a review of others factors which have contributed to a decline in manufacturers' strength relative to other traders.

inflation, since retailers "were pushed to generate new income streams" whereas previously they were able to stock only more lucrative branded products[112]:

> "Own-label products could be said to have begun as a cost-cutting response to inflation with prices typically twenty per cent below branded items. This was achieved through bulk purchasing, zero to low advertising and a product quality that was clearly inferior to branded lines. Whereas in 1971, own-label accounted for twenty per cent of all sales, own-label now accounts for a third of all sales, and higher in the case of Waitrose (forty per cent) and Sainsburys (fifty per cent)."[113]

Of course, own-brands have been only one of several factors responsible for the increasing power of retailers. For example, "it is shopkeepers who meet consumers [so] they are best placed to respond to changing tastes"[114] after all, and, more recently, it has been retailers who have been able to take advantage of new Electronic Point of Sale technology.[115] Control over the chain of distribution, however, has been the key distinguishing feature of own-label products[116] and reason for the growth in retailer power, since this leaves the retailer in charge of the destiny of his product, whereas once producers' branded goods (which are available to all retailers) pass into the retailer's hands, the producer loses any control over how the product is finally marketed. It is up to the retailer how each brand is displayed, and even the extent to which the particular brand is promoted.[117] The market dominance which retailers have gained is quite legitimate, in part because it has been the result of the manner in which retailing has developed. It is consequently something which the manufacturers have had to accept albeit unwillingly. Furthermore, the competition that has been engendered can only be in the interests of consumers who have come to expect the variety of choice which they are now offered.[118] However, manufacturers now believe that the retailers, in attempting to consolidate their position, have overstepped the mark.

Own-label products can take several forms. Most important for our purposes are *generic brands* which are goods sold as commodities with a minimum of additional costs under names such as Tesco VALUE or Safeway SAVERS to enable them to be sold at the lowest price for that type of product in the store and *store brands* which are marketed in a far more sophisticated manner so that they will compete directly with the branded product, for example Sainsbury's CLASSIC

[112] Mills, n. 97 above, 117–8.

[113] Hankinson and Cowking, *Branding in Action* (1993), 107 quoted in *ibid.*

[114] *The Economist*, "Knocking brands off the shelf", 24 Feb. 1990.

[115] *The Economist*, "The Year of the Brand", 24 Dec. 1988, notes that "[o]ne British drinks manufacturer is proud that it can work its retail sales within six weeks; Sainsburys knows its figures in four hours".

[116] See Mills, n. 97 above, 116–7. The other forms are non-store brands that are similar to store brands, but the name is chosen so that it does not necessarily rely on the retailer's reputation, examples are ST. MICHAEL for Marks and Spencer and KEYNOTE for Littlewoods; and private or exclusive brands are used by a manufacturer producing branded goods but for one particular retailer only such as NO.7 cosmetics at Boots.

[117] A. Y. Spencer, "Look-alikes and Private Label Competition", Sept. 1994, *TW* 14.

[118] *Ibid.*, 14–15.

COLA or, to use an example from less controversial sector, NEXT clothing.[119] Initially, supermarkets' own-label goods tended to correspond to the former category, but, as *The Economist* observes:

> "If competitive, branded products are on the shelves . . . shoppers are not easily persuaded to buy own-label products on price alone. They must be able to tell if it is as good as or better than its branded equivalent. Where the two are indistinguishable, shoppers tend to buy on image."[120]

The problems therefore started when the retailers sought to move up-market from their original generic brands and so tap the greater profit margins available. The retailers needed to differentiate their own-label product on the same basis as the branded product, that is to say, superior quality rather than just price and even establish a true brand identity. In order to indicate this to consumers, as well as the fact that the own-label product is situated in the same category as its branded competitor, the temptation arises to make the product *look* like the brand leader "which has achieved that elusive combination of widespread pubic recognition and an uncompromising image of exclusivity"[121]; so came about the own-label look-alike phenomenon which is the aspect of own-labelling that the manufacturers find so objectionable. Some recent examples have been reproduced in Appendix B.

Assuming, for the reasons mentioned above, that design and trade mark registration cannot provide a remedy, the aggrieved producer confronted by a supermarket product with trade dress not so different from that of his own competing product must rely on an action in passing-off. The pivotal question is whether, in marketing the look-alike product, the retailer has made an actionable misrepresentation. Obviously, each instance must be judged on its merits by reference to evidence of consumers' perception of the products in dispute,[122] but unless the retailer's efforts have been spectacularly crude and thus inept, consumers will not generally believe that the own-label product is in fact the produce of the manufacturer. This is because, although the own-label may imitate the branded product, it will also generally have the retailer's own trade mark prominently displayed. Note, however, that it was seen in *JIF Lemon* that there is no presumption that a product's trade dress is always subordinate to its brand name and indeed this is no less than how a consumer or product may view a product. This confirms the view in *Edge* v. *Niccolls*[123] that "even if the defendant puts his name on the goods this will not suffice if the only effect is that the customer thinks that he is the same person as the plaintiff".[124] Therefore own-label look-alikes will tend not to constitute "classic" passing-off in the sense of

[119] Mills, n. 97 above, 117.
[120] *The Economist*, "Knocking brands off the shelf", 24 Feb. 1990.
[121] See Wadlow, n. 101 above, 106.
[122] *Ibid.*, 105–6.
[123] [1911] AC 693.
[124] Lahore, n. 93 above.

"counterfeiting"[125]; this, though, is not really the manufacturers' primary complaint nor the retailers' motive.

More pressing is when "the public is induced to believe that the own-label product is the same as the branded product, but bought from the manufacturer at a preferential price which allow for the own-label 'version' to be sold at a discount".[126] This belief is quite credible when one considers that it is often true or, more importantly, had once been true; the problem is that consumers are unable to know whether this is in fact the case.[127] This argument was advanced in *Beecham Group plc* v. *J. Sainsbury plc*[128] where the defendant supermarket suddenly changed the trade dress of its own-label product to resemble that of the plaintiff manufacturer (in this case, BOVRIL) where previously it had been different.[129] It was submitted that whilst consumers would not think that the own-label product *was* BOVRIL, they would believe the two products came from the same source. Unfortunately, the judge did not for various reasons ultimately resolve the issue as to whether this constituted the necessary misrepresentation.[130]

The principal objection by manufacturers is not that retailers are making out that their product is the branded product or that the own-label is made by the manufacturer of the branded product and is therefore the same, but rather the "subtle goal of 'lookalike' packaging is to hijack the reputation and symbolism of the famous brand. To give two products a virtually identical visual appearance is to *imply a similarity of quality, taste or efficiency*."[131] Although on closer examination, the two complaints just mentioned are negated, given for example the strength of the retailer's trade mark, a busy consumer is still likely to make the mental association between the two products with a similar result in fact to the associative comparative advertising described above. Is this type of misrepresentation actionable? Since consumers are patently not deceived as to product source (in the trade mark sense), an orthodox interpretation of passing-off, supported by recent *dicta*,[132] would say no. Having said that, the plaintiff in *JIF Lemon*, who admittedly had a very strong case evidentially, was nonetheless thought to be bound to fail in law,[133] but eventually succeeded; equally, Sainsbury's eventually agreed to alter its controversial CLASSIC COLA trade dress

125 D. M. Franklin, "Brands versus Look-alikes in the UK", July/Aug. 1994, *TW* 10, 11.

126 Spencer, n. 116 above, 15. Note, though, that certainly for the purposes of a passing-off action it is not possible to make universal presumptions of fact as to what consumers seek (see Laddie J.'s comments in *ELVIS PRESLEY Trade Marks* [1997] RPC 543).

127 Mills, n. 97 above, 121. Spencer (n. 116 above, 15) thinks that where manufacturers do produce own-label goods for retailers, they deserve little sympathy when "the boot is on the other foot". Kellogg's, however, are constantly at pains to tell consumers that they "don't make cereals for anybody else" (see Appendix B below, fig.5 and *Daily Telegraph*, "Tesco corn flake packs get frosty response", 16 Aug. 1996).

128 Unreported (1987).

129 See Appendix B below, fig.7.

130 Mills, n. 97 above, 123.

131 *The Times*, "Brand of logic", 20 Apr. 1994 (emphasis added).

132 In *Hodgkinson and Corby* and *Harrods Ltd.* v. *Harrodian School* [1996] RPC 697.

133 See Wadlow n. 101 above.

which may be seen as a tacit admission that what it was doing could be seen as passing-off.[134]

Is Specific Protection Necessary?

Regardless of the latter two rather indecisive factors, it seems that passing-off is inadequate in this context and understandably there have been calls for legal protection against the practice of own-label look-alikes, either by extending the passing-off definition to include this "likelihood of association"[135] or, more likely given the current judicial climate, by some form of unfair competition law.[136] The arguments advanced by manufacturers in favour of protection are familiar and straightforward. They claim that the retailers' actions unfairly exploit their product "goodwill" which has been established through investment in the brand, its advertising and marketing. The trade dress, no less so than the product's trade mark, communicates information about the product and the value, in this that has been established in the brand identity is being taken by the retailer. This may even cause consumers to infer characteristics that the own-label may not possess, thereby adding to the confusion.[137] Although the effect on consumers is psychologically more subtle than where a trader makes a misrepresentation of a blatant nature as to the identity of the goods, it is still quite real and susceptible to proof. Retailers are effectively preying on the minimal time that many consumers have to spend in a supermarket. The manufacturers (contrary to how they may have presented their case[138]) have no quarrel with own-labelling in general; but in their brand identities, they believe that they have an interest worthy of protection. In reply, retailers seek to *justify* their actions on the basis that they are not confusing consumers[139] as to the manufacture of

[134] *The Economist*, "Unreal", 14 May 1994.

[135] In the Benelux sense, as exemplified by the ALWAYS/REGINA case, n. 96 above. Support for this approach is encouraged by the developments made in *Taittinger* v. *Allbev* [1993] FSR 641.

[136] It has (predictably) been suggested that trade dress is in need of protection against dilution (Mills, n. 97 above, 124–8), but although "fear of drawing the line (as to where protection should cease) should not preclude any consideration or application of the doctrine *per se*" (*ibid.*, 128), protection against dilution is only available to registered trade marks in respect of dissimilar goods (and this does not look set to change) and the trade dress must be first registered as a trade mark which is generally quite difficult.

[137] Franklin, n. 124 above, 12.

[138] Mills, n. 97 above, 124. The manufacturers only organised themselves into the British Producers and Brand Owners Group fairly late on in order to respond to failings they saw in the Trade Marks Bill 1993 (Franklin, n. 124 above, 12) and so their message was not put across as clearly as it might have been. Their reluctance to do anything about the problem was said to be due to the reluctance of manufacturers to sue a major customer (Spencer, n. 116 above, 15) and the ability of retailers to "de-list" punitively a particular brand (Mills, n. 97 above, 120). Other disincentives to act were said to be the time, difficulty and cost of legal action, but if new rights were introduced, the fact of their presence would arguably *discourage* retailers from more dubious conduct and so reduce the need to go to court in the first place.

[139] Although this is debatable, given the way that retailers are known to adjust the presentation of goods on shelves in order to manipulate consumer attention.

goods, and in fact are assisting consumers by positioning the own-label products relative to the brand leaders whilst distinguishing their products by using their own trade mark, normally the store name. A further argument given in support of their use of the colours of the branded product's packaging is that particular colours are associated by consumers with certain products[140] "as a form of generic code or visual cue".[141] This particular justification is unsatisfactory because of its circularity: Sainsbury's would argue that they chose gold as the colour for the lid on their premium instant coffee because this is what is connoted by a gold lid, but why does a gold lid connote this? The answer is because NESCAFÉ, which just happens to be the brand leader, originally used a lid of that colour.[142] Retailers are correct to comment that "no one retailer has a monopoly over which colours are used"[143] but their arguments seem to ignore a basic principle of the law protecting trade symbols that *once* a sign, be it a trade mark, a colour or whatever, becomes distinctive in the eyes of consumers of a product or producer, the situation changes and the producer then has a legitimate expectation that the sign will be protected. Furthermore, and this is the essence of the objections to the lookalikes, as Mills points out:

> "A parallel might . . . be drawn with the protection granted to musical compositions under copyright law; after all musicians have only a limited number of notes and instruments from which to choose. It is surely the 'selection and arrangement' of these ingredients that should be protected, or the 'skill and labour' of those involved with the creation of the final work."[144]

From the discussion so far, it would seem that the difficulty is not a lack of trade dress protection in general; on the contrary, the three methods suggested, design and trade mark registration as well as passing-off, seem quite adequate so long as the complaint falls into the traditional form of deception as to source. As far as securing the protection in the first place is concerned, it will always be inherently more difficult to show that trade dress falls within either the criteria for registration or otherwise for proving goodwill because of the naturally more complex design of trade dress on the one hand and functionality on the other. Rather the issue of own-label look-alikes is a specific problem about which it must be decided whether there is a need for legislative provision to resolve it. Of course, it is not appropriate to see the solution as an exercise in distributive justice. In other words, one must resist the inducement to see the situation as one

[140] E.g., "People will identify red as being corn flakes and blue as being frosted flakes" (*Daily Telegraph*, "Tesco corn flake packs get frosty response", 16 Aug. 1996) and the NESCAFÉ range has different coloured jar caps to signify the various blends (Annand and Norman, n. 71 above, 62).

[141] Mills, n. 97 above, 131.

[142] *Ibid*. Interestingly, Mills comments that although retailers advance this argument which presumes that consumers do not pay attention to the "fine print" on packaging, they are also quick to point out that consumers are nevertheless observant enough to distinguish between the own-label and branded product. This latter point is illustrated by WALKER'S crisps which use different colouring for their packaging from the arguably generic colours used by the other manufacturers.

[143] *Daily Telegraph*, "Tesco corn flake packs get frosty response", 16 Aug. 1996.

[144] Mills, n. 97 above, 128.

in which the retailers have gained too much market influence at the expense of the manufacturers and consequently the balance must be redressed by outlawing the activities complained of.

Two, in the event unsuccessful, legislative attempts were made to resolve the problem in response to pressure from the British Producers and Brand Owners Group during the passage of what is now the Trade Marks Act 1994. First, an additional head of infringement was sought to protect unregistered trade dress (presumably in a similar fashion to section 56), but this was rejected as being contrary to the Directive; secondly, it was attempted to secure an action for unfair competition based on Article 10*bis* of the Paris Convention, but this foundered in the face of opposition from the Consumers Association.[145] However, these efforts were notable for the sympathy they attracted in particular from the House of Lords where the amendments were originally introduced,[146] from the Department of Trade and Industry Standing Advisory Committee on Intellectual Property and from the government minister responsible, who indicated that the matter was under review.[147] It was thought that since a new unfair competition law would have an ambit wider than simply the field of trade marks and trade dress, it was inappropriate to legislate within the framework of the Trade Marks Act.[148]

The view has been expressed that seeking to resolve the matter through legal means is the wrong approach entirely and that the current law is adequate; any loss should lie with the manufacturers and they should concentrate on product development rather than seek to rest on their laurels of past branding achievements.[149] Given the legislative impasse, moves were made to establish a voluntary dispute resolution procedure in the form of the Institute of Grocery Distribution's code of practice, one principle of which is to "encourage competition but avoid commercial plagiarism", and both parties to the recent breakfast cereal dispute are said to be keen to address the dispute in this way rather than having to resort to litigation.[150] It has even been suggested that own-label look-alikes are quite needless: "how can you overtake a branded product and become brand leader if you are always looking over your shoulder to copy the branded product?"[151] However, this does not answer the fact that a situation will arise sooner or later that will require some form of legal resolution.

The phenomenon of own-label look-alikes illustrates well the need for protection against unfair competition in English law. The problem highlighted does not,

[145] Annand and Norman, n. 71 above, 160–1.

[146] *Ibid.*

[147] Franklin, n. 124 above, 12.

[148] Mills, n. 97 above. 129.

[149] *The Economist*, "Unreal", 14 May 1994; *The Times*, "Brand of logic", 20 Apr. 1994.

[150] *The Times*, "The £903 million story behind big names in daily cereal", 16 Aug. 1996; *Daily Telegraph*, "Tesco corn flake packs get frosty response", 16 Aug. 1996.

[151] Mills, n. 97 above, 130 citing the success of store brands developed without any reference to competing branded products, e.g. Sainsbury's NOVON detergent or GIO soft drink, which are regarded, and indeed respected, by manufacturers as fair competition.

it is submitted, result from a lack of protection for distinctive trade dress, but rather an unwillingness on the part of the law (by which we mean the judiciary) to assess anything less tangible than "confusion as to source" and thus to recognise, evaluate or protect "the fruit of one's labours". Trade dress that is distinctive of a producer must be and is protected for the same reasons as trade marks, of which trade dress is arguably a species; it is inherent in its nature, though, that its distinctiveness is more difficult to prove. The obstacles facing manufacturers and their consequent misfortune are not sufficient to justify specific law reform, but it is symptomatic of the need for a "level playing field" supplied by the law upon which the more conciliatory measures suggested above may rest in the first place.

CONCLUSION: TOWARDS GENERAL PROTECTION AGAINST UNFAIR COMPETITION

It is no coincidence that a leading article in *The Economist*[152] published four years ago should choose to comment on the controversy surrounding Unilever's PERSIL POWER as well as Sainsbury's CLASSIC COLA, incidents concerning a comparative advertisement and an own-label look-alike respectively since they are both illustrations of how the law may have failed to keep up with developments in the realm of commerce. Although it concludes that "this courtroom soap opera is a sign of just how rare genuine innovations have become . . . the verdict that will matter in the long run will be that of consumers in the market place, not that of judges in courts", it seems that the consumers' verdict will not be reached fairly unless the rules are initially made clear. Whether it suits producers or not, comparative advertising is now regarded, as demonstrated by the enactment of section 10(6) of the Trade Marks Act, as a legitimate aspect of commercial dealings; the extent to which this is the case, though, has not yet been settled. One reason for this must be the fact that it is clear that producers whose goods feature in another's comparative advertisement do stand to be affected adversely. Since it is still not completely certain how great is the benefit to consumers, it is not justifiable to remove all protection from producers' interests until such a conclusive countervailing interest can be shown.[153] It is also not clear that the law of trade marks in practice is the most appropriate way of safeguarding the producers' interest, despite the fact the trade mark right is indisputably affected by trade mark use in a comparative advertisement. Now that the comparative advertising Directive has been adopted, the opportunity must be taken to review the implications of *Barclays Bank plc* v. *RBS Advanta*[154] and the alternatives for implementing the balancing of claims struck by the Directive.

[152] *The Economist*, "Unreal", 14 May 1994. See generally G. Dworkin, "Unfair Competition: Is the Common Law Developing a New Tort?" [1979] *EIPR* 241; A. Terry, "Unfair Competition and the Misappropriation of a Competitor's Trade Values" (1988) 51 *MLR* 296; D. Harms, "Hark! There Goes a Tort" [1995] *EIPR* 453, Robertson and Horton, n. 83 above; and M. Spence, "Passing-off and the Misappropriation of Valuable Intangibles" (1996) 112 *LQR* 472.

[153] Mills, n. 97 above, 428.

[154] [1966] *RPC* 307.

The element shared by trade marks used in comparative advertisements and trade dress imitated by own-label products is the exploitation, intentionally or otherwise, of the associations surrounding the underlying product. This is conduct that many would regard as unfairly competitive, and moreover it is conduct that cannot be dismissed as simply breaking down product differentiation on the basis of spurious images. In the context of trade dress protection, this does not justify intervention with specific respect to own-label look-alikes, but it does strengthen the case for a general unfair competition law. Although examining the merits of this case are beyond the scope of this book, it worth taking on board the World Intellectual Property Organisation's comment that:

> "Experience has shown that there is little hope of fairness in competition being achieved solely by the free play of market forces."[155]

Instead, as Mills has observed,[156] moves must be made to "reintroduce standards of morality and integrity into the business world by providing incentives for investment in the use of creative skill and labour and by apparently encouraging competitors to trade off the work and investment of others"; we must reassess the minimum standard of conduct which the law is prepared to tolerate.

[155] *Report on Protection Against Unfair Competition* quoted in Mills, n. 97 above, 129.
[156] *Ibid.*

6

Conclusions on the Rationale of Trade Mark Protection

The practice of marketing goods and services under a manufacturer's trade mark has now become firmly entrenched in our society. According protection to trade marks serves no lesser purpose than to secure the benefits of the practice to those who encounter trade marks in the modern chain of distribution. Far from being an unobtrusive marking relevant only after sale in cases of complaint (such as historic marks were), the modern trade mark is often as relevant to the consumer's purchasing decision as the characteristics of the product that bears it; it is arguably capable of imparting to the product in question additional value for the purchaser and could even be said to be part of the product itself. This is nothing more than what consumers have been conditioned to expect.[1] In pre-industrial times, it was common knowledge that if a product was unsatisfactory, the authority responsible for ensuring quality within a particular trade was able to identify the product's manufacturer through its trade mark. The complete reorganisation of commerce, and in particular the separation of the consumer from the producer, meant that different ways of selling products had to be found. Instrumental in this was the advertising of a product through a key marketing tool, the product's brand name or trade mark. Consumers therefore became accustomed to *identifying* a product by reference to their trade marks. Indeed, the enduring presence of a handful of brand names in the consumer's consciousness has reached such an extent that it is possible to say that certain trade marks have assumed a wider cultural significance and meaning outside of the commercial context in which they were first created; consider BARBIE doll, ROLLS-ROYCE, MCDONALD'S, COCA-COLA or ROLEX. Marketing centres on causing consumers to purchase products by reference to trade marks. It is therefore understandable that if the meaning of a word becomes so strong, it will outgrow its original context. On reflection, it is not surprising that trade marks have become so whole-heartedly accepted by our modern consumer society given that it is a "society accustomed to receiving information in easily swallowed 'sound bites' "[2]; trade marks are no more than the merchants' equivalent.

[1] Having said this, one of the problems evident in the literature is that a large proportion of the theory of trade mark law is based on presumption concerning consumer psychology. However, there is very little empirical evidence of how consumer decision-making takes places which can confirm or dispute such presumptions.

[2] R. C. Dreyfuss, "Expressive Genericity: Trade Marks as Language in the PEPSI Generation" (1990) 65 *Notre Dame LR* 397, 413.

This acceptance or entrenchment to which we have just referred is one reason that explains why challenges to the economic efficiency of trade mark use that were discussed in Chapter 3 have been unsuccessful. The second reason is that the use of legally protected trade marks in the resource allocation process (taking place by way of consumer transactions in the market place) is actually perceived as being economically beneficial. Since trade marks convey information about the underlying product gained commonly through previous experience or advertising, this will enable consumers to economise on the search costs that would otherwise be incurred in finding the most suitable product for their needs. Furthermore, consumers are thought to be prepared to pay a premium for branded goods, since the trade mark gives them the assurance that the product will be of a consistent quality. In turn the producer gains a incentive to continue maintaining product quality. It is not thought that there is any other way of satisfactorily facilitating these twin benefits. Thirdly, and again reflecting the development of trade marks over the last 100 years, the trade mark has gone from being something of a hindrance to the producer to being an asset, the value of which no producer would now wish to be deprived of.

Thus we have trade mark protection, primarily through the law of trade mark registration and supplemented by the tort of passing-off. Both of these enable a producer to object to third party interference with his trade mark in circumstances when this would be injurious to his own and consumers' interests *in that order*. It will always be fundamental to trade mark law that trade mark infringement is prevented, so that consumers' freedom of choice will not be jeopardised. After all, if a trader were able to use a trade mark that consumers had already been conditioned to associate with another trader, their ability to make informed purchasing decisions would be impaired because of their resulting inability to relate a particular mark to a particular expectation. Consumer protection is therefore an important motivation in trade mark law, since, were it not for consumers purchasing goods and services with reference to brand names, trade marks and trade mark protection would have no purpose. An examination of the structure of trade mark law, however, revealed that the dominant interest is that of the producer. A trade mark-using producer is concerned to see both that custom is not diverted away from him by another's use of his trade mark or one similar and moreover that the often substantial investment in his brand is not undermined.

In appreciating what is arguably the driving force in modern trade mark law, mention must be made of whether it is helpful to characterise trade marks as property (whatever that implies[3]). Although this book has not carried out a detailed consideration of this question, it suffices to say that the concept of property is more useful as a conclusion[4] than as an analytical starting

[3] See e.g. K. Grey, *Elements of Land Law* (London, 1987), ch.1; D. F. Libling, "The Concept of Property: Property in Intangibles" (1978) 94 *LQR* 103.

[4] Since to say that something is "property" is simply to state that the law has protected a certain interest in a particular way. As E. J. Weinrib, "The Fiduciary Obligation" (1975) 25 *UTLJ* 1, 10–1,

point[5] and, most importantly for our purposes, it is a useful rhetorical device in that by stating a conclusion about the nature of the trade mark right, it emphasises, not that any particular rights attach to the mark, but that the mark is an important *asset* belonging to the producer making use of it.[6] As has just been observed, a producer is likely to have invested heavily in making his brand successful both in developing the product and marketing it, and it seems only that natural that he will want this recognised through his trade mark. It is for this reason that the trade mark can be said to be an asset belonging to him. Moreover, the law is increasingly willing to accept this fact. Consider, for example, the freedom with which a trade mark may now be licensed or even assigned, normally at a profit for the owner. Indeed, when section 2(1) Trade Marks Act 1994 confronts us with the bald statement that:

> "a registered trade mark is a property right obtained by the registration of the trade mark under this Act and the proprietor of a registered trade mark has the rights and remedies provided by this Act"

which is then "amplified" by the assertion in section 22 that "a registered trade mark is personal property", it is merely facilitating dealings in marks that are consistent with their status as producers' assets, "which are exploitable in the owner's discretion".[7] The expanded scope of the trade mark right, notwithstanding the effect of recent decisions, is no more than an acceptance of the meaning that a trade mark may potentially convey. The fact also that a trade mark is capable of a broad spectrum of meaning is acknowledged both by the new dilution provision and, in the Trade Marks Directive at least, by the inclusion of a mark's strength as a factor in determining whether a sign will infringe for likelihood of confusion.[8] Not all marks will qualify for the full ambit of

observed, "property is itself merely a label for that crystallised bundle of economic interests which the law deems worthy of protection. When intangibles such as (trade marks) are at stake, affixing the label of property constitutes a conclusion not a reason. The difficulty is not to supply a label but to identify the protected interest."

[5] This analysis is problematic because it presents a *fait accompli*—it implies a right of total exclusion—which does not admit the wide range of circumstances when third parties may legitimately use another's trade mark, and moreover clouds the issues underlying the reasons for protecting trade marks in the first place. Cohen, writing in the 1930s, criticised courts for seeking refuge in such analysis because of their fear of being seen to "take sides upon controversial issues of politics and economics" (F. Cohen, "Transcendental Nonsense and the Functional Approach" (1935) 35 *Columbia LR* 809, 815). It must therefore be assumed that the issues of the extent of trade marks' legal protection and the question of their status as property are necessarily independent of one another. This view is supported by F. I. Schechter, *The Historical Foundations of the Law Relating to Trade Marks* (New York, 1925), 171 and R. C. Denicola, "Trade Marks as Speech: Constitutional Implications of the Emerging Rationales for the Protection of Trade Symbols" [1982] *Wisconsin LR* 158, 165.

[6] "The basic fact is that many trade marks are no longer mere words indicating source but are symbols with independent value and are entitled to be protected like any other corporate asset." (J. B. Swann and T. H. Davis, "Dilution, an Idea Whose Time has Gone; Brand Equity as Protectable Property, the New/Old Paradigm" (1994) 84 *TMR* 267, 282).

[7] K. Parks, "'Naked' is not a Four Letter Word: Debunking the Myth of the 'Quality Control Requirement' in Trade Mark Licensing" (1992) 82 *TMR* 531, 567.

[8] 10th Recital of the Preamble to the Directive.

protection. Robert Denicola expresses the role of the property conception in trade mark law well:

> "To say that the law appears increasingly willing to accord trade marks the status of property may not be a particularly helpful characterisation of modern trade mark law, but it does emphasise that today's doctrine somehow differs from yesterday's."[9]

The doctrine differs because of the primacy of the producers' interests. Given that merchandising properties are also symbols that are being exploited at the owner's discretion, it is not surprising that merchandising has gained a hold within trade mark law. The repeal of the "trafficking" prohibition, for example, did nothing to discourage use by producers of their trade marks in merchandising ventures, or indeed the use of trade mark law to protect symbols and images that have never functioned as trade marks. The issue must still however be expressly addressed whether merchandising should, as a matter of policy, be protected within trade mark law or whether this could be done more satisfactorily elsewhere.

Another factor underlying trade mark law is the need to provide protection against unfairly competitive practices. Although it may once have been possible to conceive of trade mark law as being aimed at one specific wrong, namely a straightforward deception that one manufacturer's goods were in fact those of another, trade mark protection now has a far broader constituency. In Chapter 4, it was seen how it is possible to characterise trade mark infringement as a form of unfair competition because of the broadening bases of protection, particularly with respect to dilution, and, in Chapter 5, it was seen that the trade mark right may (in limited circumstances) be used to regulate comparative advertising even though this practice cannot strictly be said to affect a producer's trade identity. These considerations have already caused practical difficulties in some of the cases[10] so far decided under the new Trade Marks Act. Although these difficulties may be partially attributed to a (possibly misplaced) judicial antipathy towards a wider trade mark right, it may also be argued that, presuming that there is a case for more generally protecting one trader against another's unfairly competitive practices, such protection should be given outside the law of trade marks through an unfair competition law of general application. Traditionally the law has been loath to intervene on behalf of one trader against another when competition from the latter injures the first trader (compare this with competition law which intervenes in the public rather than a private interest). Courts felt unable to adjudicate effectively on intervention of this nature which, in any event, was also thought to be anathema to the functioning of the free market. Market forces could resolve any irregularities. However, many writers recently have pointed to the changing conditions in which trade marks, for example, are required to function in the shape of the changed busi-

[9] Denicola, n. 5 above, 159.

[10] Namely WAGAMAMA [1995] FSR 713 and *Barclays Bank plc* v. *RBS Advanta* [1996] RPC 307.

ness morality and the ever increasing competitiveness evident in the market place; they argue that it is no longer possible to abdicate protection of private interests to the market and the law must provide active incentives and a coherent policy so as to secure a sounder ethical basis in the market place.[11] Achieving this within trade mark law may be problematic in so far as historical preconceptions as the function of trade mark protection linger. This is because trade mark protection is rooted in the nineteenth century, a time of *laissez-faire* competition policy when only minimal legal intervention with respect to trade marks, in order only to safeguard trade identity, was thought necessary. Therefore the undoubted moves within modern trade mark law in the direction of giving priority to producers' interests as against other producers must be supplemented in some way external to trade mark law.

Although this book has attempted to identify and understand the rationale underlying trade mark law, it has in the process also identified areas where only empirical research will enable a full and proper understanding of the assumptions concerning consumer behaviour upon which trade mark law is based. In particular not enough is generally understood, I would suggest, about the consumer purchasing decision making process in relation to experience goods or about the damage done to a (well-known) trade mark and its underlying product where a mere association is made between it and a new mark. These are two potential areas for further useful study.

My final observation in conclusion is that the trade mark as a legal institution is now a mature and firmly established intellectual property right of equal status to patents and copyright. It must follow from this that any trade mark should be recognised for what it is, namely a vital asset of its owner and an important symbol to consumers in the market place which should receive the full protection that the law is now prepared to allow; this will only happen if the rationale of such protection is fully understood. What does *not* follow from this is that trade marks are "tarred with same brush" as the other intellectual property rights. It sometimes appears that trade marks are the poor relations of the intellectual property family on the one hand, but that, on the other, misunderstanding of their nature and function stems from this very grouping when their underlying rationale is quite different. The rationale of trade mark protection will never be properly understood as long as preconceptions about the theoretical bases of patents and copyright are allowed to obscure one's thinking, for the rationale of trade mark protection is quite different. Trade marks are *not* protected to create incentives to invent new brand names or symbols. Trade marks are *not* protected so that one person may gain a monopoly in using a word or symbol in certain context. Trade marks *are* protected because of the significance that they acquire in the course of trade through the trade mark owner's investment in the quality and presentation of the underlying product as well as the need to ensure that the resulting benefits continue. It must always be

[11] See articles cited at Ch.5, n. 151 above, as well as the accompanying text.

remembered that the trade mark is a marketing symbol and its purpose comes from how it is used in the market place. Although the manner in which marks are protected through registration may obscure this, any strength or value that a mark will have to its owner will come from the use to which it is put, not directly from any legal protection. The law has, perhaps irrevocably, recognised the commercial practice of trade marking and we must accept any consequences that may ensue without frustrating the legitimate expectations of those who have come to rely on its protection.

Appendix A—Brand Equity

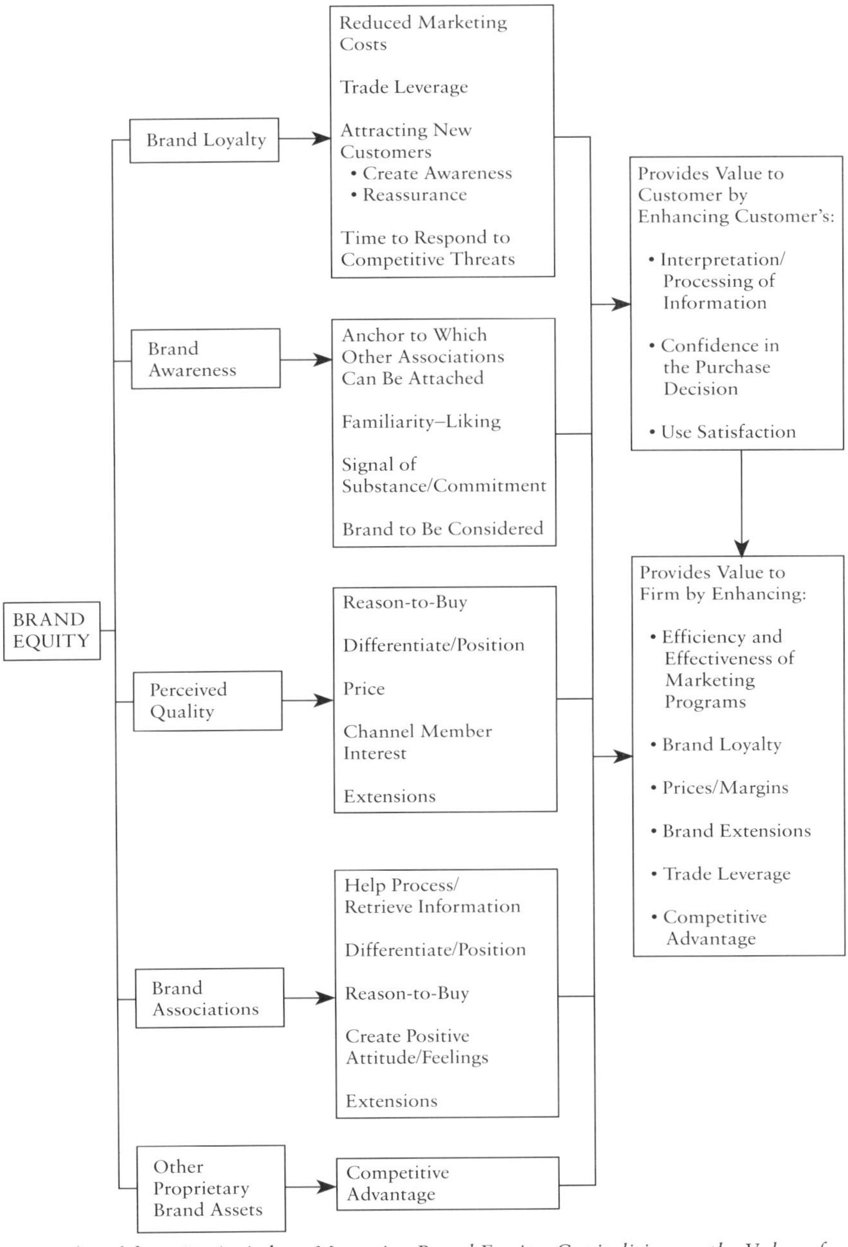

Reproduced from D. A. Aker, *Managing Brand Equity: Capitalising on the Value of a Brand Name* (New York, 1991)

Appendix B—Examples of Own-brand Look-alikes

Figure 1 *Own Brand and Branded Soap*

Figure 2 *Own Brand and Branded Wine*

Figure 3 *Own Brand and Branded Schnapps*

Figure 4 *Coca Cola and Sainsbury's Classic Cola*

Figure 5 *Kellogg's Corn Flakes*
The warning notice is at the top

Figure 6 *JPS and Raffles Cigarettes*

Figure 7 *The Marmite Case*
At the time of the hearing the cap of Sainsbury's product was yellow

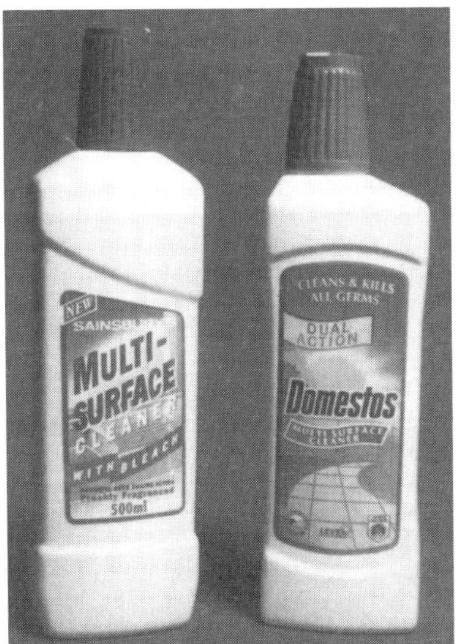

Figure 8 *Own Brand and Branded Cleaner*

Figure 9 *Sainsbury's Full Roast and Nescafé*

Reproduced from B. Mills, "Own Label Products and the Look-alike Phenomenon: A Lack of Trade Dress and Unfair Competition Protection?" [1995] EIPR 116

Appendix C—First Trade Marks Directive

First Council Directive 89/104/EEC of 21 December 1988 to approximate the laws of the Member States relating to trade marks (OJ [1989] L40/1)

THE COUNCIL OF THE EUROPEAN COMMUNITIES,

Having regard to the Treaty establishing the European Economic Community, and in particular Article 100a thereof,

Having regard to the proposal from the Commission,[1]

In co-operation with the European Parliament,[2]

Having regard to the opinion of the Economic and Social Committee,[3]

Whereas the trade mark laws at present applicable in the Member States contain disparities which may impede the free movement of goods and freedom to provide services and may distort competition within the common market; whereas it is therefore necessary, in view of the establishment and functioning of the internal market, to approximate the laws of Member States;

Whereas it is important not to disregard the solutions and advantages which the Community trade mark system may afford to undertakings wishing to acquire trade marks;

Whereas it does not appear to be necessary at present to undertake full-scale approximation of the trade mark laws of the Member States and it will be sufficient if approximation is limited to those national provisions of law which most directly affect the functioning of the internal market;

Whereas the Directive does not deprive the Member States of the right to continue to protect trade marks acquired through use but takes them into account only in regard to the relationship between them and trade marks acquired by registration;

Whereas Member States also remain free to fix the provisions of procedure concerning the registration, the revocation and the invalidity of trade marks acquired by registration; whereas they can, for example, determine the form of trade mark registration and invalidity procedures, decide whether earlier rights should be invoked either in the registration procedure or in the invalidity procedure or in both and, if they allow earlier rights to be invoked in the registration procedure, have an opposition procedure or an *ex officio* examination procedure or both; whereas Member States remain free to determine the effects of revocation or invalidity of trade marks;

[1] OJ [1980] C351/1 and [1985] C351/4.
[2] OJ [1983] C307/66 and [1988] C309.
[3] OJ [1981] C310/22.

Whereas this Directive does not exclude the application to trade marks of provisions of law of the Member States other than trade mark law, such as the provisions relating to unfair competition, civil liability or consumer protection;

Whereas attainment of the objectives at which this approximation of laws is aiming requires that the conditions for obtaining and continuing to hold a registered trade mark are, in general, identical in all Member states; whereas, to this end, it is necessary to list examples of signs which may constitute a trademark, provided that such signs are capable of distinguishing the goods or services of one undertaking from those of other undertakings; whereas the grounds for refusal or invalidity concerning the trade mark itself, for example, the absence of any distinctive character, or concerning conflicts between the trade mark and earlier rights, are to be listed in an exhaustive manner, even if some of these grounds are listed as an option for the Member States which will therefore be able to maintain or introduce those grounds in their legislation; whereas Member States will be able to maintain or introduce into their legislation grounds of refusal or invalidity linked to conditions for obtaining and continuing to hold a trade mark for which there is no provision of approximation, concerning, for example, the eligibility for the grant of a trade mark, the renewal of the trade mark or rules on fees, or related to the non-compliance with procedural rules;

Whereas in order to reduce the total number of trade marks registered and protected in the Community and, consequently, the number of conflicts which arise between them, it is essential to require that registered trade marks must actually be used or, if not used, be subject to revocation; whereas it is necessary to provide that a trade mark cannot be invalidated on the basis of the existence of a non-used earlier trade mark, while the Member States remain free to apply the same principle in respect of the registration of a trade mark or to provide that a trade mark may not be successfully invoked in infringement proceedings if it is established as a result of a plea that the trade mark could be revoked; whereas in all these cases it is up to the Member States to establish the applicable rules of procedure;

Whereas it is fundamental, in order to facilitate the free circulation of goods and services, to ensure that henceforth registered trade marks enjoy the same protection under the legal systems of all the Member States; whereas this should however not prevent the Member States from granting at their option extensive protection to those trade marks which have a reputation;

Whereas the protection afforded by the registered trade mark, the function of which is in particular to guarantee the trade mark as an indication of origin, is absolute in the case of identity between the mark and the sign and goods or services; whereas the protection applies also in case of similarity between the mark and the sign and the goods or services; whereas it is indispensable to give an interpretation of the concept of similarity in relation to the likelihood of confusion; whereas the likelihood of confusion, the appreciation of which depends on numerous elements and, in particular, on the recognition of the trade mark on the market, of the association which can be made with the used or registered sign, of the degree of similarity between the trade mark and the sign and between the goods or services identified, constitutes the specific condition for such protection; whereas the ways in which likelihood of confusion may be established, and in particular the onus of proof, are a matter for national Procedural rules which are not prejudiced by the Directive;

Whereas it is important, for reasons of legal certainty and without inequitably prejudicing the interests of a proprietor of an earlier trade mark, to provide that the latter may no longer request a declaration of invalidity nor may he oppose the use of a trade mark subsequent to his own of which he has knowingly tolerated the use for a substantial length of time, unless the application for the subsequent trade mark was made in bad faith:

Whereas all Member States of the Community are bound by the Paris Convention for the Protection of Industrial Property; whereas it is necessary that the provisions of this Directive are entirely consistent with those of the Paris Convention; whereas the obligations of the Member States resulting from this Convention are not affected by this Directive; whereas, where appropriate, the second subparagraph of Article 234 of the Treaty is applicable,

HAS ADOPTED THIS DIRECTIVE:

Article 1

Scope

This Directive shall apply to every trade mark in respect of goods or services which is the subject of registration or of an application in a Member State for registration as an individual trade mark, a collective mark or a guarantee or certification mark, or which is the subject of a registration or an application for registration in the Benelux Trade Mark Office or of an international registration having effect in a Member State.

Article 2

Signs of which a trade mark may consist

A trade mark may consist of any sign capable of being represented graphically, particularly words, including personal names, designs, letters, numerals, the shape of goods or of their packaging, provided that such signs are capable of distinguishing the goods or services of one undertaking from those of other undertakings.

Article 3

Grounds for refusal or invalidity

1. the following shall not be registered or if registered shall be liable to be declared invalid:

- (a) signs which cannot constitute a trade mark;
- (b) trade marks which are devoid of any distinctive character;
- (c) trade marks which consist exclusively of signs or indications which may serve, in trade, to designate the kind, quality, quantity, intended purpose, value, geographical origin, or the time of production of the goods or of rendering of the service, or other characteristics of the goods
- (d) trade marks which consist exclusively of signs or indications which have become customary in the current language or in the bona fide and established practices of the trade;

(e) signs which consist exclusively of:
—the shape which results from the nature of the goods themselves, or
—the shape of goods which is necessary to obtain a technical result, or
—the shape which gives substantial value to the goods;
(f) trade marks which are contrary to public policy or to accepted principles of morality;
(g) trade marks which are of such a nature as to deceive the public, for instance as to the nature, quality or geographical origin of the goods or service;
(h) trade marks which have not been authorized by the competent authorities and are to be refused or invalidated pursuant to Article 6 *ter* of the Paris Convention for the Protection of Industrial Property, hereinafter referred to as the "Paris Convention".

2. Any Member State may provide that a trade mark shall not be registered or, if registered, shall be liable to be declared invalid where and to the extent that:

(a) the use of that trade mark may be prohibited pursuant to provisions of law other than trade mark law of the Member State concerned or of the Community;
(b) the trade mark covers a sign of high symbolic value, in particular a religious symbol;
(c) the trade mark includes badges, emblems and escutcheons other than those covered by Article 6*ter* of the Paris Convention and which are of public interest, unless the consent of the appropriate authorities to its registration has been given in conformity with the legislation of the Member State;
(d) the application for registration of the trade mark was made in bad faith by the applicant.

3. A trade mark shall not be refused registration or be declared invalid in accordance with paragraph 1(b), (c) or (d) if, before the date of application for registration and following the use which has been made of it, it has acquired a distinctive character. Any Member State may in addition provide that this provision shall also apply where the distinctive character was acquired after the date of application for registration or after the date of registration.

4. Any Member state may provide that, by derogation from the preceding paragraphs, the grounds of refusal of registration or invalidity in force in that State prior to the date on which the provisions necessary to comply with this Directive enter into force, shall apply to trade marks for which application has been made prior to that date.

Article 4

Further grounds for refusal or invalidity concerning conflicts with earlier rights

1. A trade mark shall not be registered or, if registered, shall be liable to be declared invalid:

(a) if it is identical with an earlier trade mark, and the goods or services for which the trade mark is applied for or is registered are identical with the goods or services for which the earlier trade mark is protected;

(b) if because of its identity with, or similarity to, the earlier trade mark and the identity or similarity of the goods or services covered by the trade marks, there exists a likelihood of confusion on the part of the public, which includes the likelihood of association with the earlier trade mark.

2. "Earlier trade marks" within the meaning of paragraph 1 means:

(a) trade marks of the following kinds with a date of application for registration which is earlier than the date of application for registration of the trade mark, taking account, where appropriate, of the priorities claimed in respect of those trade marks;
  (i) Community trade marks;
  (ii) trade marks registered in the Member State or, in the case of Belgium, Luxembourg or the Netherlands, at the Benelux Trade Mark Office;
  (iii) trade marks registered under international arrangements which have effect in the Member State;

(b) Community trade marks which validly claim seniority, in accordance with the Regulation on the Community trade mark, from a trade mark referred to in (a)(ii) and (iii), even when the latter trade mark has been surrendered or allowed to lapse;

(c) applications for the trade marks referred to in (a) and (b), subject to their registration;

(d) trade marks which, on the date of application for registration of the trade mark, or, where appropriate, of the priority claimed in respect of the application for registration of the trade mark, are well known in a Member State, in the sense in which the words "well known" are used in Article 6 bis of the Paris Convention.

3. A trade mark shall furthermore not be registered or, if registered, shall be liable to be declared invalid if it is identical with, or similar to, an earlier Community trade mark within the meaning of paragraph 2 and is to be, or has been, registered for goods or services which are not similar to those for which the earlier Community trade mark is registered, where the earlier Community trade mark has a reputation in the Community and where the use of the later trade mark without due cause would take unfair advantage of, or be detrimental to, the distinctive character or the repute of the earlier Community trade mark.

4. Any Member State may furthermore provide that a trade mark shall not be registered or, if registered, shall be liable to be declared invalid where, and to the extent that:

(a) the trade mark is identical with, or similar to, an earlier national trade mark within the meaning of paragraph 2 and is to be, or has been, registered for goods or services which are not similar to those for which the earlier trade mark is registered, where the earlier trade mark has a reputation in the Member State concerned and where the use of the later trade mark without due cause would take unfair advantage of, or be detrimental to, the distinctive character of che repute of the earlier trade mark;

(b) rights to a non-registered trade mark or to another sign used in the course of trade were acquired prior to the date of application for registration of the subsequent trade mark, or the date of the priority claimed for the application for registration of the subsequent trade mark and that non-registered trade mark or other sign confers on its proprietor the right to prohibit the use of a subsequent trade mark;

(c) the use of the trade mark may be prohibited by virtue of an earlier right other than the rights referred to in paragraphs 2 and 4 (b) and in particular:
  (i) a right to a name;
  (ii) a right of personal portrayal;
  (iii) a copyright;
  (iv) an industrial property right;

(d) the trade mark is identical with, or similar to, an earlier collective trade mark conferring a right which expired within a period of a maximum of three years preceding application;

(e) the trade mark is identical with, or similar to, an earlier guarantee or certification mark conferring a right which expired within a period preceding application the length of which is fixed by the Member State;

(f) the trade mark is identical with, or similar to, an earlier trade mark which was registered for identical or similar goods or services and conferred on them a right which has expired for failure to renew within a period of a maximum of two years preceding application, unless the proprietor of the earlier trade mark gave his agreement for the registration of the later mark or did not use his trade mark;

(g) the trade mark is liable to be confused with a mark which was in use abroad on the filing date of the application and which is still in use there, provided that at the date of the application the applicant was acting in bad faith?

5. The Member States may permit that in appropriate circumstances registration need not be refused or the trade mark need not be declared invalid where the proprietor of the earlier trade mark or other earlier right consents to the registration of the later trade mark.

6. Any Member State may provide that, by derogation from paragraphs 1 to S, the grounds for refusal of registration or invalidity in force in that State prior to the date on which the provisions necessary to comply with this Directive enter into force, shall apply to trade marks for which application has been made prior to that date.

Article 5

Rights conferred by a trade mark

1. The registered trade mark shall confer on the proprietor exclusive rights therein. The proprietor shall be entitled to prevent all third parties not having his consent from using in the course of trade:

(a) any sign which is identical with the trade mark in relation to goods or services which are identical with those for which the trade mark is registered;

(b) any sign where, because of its identity with, or similarity to, the trade mark and the identity or similarity of the goods or services covered by the trade mark and the sign, there exists a likelihood of confusion on the part of the public, which includes the likelihood of association between the sign and the trade mark.

2. Any Member State may also provide that the proprietor shall be entitled to prevent all third parties not having his consent from using in the course of trade any sign which is

identical with, or similar to, the trade mark in relation to goods or services which are not similar to those for which the trade mark is registered, where the latter has a reputation in the Member State and where use of that sign without due cause takes unfair advantage of, or is detrimental to, the distinctive character or the repute of the trade mark.

3. The following, *inter alia*, may be prohibited under paragraphs 1 and 2:

(a) affixing the sign to the goods or to the packaging thereof;
(b) offering the goods, or putting them on the market or stocking them for these purposes under that sign, or offering or supplying services thereunder;
(c) importing or exporting the goods under the sign;
(d) using the sign on business papers and in advertising.

4. Where, under the law of the Member State, the use of a sign under the conditions referred to in 1(b) or 2 could not be prohibited before the date on which the provisions necessary to comply with this Directive entered into force in the Member State concerned, the rights conferred by the trade mark may not be relied on to prevent the continued use of the sign.

5. Paragraphs 1 to 4 shall not affect provisions in any Member State relating to the protection against the use of a sign other than for the purposes of distinguishing goods or services, where use of that sign without due cause takes unfair advantage of, or is detrimental to, the distinctive character or the repute of the trade mark.

Article 6

Limitation of the effects of a trade mark

1. The trade mark shall not entitle the proprietor to prohibit a third party from using, in the course of trade,

(a) his own name or address;
(b) indications concerning the kind, quality, quantity, intended purpose, value, geographical origin, the time of production of goods or of rendering of the service, or other characteristics of goods or services;
(c) the trade mark where it is necessary to indicate the intended purpose of a product or service, in particular as accessories or spare parts;

provided he uses them in accordance with honest practices in industrial or commercial matters.

2. The trade mark shall not entitle the proprietor to prohibit a third party from using, in the course of trade, an earlier right which only applies in a particular locality if that right is recognized by the laws of the Member State in question and within the limits of the territory in which it is recognized.

Article 7

Exhaustion of the rights conferred by a trade mark

1. The trade mark shall not entitle the proprietor to prohibit its use in relation to goods which have been put on the market in the Community under that trade mark by the proprietor or with his consent.

2. Paragraph 1 shall not apply where there exist legitimate reasons for the proprietor to oppose further commercialization of the goods, especially where the condition of the goods is changed or impaired after they have been put on the market.

Article 8

Licensing

1. A trade mark may be licensed for some or all of the goods or services for which it is registered and for the whole or part of the Member State concerned. A license may be exclusive or non-exclusive.

2. The proprietor of a trade mark may invoke the rights conferred by that trade mark against a licensee who contravenes any provision in his licensing contract with regard to its duration, the form covered by the registration in which the trade mark may be used, the scope of the goods or services for which the licence is granted, the territory in which the trade mark may be affixed, or the quality of the goods manufactured or of the services provided by the licensee.

Article 9

Limitation in consequence of acquiescence

1. Where, in a Member State, the proprietor of an earlier trade mark as referred to in Article 4(2) has acquiesced, for a period of five successive years, in the use of a later trade mark registered in that Member State while being aware of such use, he shall no longer be entitled on the basis of the earlier trade mark either to apply for a declaration that the later trade mark is invalid or to oppose the use of the later trade mark in respect of the goods or services for which the later trade mark has been used, unless registration of the later trade mark was applied for in bad faith.

2. Any Member State may provide that paragraph 1 shall apply *mutatis mutandis* to the proprietor of an earlier trade mark referred to in Article 4(4)(a) or another earlier right referred to in Article 4(4)(b) or (c).

3. In the cases referred to in paragraphs 1 and 2, the proprietor of a later registered trade mark shall not be entitled to oppose the use of the earlier right, even though that right may no longer be invoked against the later trade mark.

Article 10

Use of trade marks

1. If, within a period of five years following the date of the completion of the registration procedure, the proprietor has not put the trade mark to genuine use in the Member State in connection with the goods or services in respect of which it is registered, or if such use has been suspended during an uninterrupted period of five years, the trade mark shall be subject to the sanctions provided for in this Directive, unless there are proper reasons for non-use.

2. The following shall also constitute use within the meaning of paragraph 1:

(a) use of the trade mark in a form differing in elements which do not alter the distinctive character of the mark in the form in which it was registered;
(b) affixing of the trade mark to goods or to the packaging thereof in the Member State concerned solely for export purposes.

3. Use of the trade mark with the consent of the proprietor or by any person who has authority to use a collective mark or a guarantee or certification mark shall be deemed to constitute use by the proprietor.

4. In relation to trade marks registered before the date on which the provisions necessary to comply with this Directive enter into force in the Member State concerned:

(a) where a provision in force prior to that date attaches sanctions to non-use of a trade mark during an uninterrupted period, the relevant period of five years mentioned in paragraph 1 shall be deemed to have begun to run at the same time as any period of non-use which is already running at that date;
(b) where there is no use provision in force prior to that date, the periods of five years mentioned in paragraph 1 shall be deemed to run from that date at the earliest.

Article 11

Sanctions for non-use of a trade mark in legal or administrative proceedings

1. A trade mark may not be declared invalid on the ground that there is an earlier conflicting trade mark if the latter does not fulfil the requirements of use set out in Article 10(1), (2) and (3) or in Article 10(4), as the case may be.

2. Any Member State may provide that registration of a trade mark may not be refused on the ground that there is an earlier conflicting trade mark if the latter does not fulfil the requirements of use set out in Article 10(1), (2) and (4) or in Article 10(4), as the case may be.

3. Without prejudice to the application of Article 12, where a counter-claim for revocation is made, any Member State may provide that a trade mark may not be successfully invoked in infringement proceedings if it is established as a result of a plea that the trade mark could be revoked pursuant to Article 12(1).

4. If the earlier trade mark has been used in relation to part only of the goods or services for which it is registered, it shall, for purposes of applying paragraphs 1, 2 and 3, be deemed to be registered in respect only of that part of the goods or services.

Article 12

Grounds for revocation

1. A trade mark shall be liable to revocation if, within a continuous period of five years, it has not been put to genuine use in the Member State in connection with the goods or services in respect of which it is registered, and there are no proper reasons for non-use; however, no person may claim that the proprietor's rights in a trade mark should be revoked where, during the interval between expiry of the five-year period and filing of the application for revocation, genuine use of the trade mark has been started or resumed; the commencement or resumption of use within a period of three months preceding the filing of the application for revocation which began at the earliest on expiry of the continuous period of five years of non-use shall, however, be disregarded where preparations for the commencement or resumption occur only after the proprietor becomes aware that the application for revocation may be filed.

2. A trade mark shall also be liable to revocation if, after the date on which it was registered,

(a) in consequence of acts or inactivity of the proprietor, it has become the common name in the trade for a product or service in respect of which it is registered;

(b) in consequence of the use made of it by the proprietor of the trade mark or with his consent in respect of the goods or services for which it is registered, it is liable to mislead the public, particularly as to the nature, quality or geographical origin of those goods or services.

Article 13

Grounds for refusal or revocation or invalidity relating to only some of the goods or services

Where grounds for refusal of registration or for revocation or invalidity of a trade mark exist in respect of only some of the goods or services for which that trade mark has been applied for or registered, refusal of registration or revocation or invalidity shall cover those goods or services only.

Article 14

Establishment a posteriori of invalidity or revocation of a trade mark

Where the seniority of an earlier trade mark which has been surrendered or allowed to lapse, is claimed for a Community trade mark, the invalidity or revocation of the earlier trade mark may be established *a posteriori.*

Article 15

Special provisions in respect of collective marks, guarantee marks and certification marks

1. Without prejudice to Article 4, Member States whose laws authorize the registration of collective marks or of guarantee or certification marks may provide that such marks shall not be registered, or shall be revoked or declared invalid, on grounds additional to those specified in Articles 3 and 12 where the function of those marks so requires.

2. By way of derogation from Article 3(1)(c), Member States may provide that signs or indications which may serve, in trade, to designate the geographical origin of the goods or services may constitute collective, guarantee or certification marks. Such a mark does not entitle the proprietor to prohibit a third party from using in the course of trade such signs or indications, provided he uses them in accordance with honest practices in industrial or commercial matters; in particular, such a mark may not be invoked against a third party who is entitled to use a geographical name.

Article 16

National provisions to be adopted pursuant to this Directive

1. The Member States shall bring into force the laws, regulations and administrative provisions necessary to comply with this Directive not later than 28 December 1991. They shall immediately inform the Commission thereof.

2. Acting on a proposal from the Commission, the Council, acting by qualified majority, may defer the date referred to in paragraph 1 until 31 December 1992 at the latest.

3. Member States shall communicate to the Commission the text of the main provisions of national law which they adopt in the field governed by this Directive.

Article 17

Addressees

This Directive is addressed to the Member States.

Done at Brussels, 21 December 1988.

For the Council
The President
V. PAPANDREOU

Appendix D—Extracts from the Trade Marks Act 1938 (repealed)

. . .

4 Right given by registration in Part A, and infringement thereof

(1) Subject to the provisions of this section, and of sections seven and eight of this Act, the registration (whether before or after the commencement of this Act) of a person in Part A of the register as proprietor of a trade mark (other than a certification trade mark) in respect of any goods shall, if valid, give or be deemed to have given to that person the exclusive right to the use of the trade mark in relation to those goods and, without prejudice to the generality of the foregoing words, that right shall be deemed to be infringed by any person who, not being the proprietor of the trade mark or a registered user thereof using by way of the permitted use, uses [in the course of trade a mark identical with or nearly resembling it], in relation to any goods in respect of which it is registered, and in such manner as to render the use of the mark likely to be taken either—

(a) as being use as a trade mark; or
(b) in a case in which the use is use upon the goods or in physical relation thereto or in an advertising circular or other advertisement issued to the public, as importing a reference to some person having the right either as proprietor or as registered user to use the trade mark or to goods with which such a person as aforesaid is connected in the course of trade.

. . .

5 Right given by registration in Part B, and infringement thereof

(1) Except as provided by subsection (2) of this section, the registration (whether before or after the commencement of this Act) of a person in Part B of the register as proprietor of a trade mark in respect of any goods shall, if valid, give or be deemed to have given to that person the like right in relation to those goods as if the registration had been in Part A of the register, and the provisions of the last foregoing section shall have effect in like manner in relation to a trade mark registered in Part B of the register as they have effect in relation to a trade mark registered in Part A of the register.

(2) In any action for infringement of the right to the use of a trade mark given by registration as aforesaid in Part B of the register, otherwise than by an act that is deemed to be an infringement by virtue of the next succeeding section, no injunction or other relief shall be granted to the plaintiff if the defendant establishes to the satisfaction of the court that the use of which the plaintiff complains is not likely to deceive or cause confusion or to be taken as indicating a connection in the course of trade between the goods and some person having the right either as proprietor or as registered user to use the trade mark.

. . .

Registrability and validity of registration

9 Distinctiveness requisite for registration in Part A

(1) In order for a trade mark (other than a certification trade mark) to be registrable in Part A of the register, it must contain or consist of at least one of the following essential particulars:—

(a) the name of a company, individual, or firm, represented in a special or particular manner;
(b) the signature of the applicant for registration or some predecessor in his business;
(c) an invented word or invented words;
(d) a word or words having no direct reference to the character or quality of the goods, and not being according to its ordinary signification a geographical name or a surname;
(e) any other distinctive mark, but a name, signature, or word or words, other than such as fall within the descriptions in the foregoing paragraphs (a), (b), (c) and (d), shall not be registrable under the provisions of this paragraph except upon evidence of its distinctiveness.

(2) For the purposes of this section "distinctive" means adapted, in relation to the goods in respect of which a trade mark is registered or proposed to be registered, to distinguish goods with which the proprietor of the trade mark is or may be connected in the course of trade from goods in the case of which no such connection subsists, either generally or, where the trade mark is registered or proposed to be registered subject to limitations, in relation to use within the extent of the registration.

(3) In determining whether a trade mark is adapted to distinguish as aforesaid the tribunal may have regard to the extent to which:—

(a) the trade mark is inherently adapted to distinguish as aforesaid; and
(b) by reason of the use of the trade mark or of any other circumstances, the trade mark is in fact adapted to distinguish as aforesaid.

10 Capability of distinguishing requisite for registration in Part B

(1) In order for a trade mark to be registrable in Part B of the register it must be capable, in relation to the goods in respect of which it is registered or proposed to be registered, of distinguishing goods with which the proprietor of the trade mark is or may be connected in the course of trade from goods in the case of which no such connection subsists, either generally or, where the trade mark is registered or proposed to be registered subject to limitations, in relation to use within the extent of the registration.

(2) In determining whether a trade mark is capable of distinguishing as aforesaid the tribunal may have regard to the extent to which—

(a) the trade mark is inherently capable of distinguishing as aforesaid; and
(b) by reason of the use of the trade mark or of any other circumstances, the trade mark is in fact capable of distinguishing as aforesaid.

(3) A trade mark may be registered in Part B notwithstanding any registration in Part A in the name of the same proprietor of the same trade mark or any part or parts thereof.

11 Prohibition of registration of deceptive, etc, matter

It shall not be lawful to register as a trade mark or part of a trade mark any matter the use of which would, by reason of its being likely to deceive or cause confusion or otherwise, be disentitled to protection in a court of justice, or would be contrary to law or morality, or any scandalous design.

12 Prohibition of registration of identical and resembling trade marks

(1) Subject to the provisions of subsection (2) of this section, no trade mark shall be registered in respect of any goods or description of goods that is identical with [or nearly resembles a mark belonging to a different proprietor and already on the register in respect of—

(a) the same goods,
(b) the same description of goods, or
(c) services or a description of services which are associated with those goods or goods of that description.]

(2) In case of honest concurrent use, or of other special circumstances which in the opinion of the Court or the Registrar make it proper so to do, the Court or the Registrar may permit the registration [by more than one proprietor, in respect to—

(a) the same goods,
(b) the same description of goods, or
(c) goods and services or descriptions of goods and services which are associated with each other,

of marks that are identical or nearly resemble each other,] subject to such conditions and limitations, if any, as the Court or the Registrar, as the case may be, may think it right to impose.

(3) Where separate applications are made by different persons to be registered as proprietors respectively of [marks that are identical or nearly resemble each other, in respect of—

(a) the same goods,
(b) the same description of goods, or
(c) goods and services or descriptions of goods and services which are associated with each other,]

the Registrar may refuse to register any of them until their rights have been determined by the Court, or have been settled by agreement in a manner approved by him or on an appeal (which may be brought either to the Board of Trade or to the Court at the option of the appellant) by the Board or the Court, as the case may be.

. . .

Assignment and transmission

22 Powers of, and restrictions on, assignment and transmission

(1) Notwithstanding any rule of law or equity to the contrary, a registered trade mark shall be, and shall be deemed always to have been, assignable and transmissible either in connection with the goodwill of a business or not.

. . .

(4) Notwithstanding anything in the foregoing subsections, a trade mark shall not be, or be deemed to have been, assignable or transmissible in a case in which as a result of an assignment or transmission there would in the circumstances subsist, or have subsisted, whether under the common law or by registration, exclusive rights in more than one of the persons concerned to the use, in relation to

[(a) the same goods,
(b) the same description of goods, or
(c) goods and services or descriptions of goods and services which are associated with each other]

of trade marks nearly resembling each other or of identical trade marks, if, having regard to the similarity of the goods [or the association of the goods and services or description of goods and services and to the similarity of the trade marks], the use of the trade marks in exercise of those rights would be, or have been, likely to deceive or cause confusion:

Provided that, where a trade mark is, or has been, assigned or transmitted in such a case as aforesaid, the assignment or transmission shall not be deemed to be, or to have been, invalid under this subsection if the exclusive rights subsisting as a result thereof in the persons concerned respectively are, or were, having regard to limitations imposed thereon, such as not to be exercisable by two or more of those persons in relation to goods to be sold, or otherwise trade in, within the United Kingdom (otherwise than for export therefrom) or in relation to goods to be exported to the same market outside the United Kingdom.

. . .

Use and non-use

26 Removal from register and imposition of limitations on ground of non-use

(1) Subject to the provisions of the next succeeding section, a registered trade mark may be taken off the register in respect of any of the goods in respect of which it is registered on application by any person aggrieved to the Court or, at the option of the applicant and subject to the provisions of section fifty-four of this Act, to the Registrar, on the ground either—

(a) that the trade mark was registered without any bona fide intention on the part of the applicant for registration that it should be used in relation to those goods by him, and that there has in fact been no bona fide use of the trade mark in relation to those goods by any proprietor thereof for the time being up to the date one month before the date of the application; or

(b) that up to the date one month before the date of the application a continuous period of five years or longer elapsed during which the trade mark was a registered trade mark and during which there was no bona fide use thereof in relation to those goods by any proprietor thereof for the time being:

Provided that (except where the applicant has been permitted under subsection (2) of section twelve of this Act to register an identical or nearly resembling trade mark in respect of the goods in question or where the tribunal is of opinion that he might properly be permitted so to register such a trade mark) the tribunal may refuse an application made under paragraph (a) or (b) of this subsection in relation to any goods, if it is shown that there has been, before the relevant date or during the relevant period, as the case may be, bona fide use [of the mark by the proprietor thereof for the time being in relation to—

(i) goods of the same description; or

(ii) services associated with those goods or goods of that description,

being goods or, as the case may be, services in respect of which the mark is registered.].

(2) Where in relation to any goods in respect of which a trade mark is registered—

(a) the matters referred to in paragraph (b) of the foregoing subsection are shown so far as regards non-use of the trade mark in relation to goods to be sold, or otherwise traded in, in a particular place in the United Kingdom (otherwise than for export from the United Kingdom), or in relation to goods to be exported to a particular market outside the United Kingdom; and
(b) a person has been permitted under subsection (2) of section twelve of this Act to register an identical or nearly resembling trade mark in respect of those goods under a registration extending to use in relation to goods to be sold, or otherwise traded in, in that place (otherwise than for export from the United Kingdom), or in relation to goods to be exported to that market, or the tribunal is of opinion that he might properly be permitted so to register such a trade mark.

on application by that person to the Court or, at the option of the applicant and subject to the provisions of section fifty-four of this Act, to the Registrar, the tribunal may impose on the registration of the first-mentioned trade mark such limitations as the tribunal thinks proper for securing that that registration shall cease to extend to such use as last aforesaid.

(3) An applicant shall not be entitled to rely for the purposes of paragraph (b) of subsection (1), or for the purposes of subsection (2), of this section on any non-use of a trade mark that is shown to have been due to special circumstances in the trade and not to any intention not to use or to abandon the trade mark in relation to the goods to which the application relates.

27 Defensive registration of well known trade marks

(1) Where a trade mark consisting of an invented word or invented words has become so well known as respects any goods in respect of which it is registered and in relation to which it has been used that the use thereof in relation to other goods would be likely to be taken as indicating a connection in the course of trade between those goods and a person entitled to use the trade mark in relation to the first-mentioned goods, then, notwithstanding that the proprietor registered in respect of the first-mentioned goods does not use or propose to use the trade mark in relation to those other goods and notwithstanding anything in the last foregoing section, the trade mark may, on the application in the prescribed manner of the proprietor registered in respect of the first-mentioned goods, be registered in his name in respect of those other goods as a defensive trade mark and, while so registered, shall not be liable to be taken off the register in respect of those goods under the last foregoing section.

(2) The registered proprietor of a trade mark may apply for the registration thereof in respect of any goods as a defensive trade mark notwithstanding that it is already registered in his name in respect of those goods otherwise than as a defensive trade mark, or

may apply for the registration thereof in respect of any goods otherwise than as a defensive trade mark notwithstanding that it is already registered in his name in respect of those goods as a defensive trade mark, in lieu in each case of the existing registration.

(3) A trade mark registered as a defensive trade mark and that trade mark as otherwise registered in the name of the same proprietor shall, notwithstanding that the respective registrations are in respect of different goods, be deemed to be, and shall be registered as, associated trade marks.

(4) On application by any person aggrieved to the Court or, at the option of the applicant and subject to the provisions of section fifty-four of this Act, to the Registrar, the registration of a trade mark as a defensive trade mark may be cancelled on the ground that the requirements of subsection (1) of this section are no longer satisfied in respect of any goods in respect of which the trade mark is registered in the name of the same proprietor otherwise than as a defensive trade mark, or may be cancelled as respects any goods in respect of which it is registered as a defensive trade mark on the ground that there is no longer any likelihood that the use of the trade mark in relation to those goods would be taken as giving the indication mentioned in subsection (1) of this section.

(5) The Registrar may at any time cancel the registration as a defensive trade mark of a trade mark of which there is no longer any registration in the name of the same proprietor otherwise than as a defensive trade mark.

(6) Except as otherwise expressly provided in this section, the provisions of this Act shall apply in respect of the registration of trade marks as defensive trade marks and of trade marks so registered as they apply in other cases.

28 Registered users

(1) Subject to the provisions of this section, a person other than the proprietor of a trade mark may be registered as a registered user thereof in respect of all or any of the goods in respect of which it is registered (otherwise than as a defensive trade mark) and either with or without conditions or restrictions.

The use of a trade mark by a registered user thereof in relation to goods with which he is connected in the course of trade and in respect of which for the time being the trade mark remains registered and he is registered as a registered user, being use such as to comply with any conditions or restrictions to which his registration is subject, is in this Act referred to as the "permitted use" thereof.

(2) The permitted use of a trade mark shall be deemed to be use by the proprietor thereof, and shall be deemed not to be use by a person other than the proprietor, for the purposes of section twenty-six of this Act and for any other purpose for which such use is material under this Act or at common law.

(3) Subject to any agreement subsisting between the parties, a registered user of a trade mark shall be entitled to call upon the proprietor thereof to take proceedings to prevent infringement thereof, and, if the proprietor refuses or neglects to do so within two months after being so called upon, the registered user may institute proceedings for infringement in his own name as if he were the proprietor, making the proprietor a defendant.

A proprietor so added as defendant shall not be liable for any costs unless he enters an appearance and takes part in the proceedings.

(4) Where it is proposed that a person should be registered as a registered user of a

trade mark, the proprietor and the proposed registered user must apply in writing to the Registrar in the prescribed manner and must furnish him with a statutory declaration made by the proprietor, or by some person authorised to act on his behalf and approved by the Registrar,—

(a) giving particulars of the relationship, existing or proposed, between the proprietor and the proposed registered user, including particulars showing the degree of control by the proprietor over the permitted use which their relationship will confer and whether it is a term of their relationship that the proposed registered user shall be the sole registered user or that there shall be any other restriction as to persons for whose registration as registered users application may be made;
(b) stating the goods in respect of which registration is proposed;
(c) stating any conditions or restrictions proposed with respect to the characteristics of the goods, to the mode or place of permitted use, or to any other matter; and
(d) stating whether the permitted use is to be for a period or without limit of period, and, if for a period, the duration thereof;

and with such further documents, information or evidence as may be required under the rules or by the Registrar.

(5) When the requirements of the last foregoing subsection have been complied with, if the Registrar, after considering the information furnished to him under that subsection, is satisfied that in all the circumstances the use of the trade mark in relation to the proposed goods or any of them by the proposed registered user subject to any conditions or restrictions which the Registrar thinks proper would not be contrary to the public interest, the Registrar may register the proposed registered user as a registered user in respect of the goods as to which he is so satisfied subject as aforesaid.

(6) The Registrar shall refuse an application under the foregoing provisions of this section if it appears to him that the grant thereof would tend to facilitate trafficking in a trade mark.

(7) The Registrar shall, if so required by an applicant, take steps for securing that information given for the purposes of an application under the foregoing provisions of this section (other than matter entered in the register) is not disclosed to rivals in trade.

(8) Without prejudice to the provisions of section thirty-two of this Act, the registration of a person as a registered user—

(a) may be varied by the Registrar as regards the goods in respect of which, or any conditions or restrictions subject to which, it has effect, on the application in writing in the prescribed manner of the registered proprietor of the trade mark to which the registration relates;
(b) may be cancelled by the Registrar on the application in writing in the prescribed manner of the registered proprietor or of the registered user or of any other registered user of the trade mark; or
(c) may be cancelled by the Registrar on the application in writing in the prescribed manner of any person on any of the following grounds, that is to say,—
    (i) that the registered user has used the trade mark otherwise than by way of the permitted use, or in such a way as to cause, or to be likely to cause, deception or confusion;

(ii) that the proprietor or the registered user misrepresented, or failed to disclose, some fact material to the application for the registration, or that the circumstances have materially changed since the date of the registration;

(iii) that the registration ought not to have been effected having regard to rights vested in the applicant by virtue of a contract in the performance of which he is interested.

(9) Provision shall be made by the rules for the notification of the registration of a person as a registered user to any other registered user of the trade mark, and for the notification of an application under the last foregoing subsection to the registered proprietor and each registered user (not being the applicant) of the trade mark, and for giving to the applicant on such an application, and to all persons to whom such an application is notified and who intervene in the proceedings in accordance with the rules, an opportunity of being heard.

(10) The Registrar may at any time cancel the registration of a person as a registered user of a trade mark in respect of any goods in respect of which the trade mark is no longer registered.

(11) Any decision of the Registrar under the foregoing provisions of this section shall be subject to appeal to the Court.

(12) Nothing in this section shall confer on a registered user of a trade mark any assignable or transmissible right to the use thereof.

. . .

Supplemental

68 Interpretation

(1) In this Act, unless the context otherwise requires, the following expressions have the meanings hereby assigned to them respectively, that is to say:—

. . .

"trade mark" means, except in relation to a certification trade mark, a mark used or proposed to be used in relation to goods for the purpose of indicating, or so as to indicate, a connection in the course of trade between the goods and some person having the right either as proprietor or as registered user to use the mark, whether with or without any indication of the identity of that person, and means, in relation to a certification trade mark, a mark registered or deemed to have been registered under section thirty-seven of this Act;

(2) References in this Act to the use of a mark shall be construed as references to the use of a printed or other visual representation of the mark, and references therein to the use of a mark in relation to goods shall be construed as references to the use thereof upon, or in physical or other relation to, goods.

[(2A) For the purposes of this Act goods and services are associated with each other if it is likely that those goods might be sold or otherwise traded in and those services might be provided by the same business, and so with descriptions of goods and descriptions of services.

(2B) References in this Act to a near resemblance of marks are references to a resemblance so near as to be likely to deceive or cause confusion.]

. . .

Appendix E—Extracts from the Trade Marks Act 1994

An Act to make new provision for registered trade marks, implementing Council Directive No 89/104/EEC of 21st December 1988 to approximate the laws of the Member States relating to trade marks; to make provision in connection with Council Regulation (EC) No 40/94 of 20th December 1993 on the Community trade mark; to give effect to the Madrid Protocol Relating to the International Registration of Marks of 27th June 1989, and to certain provisions of the Paris Convention for the Protection of Industrial Property of 20th March 1883, as revised and amended; and for connected purposes

[21 July 1994]

Introductory

1 Trade Marks

(1) In this Act a "trade mark" means any sign capable of being represented graphically which is capable of distinguishing goods or services of one undertaking from those of other undertakings.

A trade mark may, in particular, consist of words (including personal names), designs, letters, numerals or the shape of goods or their packaging.

. . .

2 Registered trade marks

(1) A registered trade mark is a property right obtained by the registration of the trade mark under this Act and the proprietor of a registered trade mark has the rights and remedies provided by this Act.

(2) No proceedings lie to prevent or recover damages for the infringement of an unregistered trade mark as such; but nothing in this Act affects the law relating to passing off.

Grounds for refusal of registration

3 Absolute grounds for refusal of registration

(1) The following shall not be registered—

(a) signs which do not satisfy the requirements of section 1(1),
(b) trade marks which are devoid of any distinctive character,
(c) trade marks which consist exclusively of signs or indications which may serve, in trade, to designate the kind, quality, quantity, intended purpose, value, geographical origin, the time of production of goods or of rendering of services, or other characteristics of goods or services,

(d) trade marks which consist exclusively of signs or indications which have become customary in the current language or in the bona fide and established practices of the trade:

Provided that, a trade mark shall not be refused registration by virtue of paragraph (b), (c) or (d) above if, before the date of application for registration, it has in fact acquired a distinctive character as a result of the use made of it.

(2) A sign shall not be registered as a trade mark if it consists exclusively of—

(a) the shape which results from the nature of the goods themselves,
(b) the shape of goods which is necessary to obtain a technical result, or
(c) the shape which gives substantial value to the goods.

(3) A trade mark shall not be registered if it is—

(a) contrary to public policy or to accepted principles of morality, or
(b) of such a nature as to deceive the public (for instance as to the nature, quality or geographical origin of the goods or service).

(4) A trade mark shall not be registered if or to the extent that its use is prohibited in the United Kingdom by any enactment or rule of law or by any provision of Community law.

(5) A trade mark shall not be registered in the cases specified, or referred to, in section 4 (specially protected emblems).

(6) A trade mark shall not be registered if or to the extent that the application is made in bad faith.

. . .

5 Relative grounds for refusal of registration

(1) A trade mark shall not be registered if it is identical with an earlier trade mark and the goods or services for which the trade mark is applied for are identical with the goods or services for which the earlier trade mark is protected.

(2) A trade mark shall not be registered if because—

(a) it is identical with an earlier trade mark and is to be registered for goods or services similar to those for which the earlier trade mark is protected, or
(b) it is similar to an earlier trade mark and is to be registered for goods or services identical with or similar to those for which the earlier trade mark is protected,

there exists a likelihood of confusion on the part of the public, which includes the likelihood of association with the earlier trade mark.

(3) A trade mark which—

(a) is identical with or similar to an earlier trade mark, and
(b) is to be registered for goods or services which are not similar to those for which the earlier trade mark is protected,

shall not be registered if, or to the extent that, the earlier trade mark has a reputation in the United Kingdom (or, in the case of a Community trade mark, in the European Community) and the use of the later mark without due cause would take unfair advantage of, or be detrimental to, the distinctive character or the repute of the earlier trade mark.

(4) A trade mark shall not be registered if, or to the extent that, its use in the United Kingdom is liable to be prevented—

(a) by virtue of any rule of law (in particular, the law of passing off) protecting an unregistered trade mark or other sign used in the course of trade, or

(b) by virtue of an earlier right other than those referred to in subsections (1) to (3) or paragraph (a) above, in particular by virtue of the law of copyright, design right or registered designs.

A person thus entitled to prevent the use of a trade mark is referred to in this Act as the proprietor of an "earlier right" in relation to the trade mark.

(5) Nothing in this section prevents the registration of a trade mark where the proprietor of the earlier trade mark or other earlier right consents to the registration.

6 Meaning of "earlier trade mark"

(1) In this Act an "earlier trade mark" means,

(a) a registered trade mark, international trade mark (UK) or Community trade mark which has a date of application for registration earlier than that of the trade mark in question, taking account (where appropriate) of the priorities claimed in respect of the trade marks,

(b) a Community trade mark which has a valid claim to seniority from an earlier registered trade mark or international trade mark (UK), or

(c) a trade mark which, at the date of application for registration of the trade mark in question or (where appropriate) of the priority claimed in respect of the application, was entitled to protection under the Paris Convention as a well known trade mark.

(2) References in this Act to an earlier trade mark include a trade mark in respect of which an application for registration has been made and which, if registered, would be an earlier trade mark by virtue of subsection 1(a) or (b), subject to its being so registered.

(3) A trade mark within subsection (1)(a) or (b) whose registration expires shall continue to be taken into account in determining the registrability of a later mark for a period of one year after the expiry unless the registrar is satisfied that there was no bona fide use of the mark during the two years immediately preceding the expiry.

7 Raising of relative grounds in case of honest concurrent use

(1) This section applies where on an application for the registration of a trade mark it appears to the registrar—

(a) that there is an earlier trade mark in relation to which the conditions set out in section 5(1), (2) or (3) obtain, or

(b) that there is an earlier right in relation to which the condition set out in section 5(4) is satisfied,

but the applicant shows to the satisfaction of the registrar that there has been honest concurrent use of the trade mark for which registration is sought.

(2) In that case the registrar shall not refuse the application by reason of the earlier trade mark or other earlier right unless objection on that ground is raised in opposition proceedings by the proprietor of that earlier trade mark or other earlier right.

(3) For the purposes of this section "honest concurrent use" means such use in the United Kingdom, by the applicant or with his consent, as would formerly have amounted to honest concurrent use for the purposes of section 12(2) of the Trade Marks Act 1938.

(4) Nothing in this section affects—

(a) the refusal of registration on the grounds mentioned in section 3 (absolute grounds for refusal), or
(b) the making of an application for a declaration of invalidity under section 47(2) (application on relative grounds where no consent to registration).

(5) This section does not apply when there is an order in force under section 8 below.

8 Power to require that relative grounds be raised in opposition proceedings

(1) The Secretary of State may by order provide that in any case a trade mark shall not be refused registration on a ground mentioned in section 5 (relative grounds for refusal) unless objection on that ground is raised in opposition proceedings by the proprietor of the earlier trade mark or other earlier right.

(2) The order may make such consequential provision as appears to the Secretary of State appropriate—

(a) with respect to the carrying out by the registrar of searches of earlier trade marks, and
(b) as to the persons by whom an application for a declaration of invalidity may be made on the grounds specified in section 47(2) (relative grounds).

(3) An order making such provision as is mentioned in subsection (2)(a) may direct that so much of section 37 (examination of application) as requires a search to be carried out shall cease to have effect.

(4) An order making such provision as is mentioned in subsection (2)(b) may provide that so much of section 47(3) as provides that any person may make an application for a declaration of invalidity shall have effect subject to the provisions of the order.

(5) An order under this section shall be made by statutory instrument, and no order shall be made unless a draft of it has been laid before and approved by a resolution of each House of Parliament.

No such draft of an order making such provision as is mentioned in subsection (1) shall be laid before Parliament until after the end of the period of ten years beginning with the day on which applications for Community trade marks may first be filed in pursuance of the Community Trade Mark Regulation.

(6) An order under this section may contain such transitional provisions as appear to the Secretary of State to be appropriate.

Effects of registered trade mark

9 Rights conferred by registered trade mark

(1) The proprietor of a registered trade mark has exclusive rights in the trade mark which are infringed by use of the trade mark in the United Kingdom without his consent.

The acts amounting to infringement, if done without the consent of the proprietor, are specified in section 10.

. . .

10 Infringement of registered trade mark

(1) A person infringes a registered trade mark if he uses in the course of trade a sign which is identical with the trade mark in relation to goods or services which are identical with those for which it is registered.

(2) A person infringes a registered trade mark if he uses in the course of trade a sign where because—

(a) the sign is identical with the trade mark and is used in relation to goods or services similar to those for which the trade mark is registered, or
(b) the sign is similar to the trade mark and is used in relation to goods or services identical with or similar to those for which the trade mark is registered,

there exists a likelihood of confusion on the part of the public, which includes the likelihood of association with the trade mark.

(3) A person infringes a registered trade mark if he uses in the course of trade a sign which—

(a) is identical with or similar to the trade mark, and
(b) is used in relation to goods or services which are not similar to those for which the trade mark is registered,

where the trade mark has a reputation in the United Kingdom and the use of the sign, being without due cause, takes unfair advantage of, or is detrimental to, the distinctive character or the repute of the trade mark.

(4) For the purposes of this section a person uses a sign if, in particular, he—

(a) affixes it to goods or the packaging thereof;
(b) offers or exposes goods for sale, puts them on the market or stocks them for those purposes under the sign, or offers or supplies services under the sign;
(c) imports or exports goods under the sign; or
(d) uses the sign on business papers or in advertising.

(5) A person who applies a registered trade mark to material intended to be used for labelling or packaging goods, as a business paper, or for advertising goods or services, shall be treated as a party to any use of the material which infringes the registered trade mark if when he applied the mark he knew or had reason to believe that the application of the mark was not duly authorised by the proprietor or a licensee.

(6) Nothing in the preceding provisions of this section shall be construed as preventing the use of a registered trade mark by any person for the purpose of identifying goods or services as those of the proprietor or a licensee.

But any such use otherwise than in accordance with honest practices in industrial or commercial matters shall be treated as infringing the registered trade mark if the use without due cause takes unfair advantage of, or is detrimental to, the distinctive character or repute of the trade mark.

11 Limits on effect of registered trade mark

(1) A registered trade mark is not infringed by the use of another registered trade mark in relation to goods or services for which the latter is registered (but see section 47(6) (effect of declaration of invalidity of registration)).

(2) A registered trade mark is not infringed by—

(a) the use by a person of his own name or address,
(b) the use of indications concerning the kind, quality, quantity, intended purpose, value, geographical origin, the time of production of goods or of rendering of services, or other characteristics of goods or services, or
(c) the use of the trade mark where it is necessary to indicate the intended purpose of a product or service (in particular, as accessories or spare parts),

provided the use is in accordance with honest practices in industrial or commercial matters.

(3) A registered trade mark is not infringed by the use in the course of trade in a particular locality of an earlier right which applies only in that locality.

For this purpose an "earlier right" means an unregistered trade mark or other sign continuously used in relation to goods or services by a person or a predecessor in title of his from a date prior to whichever is the earlier of—

(a) the use of the first-mentioned trade mark in relation to those goods or services by the proprietor or a predecessor in title of his, or
(b) the registration of the first-mentioned trade mark in respect of those goods or services in the name of the proprietor or a predecessor in title of his;

and to an earlier right shall be regarded as applying in a locality if, or to the extent that, its use in that locality is protected by virtue of any rule of law (in particular, the law of passing off).

12 Exhaustion of rights conferred by registered trade mark

(1) A registered trade mark is not infringed by the use of the trade mark in relation to goods which have been put on the market in the European Economic Area under that trade mark by the proprietor or with his consent.

(2) Subsection (1) does not apply where there exist legitimate reasons for the proprietor to oppose further dealings in the goods (in particular, where the condition of the goods has been changed or impaired after they have been put on the market).

. . .

Registered trade mark as object of property

22 Nature of registered trade mark

A registered trade mark is personal property (in Scotland, incorporeal moveable property).

. . .

24 Assignment, &c of registered trade mark

(1) A registered trade mark is transmissible by assignment, testamentary disposition or operation of law in the same way as other personal or moveable property.

It is so transmissible either in connection with the goodwill of a business or independently.

(2) An assignment or other transmission of a registered trade mark may be partial, that is, limited so as to apply—

(a) in relation to some but not all of the goods or services for which the trade mark is registered, or
(b) in relation to use of the trade mark in a particular manner or a particular locality.

(3) An assignment of a registered trade mark, or an assent relating to a registered trade mark, is not effective unless it is in writing signed by or on behalf of the assignor or, as the case may be, a personal representative.

Except in Scotland, this requirement may be satisfied in a case where the assignor or personal representative is a body corporate by the affixing of its seal.

(4) The above provisions apply to assignment by way of security as in relation to any other assignment.

(5) A registered trade mark may be the subject of a charge (in Scotland, security) in the same way as other personal or moveable property.

(6) Nothing in this Act shall be construed as affecting the assignment or other transmission of an unregistered trade mark as part of the goodwill of a business.

25 Registration of transactions affecting registered trade mark

(1) On application being made to the registrar by—

(a) a person claiming to be entitled to an interest in or under a registered trade mark by virtue of a registrable transaction, or
(b) any other person claiming to be affected by such a transaction,

the prescribed particulars of the transaction shall be entered in the register.

(2) The following are registrable transactions—

(a) an assignment of a registered trade mark or any right in it;
(b) the grant of a licence under a registered trade mark;
(c) the granting of any security interest (whether fixed or floating) over a registered trade mark or any right in or under it;
(d) the making by personal representatives of an assent in relation to a registered trade mark or any right in or under it;
(e) an order of a court or other competent authority transferring a registered trade mark or any right in or under it.

(3) Until an application has been made for registration of the prescribed particulars of a registrable transaction—

(a) the transaction is ineffective as against a person acquiring a conflicting interest in or under the registered trade mark in ignorance of it, and
(b) a person claiming to be a licensee by virtue of the transaction does not have the protection of section 30 or 31 (rights and remedies of licensee in relation to infringement).

(4) Where a person becomes the proprietor or a licensee of a registered trade mark by virtue of a registrable transaction, then unless—

(a) an application for registration of the prescribed particulars of the transaction is made before the end of the period of six months beginning with its date, or
(b) the court is satisfied that it was not practicable for such an application to be made before the end of that period and that an application was made as soon as practicable thereafter,

he is not entitled to damages or an account of profits in respect of any infringement of the registered trade mark occurring after the date of the transaction and before the prescribed particulars of the transaction are registered.

(5) Provision may be made by rules as to—

(a) the amendment of registered particulars relating to a licence so as to reflect any alteration of the terms of the licence, and
(b) the removal of such particulars from the register—
   (i) where it appears from the registered particulars that the licence was granted for a fixed period and that period has expired, or
   (ii) where no such period is indicated and, after such period as may be prescribed, the registrar has notified the parties of his intention to remove the particulars from the register.

(6) Provision may also be made by rules as to the amendment or removal from the register of particulars relating to a security interest on the application of, or with the consent of, the person entitled to the benefit of that interest.

. . .

Licensing

28 Licensing of registered trade mark

(1) A licence to use a registered trade mark may be general or limited.

A limited licence may, in particular, apply—

(a) in relation to some but not all of the goods or services for which the trade mark is registered, or
(b) in relation to use of the trade mark in a particular manner or a particular locality.

(2) A licence is not effective unless it is in writing signed by or on behalf of the grantor.

Except in Scotland, this requirement may be satisfied in a case where the grantor is a body corporate by the affixing of its seal.

(3) Unless the licence provides otherwise, it is binding on a successor in title to the grantor's interest.

References in this Act to doing anything with, or without, the consent of the proprietor of a registered trade mark shall be construed accordingly.

(4) Where the licence so provides, a sub-licence may be granted by the licensee; and references in this Act to a licence or licensee include a sub-licence or sub-licensee.

29 Exclusive licences

(1) In this Act an "exclusive licence" means a licence (whether general or limited) authorising the licensee to the exclusion of all other persons, including the person granting the licence, to use a registered trade mark in the manner authorised by the licence.

The expression "exclusive licensee" shall be construed accordingly.

(2) An exclusive licensee has the same rights against a successor in title who is bound by the licence as he has against the person granting the licence.

30 General provisions as to rights of licensees in case of infringement

(1) This section has effect with respect to the rights of a licensee in relation to infringement of a registered trade mark.

The provisions of this section do not apply where or to the extent that, by virtue of section 31(1) below (exclusive licensee having rights and remedies of assignee), the licensee has a right to bring proceedings in his own name.

(2) A licensee is entitled, unless his licence, or any licence through which his interest is derived, provides otherwise, to call on the proprietor of the registered trade mark to take infringement proceedings in respect of any matter which affects his interests.

(3) If the proprietor—

(a) refuses to do so, or
(b) fails to do so within two months after being called upon,

the licensee may bring the proceedings in his own name as if he were the proprietor.

(4) Where infringement proceedings are brought by a licensee by virtue of this section, the licensee may not, without the leave of the court, proceed with the action unless the proprietor is either joined as a plaintiff or added as a defendant.

This does not affect the granting of interlocutory relief on an application by a licensee alone.

(5) A proprietor who is added as a defendant as mentioned in subsection (4) shall not be made liable for any costs in the action unless he takes part in the proceedings.

(6) In infringement proceedings brought by the proprietor of a registered trade mark any loss suffered or likely to be suffered by licensees shall be taken into account; and the court may give such directions as it thinks fit as to the extent to which the plaintiff is to hold the proceeds of any pecuniary remedy on behalf of licensees.

(7) The provisions of this section apply in relation to an exclusive licensee if or to the extent that he has, by virtue of section 31(1), the rights and remedies of an assignee as if he were the proprietor of the registered trade mark.

31 Exclusive licensee having rights and remedies of assignee

(1) An exclusive licence may provide that the licensee shall have, to such extent as may be provided by the licence, the same rights and remedies in respect of matters occurring after the grant of the licence as if the licence had been an assignment.

Where or to the extent that such provision is made, the licensee is entitled, subject to the provisions of the licence and to the following provisions of this section, to bring infringement proceedings, against any person other than the proprietor, in his own name.

(2) Any such rights and remedies of an exclusive licensee are concurrent with those of the proprietor of the registered trade mark; and references to the proprietor of a registered trade mark in the provisions of this Act relating to infringement shall be construed accordingly.

(3) In an action brought by an exclusive licensee by virtue of this section a defendant may avail himself of any defence which would have been available to him if the action had been brought by the proprietor of the registered trade mark.

(4) Where proceedings for infringement of a registered trade mark brought by the proprietor or an exclusive licensee relate wholly or partly to an infringement in respect of which they have concurrent rights of action, the proprietor or, as the case may be, the exclusive licensee may not, without the leave of the court, proceed with the action unless the other is either joined as a plaintiff or added as a defendant.

This does not affect the granting of interlocutory relief on an application by a proprietor or exclusive licensee alone.

(5) A person who is added as a defendant as mentioned in subsection (4) shall not be made liable for any costs in the action unless he takes part in the proceedings.

(6) Where an action for infringement of a registered trade mark is brought which relates wholly or partly to an infringement in respect of which the proprietor and an exclusive licensee have or had concurrent rights of action—

- (a) the court shall in assessing damages take into account—
  - (i) the terms of the licence, and
  - (ii) any pecuniary remedy already awarded or available to either of them in respect of the infringement;
- (b) no account of profits shall be directed if an award of damages has been made, or an account of profits has been directed, in favour of the other of them in respect of the infringement; and
- (c) the court shall if an account of profits is directed apportion the profits between them as the court considers just, subject to any agreement between them.

The provisions of this subsection apply whether or not the proprietor and the exclusive licensee are both parties to the action; and if they are not both parties the court may give directions as it thinks fit as to the extent to which the party to the proceedings is to hold the proceeds of any pecuniary remedy on behalf of the other.

(7) The proprietor of a registered trade mark shall notify any exclusive licensee who has a concurrent right of action before applying for an order under section 16 (order for delivery up); and the court may on the application of the licensee make such order under that section as it thinks fit having regard to the terms of the licence.

(8) The provisions of subsections (4) to (7) above have effect subject to any agreement to the contrary between the exclusive licensee and the proprietor.

. . .

46 Revocation of registration

(1) The registration of a trade mark may be revoked on any of the following grounds—

- (a) that within the period of five years following the date of completion of the registration procedure it has not been put to genuine use in the United Kingdom, by the proprietor or with his consent, in relation to the goods or services for which it is registered, and there are no proper reasons for non-use;
- (b) that such use has been suspended for an uninterrupted period of five years, and there are no proper reasons for non-use;
- (c) that, in consequence of acts or inactivity of the proprietor, it has become the common name in the trade for a product or service for which it is registered;
- (d) that in consequence of the use made of it by the proprietor or with his consent in relation to the goods or services for which it is registered, it is liable to mislead the public, particularly as to the nature, quality or geographical origin of those goods or services.

(2) For the purposes of subsection (1) use of a trade mark includes use in a form differing in elements which do not alter the distinctive character of the mark in the form

in which it was registered, and use in the United Kingdom includes affixing the trade mark to goods or to the packaging of goods in the United Kingdom solely for export purposes.

(3) The registration of a trade mark shall not be revoked on the ground mentioned in subsection (1)(a) or (b) if such use as is referred to in that paragraph is commenced or resumed after the expiry of the five year period and before the application for revocation is made:

Provided that, any such commencement or resumption of use after the expiry of the five year period but within the period of three months before the making of the application shall be disregarded unless preparations for the commencement or resumption began before the proprietor became aware that the application might be made.

(4) An application for revocation may be made by any person, and may be made either to the registrar or to the court, except that—

(a) if proceedings concerning the trade mark in question are pending in the court, the application must be made to the court; and
(b) if in any other case the application is made to the registrar, he may at any stage of the proceedings refer the application to the court.

(5) Where grounds for revocation exist in respect of only some of the goods or services for which the trade mark is registered, revocation shall relate to those goods or services only.

(6) Where the registration of a trade mark is revoked to any extent, the rights of the proprietor shall be deemed to have ceased to that extent as from—

(a) the date of the application for revocation, or
(b) if the registrar or court is satisfied that the grounds for revocation existed at an earlier date, that date.

47 Grounds for invalidity of registration

(1) The registration of a trade mark may be declared invalid on the ground that the trade mark was registered in breach of section 3 or any of the provisions referred to in that section (absolute grounds for refusal of registration).

Where the trade mark was registered in breach of subsection (1)(b), (c) or (d) of that section, it shall not be declared invalid if, in consequence of the use which has been made of it, it has after registration acquired a distinctive character in relation to the goods or services for which it is registered.

(2) The registration of a trade mark may be declared invalid on the ground—

(a) that there is an earlier trade mark in relation to which the conditions set out in section 5(1), (2) or (3) obtain, or
(b) that there is an earlier right in relation to which the condition set out in section 5(4) is satisfied,

unless the proprietor of that earlier trade mark or other earlier right has consented to the registration.

(3) An application for a declaration of invalidity may be made by any person, and may be made either to the registrar or to the court, except that—

(a) if proceedings concerning the trade mark in question are pending in the court, the application must be made to the court; and

(b) if in any other case the application is made to the registrar, he may at any stage of the proceedings refer the application to the court.

(4) In the case of bad faith in the registration of a trade mark, the registrar himself may apply to the court for a declaration of the invalidity of the registration.

(5) Where the grounds of invalidity exist in respect of only some of the goods or services for which the trade mark is registered, the trade mark shall be declared invalid as regards those goods or services only.

(6) Where the registration of a trade mark is declared invalid to any extent, the registration shall to that extent be deemed never to have been made:

Provided that this shall not affect transactions past and closed.

. . .

56 Protection of well-known trade marks: Article 6*bis*

(1) References in this Act to a trade mark which is entitled to protection under the Paris Convention as a well known trade mark are to a mark which is well-known in the United Kingdom as being the mark of a person who—

(a) is a national of a Convention country, or
(b) is domiciled in, or has a real and effective industrial or commercial establishment in, a Convention country,

whether or not that person carries on business, or has any goodwill, in the United Kingdom.

References to the proprietor of such a mark shall be construed accordingly.

(2) The proprietor of a trade mark which is entitled to protection under the Paris Convention as a well known trade mark is entitled to restrain by injunction the use in the United Kingdom of a trade mark which, or the essential part of which, is identical or similar to his mark, in relation to identical or similar goods or services, where the use is likely to cause confusion.

This right is subject to section 48 (effect of acquiescence by proprietor of earlier trade mark).

(3) Nothing in subsection (2) affects the continuation of any bona fide use of a trade mark begun before the commencement of this section.

. . .

Bibliography

BOOKS

AAKER, D. A., *Managing Brand Equity: Capitalising on the Value of a Brand Name* (New York, 1991)

ADAMS, J., *Merchandising Intellectual Property* (London, 1987)

ANNAND, R. E. and NORMAN, H. E., *Blackstone's Guide to the Trade Marks Act 1994* (London, 1994)

BAINBRIDGE, D. I., *Intellectual Property* (2nd edn., London, 1994)

BAKER, J. H. and MILSOM, S. F. C., *Sources of English Legal History* (London, 1986)

BENSON, J., *The Rise of the Consumer Society in Britain 1880–1980* (London, 1994)

BLANCO WHITE, T. A. and JACOB, R., *Kerly's Law of Trade Marks and Trade Names* (12th edn., London, 1986)

CHAMBERLIN, E. H., *The Theory of Monopolistic Competition* (8th edn., Cambridge, Mass., 1962)

CORNISH, W. R., *Intellectual Property: Patents, Copyrights, Trade Marks and Allied Rights* (2nd edn., London, 1989)

CORNISH, W. R., *Intellectual Property: Patents, Copyrights, Trade Marks and Allied Rights* (3rd edn., London, 1996)

CRANSTON, R., *Consumers and the Law* (2nd edn., London, 1984)

DWORKIN, G. and Taylor, R. D., *Blackstone's Guide to the Copyright, Designs and Patents Act 1988* (London, 1989)

GOWER, L. C. B., *Principles of Modern Company Law* (5th edn., London, 1992)

GREY, K., *Elements of Land Law* (London, 1987)

GUEST, A. G. (ed.), *Oxford Essays in Jurisprudence* (First Series, Oxford, 1961)

HOLYOAK, J. and TORREMANS, P., *Intellectual Property Law* (London, 1995)

LIPSEY, R. G., *An Introduction to Positive Economics* (7th edn., London, 1989)

LOCKE, J., *Two Treatises of Government* (ed. M. Goldie, London, 1993)

MARTIN, J. E., *Hanbury and Martin: Modern Equity* (13th edn., London, 1993)

MARTINO, T., *Trade Mark Dilution* (Oxford, 1996)

MILLER, C. J. and HARVEY, B. W., *Consumer and Trading Law Cases and Materials* (London, 1985)

MORCOM, C., *A Guide to the Trade Marks Act 1994* (London, 1995)

MURPHY, J. M. (ed.), *Brand Valuation* (2nd edn., London, 1991)

PARKINSON, J. E., *Corporate Power and Responsibility* (Oxford, 1993)

PEARSON, H. E. and MILLER, C. G., *Commercial Exploitation of Intellectual Property* (London, 1990)

POSNER, R. A., *Economic Analysis of Law* (4th edn., Boston, Mass., 1992)

SCHECHTER, F. I., *The Historical Foundations of the Law Relating to Trade Marks* (New York, 1925)

SCHERER, F. M. and ROSS, D., *Industrial Market Structure and Economic Performance* (3rd edn., Boston, Mass., 1990)

WADLOW, C., *The Law of Passing Off* (2nd edn., London, 1995)

WHISH, R., *Competition Law* (3rd edn., London, 1993)

ARTICLES

AKAZAKI, L., "Source Theory and Guarantee Theory in Anglo-American Trade Mark Policy: A Critical Legal Study" (1990) 72 *Journal of the Patent and Trade Mark Office Society* 255

—— "Source and Guarantee: A Critical Study of Anglo–US Trade Mark Policy" October 1989, *Trade Mark World* 40

ANSON, W., "Placing Market Values on Trade Marks and Brands", September 1995, *Trade Mark World* 27

BACKMAN, J., "The Role of Trade Marks in our Competitive Economy" (1968) 58 *Trademark Reporter* 219

BAIN, H. L. R., "The Law Affecting Comparative Advertising" (1974) 32 *University of Toronto Faculty of Law Review* 109

BANNON, E. C., "Revisiting 'The Rational Basis of Trade Mark Protection': Control of Quality and Dilution—Estranged Bedfellows?" (1990) 24 *John Marshall Law Review* 65

BEHRENDT, P. H., "Trade Marks and Monopolies: Historical and Conceptual Foundations" (1961) 51 *Trademark Reporter* 853

BEIER, F.-K., "The Law of Unfair Competition in the EC: its Development and Status" [1985] *European Intellectual Property Review* 284

—— "The Development of Trade Mark Law in the Last Twenty-Five Years" [1995] *International Review of Industrial Property and Copyright Law* 769

BORCHARD, W. M., "Stifling Creativity by Overprotecting Intellectual Property", March 1994 *Trade Mark World* 12

BRAZELL, L., "Brand Values", November/December 1997, *Trade Mark World* 24

BROWN, L. O., "Advertising Requirements of Trade Marks" (1954) 44 *Trademark Reporter* 794

BROWN, R. S., "Advertising and the Public Interest: Legal Protection of Trade Symbols" (1948) 57 *Yale Law Journal* 1165

CALLMANN, R., "Unfair Competition Without Competition?" (1947) 95 *University of Pennsylvania Law Review* 443

—— "Trade Mark Infringement and Unfair Competition" (1949) 14 *Law & Contemporary Problems* 185

CARBONI, A., "Confusion Clarified: *SABEL* v. *Puma*" [1998] *European Intellectual Property Review* 107

CARTER, S. L., "The Trouble with Trade Mark" (1990) 99 *Yale Law Journal* 759

CARTY, H., "Do Marks with a Special Reputation Merit Special Protection?" [1997] *European Intellectual Property Review* 684

CLARK, F., "*McDonald's Hamburgers Ltd.* v. *Burger King (UK) Ltd.*: '. . . a Nice Advertisement for Everybody . . .' " [1985] *European Intellectual Property Review* 264

COHEN, F., "Transcendental Nonsense and the Functional Approach" (1935) 35 *Columbia Law Review* 809

CONLON, S. B., "Comparative Advertising: Whatever Happened to 'Brand X'" (1977) 67 *Trademark Reporter* 407

CORNISH, W. R. and PHILLIPS, J., "The Economic Function of Trade Marks: An Analysis with Special Reference to Developing Countries" [1982] *International Review of Industrial Property and Copyright Law* 41

COVERDALE, J. F., "Trade Marks and Generic Words: An Effect on Competition Test" (1984) 51 *University of Chicago Law Review* 868

The Daily Telegraph, "Tesco corn flake packs get frosty response", 16 August 1996

—— "Yes, we have our own bananas", 21 August 1996

DANIEL, D., "Can the Shape of Products be Trade Marks?: A Brazilian and International Perspective" [1995] *European Intellectual Property Review* 589

DENICOLA, R. C., "Trade Marks as Speech: Constitutional Implications of the Emerging Rationales for the Protection of Trade Symbols" [1982] *Wisconsin Law Review* 158

—— "Institutional Publicity Rights: an Analysis of the Merchandising of Famous Trade Symbols" (1984) 62 *North Carolina Law Review* 603

DIAMOND, S. A., "The Public Interest and the Trade Mark System" (1980) 62 *Journal of the Patent Office Society* 528

DIETZ, A., "Intellectual Property and Desocialisation in Eastern Europe" [1995] *International Review of Industrial Property and Copyright Law* 851

DOWELL, A. E., "Trade Dress Protection of Product Design: Stifling Progress of Science and the Useful Arts for an Unlimited Time" (1994) 70 *Notre Dame Law Review* 137

DRESCHER, T. D., "The Transformation and Evolution of Trade Marks: From Signals to Symbols to Myths" (1992) 82 *Trademark Reporter* 301

DREYFUSS, R. C., "Expressive Genericity: Trade Marks as Language in the PEPSI Generation" (1990) 65 *Notre Dame Law Review* 397

DWORKIN, G., "Unfair Competition: Is the Common Law Developing a New Tort?" [1979] *European Intellectual Property Review* 241

—— " 'Knocking Copy' Comparative Advertising: a Survey of UK Practice" [1979] *European Intellectual Property Review* 41

ECONOMIDES, N. S., "The Economics of Trade Marks" (1988) 78 *Trademark Reporter* 523

The Economist, "The Year of the Brand", 24 December 1988

—— "Knocking brands off the shelf", 24 February 1990

—— "Shoot-out at the checkout", 5 June 1993

—— "Unreal", 14 May 1994

ELMSLIE, M. and LEWIS, M., "Passing-off and Image Marketing in the UK" [1992] *European Intellectual Property Review* 270

EVERTON, A. R., "Towards a Concept of Quasi-Property" [1982] *The Conveyancer and Property Lawyer* 118

The Financial Times, "Orange's campaign cleared by judge", 11 July 1996

—— " 'Lookalike' packaging leaves shoppers confused", 16 April 1998

FLETCHER, A. L., "The Defence of Functional Trade Mark Use: If what is Functional cannot be a Trade Mark, how can a Trade Mark be Functional?" (1985) 75 *Trademark Reporter* 249

FRANKLIN, D. M., "Brands versus Look-alikes in the UK", July/August 1994, *Trade Mark World* 10

GAUGHEN, L. D., "Adverts which Identify Brand 'X': a Trialogue on the Law and Policy" (1967) 57 *Trademark Reporter* 309

GETZOFF, S. M., "Anti-dilution Protects Trade Mark Goodwill", February 1990, *Trade Mark World* 20

—— "Anti-dilution and the End of Confusion", May 1992, *Trade Mark World* 40

—— "A Reply to 'Anti-dilution Protection in the US' ", October 1992, *Trade Mark World* 18

GIELEN, C., "Likelihood of Association: What Does it Mean?", December 1995/January 1996, *Trade Mark World* 20

—— "*SABEL* v. *Puma*: A Benelux Perspective" [1998] *European Intellectual Property Review* 109

GOBLE, G. W., "Where and What a Trade Mark Protects" (1927) 22 *Illinois Law Review* 379

GORDON, W. J., "A Property Right in Self-expression: Equality and Individualism in the Natural Law of Intellectual Property" (1993) 102 *Yale Law Journal* 1533

GORRINGE, P. A., "Trade Marks: An Economic Perspective", October 1988, *Trade Mark World* 28

GREIWE, N. S., "Anti-dilution Statutes: A New Attack on Comparative Advertising?" (1982) 72 *Trademark Reporter* 178

GRIMES, C. W. and BATTERSBY, G. J., "The Protection of Merchandising Properties" (1979) 69 *Trademark Reporter* 431

The Guardian, "Eric Cantona refuses label and asks court to back him", 21 June 1996

HANAK, E. W., "The Quality Assurance Function of Trade Marks" (1975) 65 *Trademark Reporter* 318

HANDLER, M. W., "Are State Anti-dilution Laws Compatible with the National Protection of Trade Marks?" (1985) 75 *Trademark Reporter* 269

—— and PICKETT, C., "Trade Marks and Trade Names: an Analysis and Synthesis" (1930) 30 *Columbia Law Review* 186, 759

HARMS, D., "Hark! There Goes a Tort" [1995] *European Intellectual Property Review* 453

HARRIS, P. A., "UK Trade Mark Law: Are You Confused?" [1995] *European Intellectual Property Review* 601

—— "WAGAMAMA: Confusion Still Reigns in the UK", October 1995, *Trade Mark World* 12

HARTMAN, S. H., "Subliminal Confusion: the Misappropriation of Advertising Values" (1988) 78 *Trademark Reporter* 506

Harvard Law Review, Note, "Dilution: Trade Mark Infringement or Will O' The Wisp" (1964) 77 *Harvard Law Review* 520

HONE, F., "The Decline and Fall of New Brands in the US", October 1989, *Trade Mark World* 13

HOWARTH, W. C., "Are Trade Marks Necessary?" (1970) 60 *Trademark Reporter* 228

HUGHES, J., "The Philosophy of Intellectual Property" (1988) 77 *Georgetown Law Journal* 287

HURDLE, H., "Can Wealthy Traders Claim Monopolies in Common English Words Under the UK Trade Marks Act 1994?", March 1996, *Trade Mark World* 20

The Independent on Sunday, "Superstores stalk the superbrands", 20 February 1994

JACOB, R., "Industrial Property—Industry's Enemy" [1997] *International Patents Quarterly* 3

JACOBACCI, G., "Trade Marks and Advertising", June 1989, *Trade Mark World* 42

JAFFEY, P., "The New European Trade Marks Regime" [1997] *International Review of Industrial Property and Copyright Law* 153

JOHNSTON, L. H., "Drifting Towards Trade Mark Rights in Gross" (1995) 85 *Trademark Reporter* 19

KAMPERMAN SANDERS, A., "The Wagamama Decision: Back to the Dark Ages of Trade Mark Law" [1996] *European Intellectual Property Review* 3

—— "The Return to Wagamama" [1996] *European Intellectual Property Review* 521

—— and MANIATIS, S., "A Consumer Trade Mark: Protection Based on Quality and Origin" [1993] *European Intellectual Property Review* 406

KLAR, L. N., "An Argument for the Restructuring of the Law of Trade Marks" (1974) 12 *Osgoode Hall Law Journal* 223

KOZINSKI, A., "Trade Marks Unplugged" (1993) 68 *New York University Law Review* 960

KRATZKE, W. P., "Normative Economic Analysis of Trade Mark Law" (1991) 21 *Memphis State University Law Review* 199

LAHORE, J., "Product Simulation and Copying the Get-up of Goods" [1979] *European Intellectual Property Review* 146

LAI, S., "The Erosion of Goodwill" (1996) 146 *New Law Journal* 874

LANDES, W. M. and POSNER, R. A., "Trade Mark Law: An Economic Perspective" [1987] *Journal of Law and Economics* 265

LEWIN, R., "The New Trade Marks Act: A Godsend for Trade Mark Owner or a Goldmine for their Lawyers?" [1994] *European Intellectual Property Review* 91

LIBLING, D. F., "The Concept of Property: Property in Intangibles" (1978) 94 *Law Quarterly Review* 103

LINK, H. C., "The Social Significance of Trade Marks" (1948) 38 *Trademark Reporter* 622

LIVERMORE, J. M., "On Uses of a Competitor's Trade Mark" (1969) 59 *Trademark Reporter* 30

LUNSFORD, J. R., "Consumers and Trade Marks: the Function of Trade Marks in the Market Place" (1974) 64 *Trademark Reporter* 75

MARTINO, T., "Trade Mark Dilution: I hear you knocking but you can't come in: *Mead Data Central* v. *Toyota*" [1990] *European Intellectual Property Review* 141

—— and GROVES, P. J., "Trade Marks: Deliver Us From Days of Old" [1991] *European Intellectual Property Review* 355

—— and ULLAH, W., "The Quality Guarantee Function of Trade Marks: an Economic Perspective" [1989] *European Intellectual Property Review* 267

MCCLURE, D. M., "Trade Marks and Unfair Competition: A Critical History of Legal Thought" (1979) 69 *Trademark Reporter* 305

MCCORMICK, G., "Updating the Intellectual Property Wardrobe: Consider Trade Dress" [1995] *Trade Mark Yearbook* 9

MCCORMICK, J., "The Future of Comparative Advertising" [1998] *European Intellectual Property Review* 41

MICHAELS, A., "The Function of Trade Marks: the Law and the Reality" [1980] *European Intellectual Property Review* 13

MIDDLETON, G. E., "Some Reflections on Dilution" (1952) 42 *Trademark Reporter* 175

—— "Some Aspects of Trade Mark Dilution" (1957) 47 *Trademark Reporter* 1023

MILLS, B., "Own Label Products and the Look-alike Phenomenon: A Lack of Trade Dress and Unfair Competition Protection?" [1995] *European Intellectual Property Review* 116

—— "Comparative Advertising: Should It Be Allowed?" [1995] *European Intellectual Property Review* 417

MIMS, P. E., "Promotional Goods and the Functionality Doctrine: an Economic Model of Trade Marks" (1984) 63 *Texas Law Review* 639

MOSKIN, J. E., "Dilution or Delusion: The Rational Limits of Trade Mark Protection" (1993) 83 *Trademark Reporter* 122
MOSTERT, F. W., "The Parasitic Use of the Commercial Magnetism of a Trade Mark on Non-competing Goods" [1986] *European Intellectual Property Review* 342
MURPHY, J. M., "Branding and Trade Marks", April 1987, *Trade Mark World* 12
MUTIMEAR, J., "Is There a Need for a Personality Right in the United Kingdom", April 1998, *Trade Mark World* 12
NYE, S., "In Defence of Truthful Comparative Advertising" (1977) 67 *Trademark Reporter* 353
ODDI, S., "Consumer Motivation in Trade Mark and Unfair Competition Law: on the Importance of Source" (1986) 31 *Villanova Law Review* 1
PALLADINO, V. N., "The Real Trouble with Trade Marks" (1991) 81 *Trademark Reporter* 154
PAPANDREOU, A. G., "The Economic Effects of Trade Marks" (1956) 44 *California Law Review* 503
PARKS, K., " 'Naked' is not a Four Letter Word: Debunking the Myth of the 'Quality Control Requirement' in Trade Mark Licensing" (1992) 82 *Trademark Reporter* 531
PARR, N. and HUGHES, M., "The Relevance of Consumer Brands and Advertising in Competition Enquiries" [1993] *European Competition Law Review* 157
PASEK, V., "Brand Success and Failure", January 1990, *Trade Mark World* 26
—— "Are Comparisons Odious?", August 1988, *Trade Mark World* 44
PASTER, B. G., "Trade Marks: Their Early History" (1969) 59 *Trademark Reporter* 551
PARKINSON, C. J., "The Re-awakening of Comparative Advertising in the UK", December 1990, *Trade Mark World* 44
PATTISHALL, B. W., "Trade Marks and the Monopoly Phobia" (1952) 50 *Michigan Law Review* 967
—— "The Dilution Rationale for Trade Marks and Trade Identity Protection: its Progress and Prospects" (1977) 71 *North Western University Law Review* 618
—— "Dawning Acceptance of the Dilution Rationale for Trade Mark and Trade Identity Protection" (1984) 74 *Trademark Reporter* 289
PORT, K. L., "The 'Unnatural' Expansion of Trade Mark Rights: Is a Federal Dilution Statute Necessary?" (1995) 85 *Trademark Reporter* 525
PRESCOTT, P., "Think Before You Waga Finger" [1996] *European Intellectual Property Review* 317
ROBERTSON, A. and HORTON, A., "Does the UK or EC Need an Unfair Competition Law?" [1995] *European Intellectual Property Review* 568
ROBIN, A. and BARNABY, H. B., "Comparative Advertising: A Sceptical View" (1977) 67 *Trademark Reporter* 358
ROGERS, E. S., "The Social Value of Trade Marks and Brands" (1947) 37 *Trademark Reporter* 249
—— "Unfair Competition" [1919] *Michigan Law Review* 490
RUIJSENAARS, H. E., "Legal Aspects of Merchandising: The AIPPI Resolution" [1996] *European Intellectual Property Review* 330
—— "The WIPO Report on Character Merchandising" [1994] *International Review of Industrial Property and Copyright Law* 532
RUSTON, G. R., "On the Origins of Trade Marks" (1955) 45 *Trademark Reporter* 127
SCHECHTER, F. I., "The Rational Basis of Trade Mark Protection" (1927) 40 *Harvard Law Review* 813

SHANAHAN, D., "The Trade Mark Right: Consumer Protection or Monopoly" (1982) 72 *Trademark Reporter* 233

SHERMAN, B., "Patent Claim Interpretation: the Impact of the Protocol on Interpretation" (1991) 54 *Modern Law Review* 499

SIMONSON, A. F., "How and When do Trade Marks Dilute: A Behavioural Framework to Judge 'Likelihood' of Dilution" (1993) 83 *Trademark Reporter* 149

SOMMERS, M. S., "The New US Trade Mark Dilution Act: Problems Lurking?", December 1995/January 1996, *Trade Mark World* 16

SPECTOR, H. M., "An Outline of a Theory Justifying Intellectual Property Rights" [1989] *European Intellectual Property Review* 270

SPENCE, M., "Passing-off and the Misappropriation of Valuable Intangibles" (1996) 112 *Law Quarterly Review* 472

SPENCER, A. Y., "Look-alikes and Private Label Competition", September 1994, *Trade Mark World* 14

STERK, S. E., "The Law of Comparative Advertising: How Much Worse is 'Better' Than 'Great' " (1977) 67 *Trademark Reporter* 368

STEWART, G. R., "The Source Theory and Trade Mark Law Reform: A Functional Analysis" (1982) 20 *University of Western Ontario Law Review* 337

The Sunday Times, "On the bratwalk", 8 May 1996

—— "A can of worms is a bad diet", 5 April 1998

SWANN, J. B., "*Anti-Monopoly*: An Exercise in Economic Futility" (1988) 78 *Trademark Reporter* 65

—— and DAVIS, T. H., "Dilution, an Idea Whose Time has Gone; Brand Equity as Protectable Property, the New/Old Paradigm" (1994) 84 *Trademark Reporter* 267

TERRY, A., "Unfair Competition and the Misappropriation of a Competitor's Trade Values" (1988) 51 *Modern Law Review* 296

TIMBERG, S., "Trade Marks, Monopoly and the Restraint of Competition" (1949) 14 *Law and Contemporary Problems* 323

The Times, "Brand of logic", 20 April 1994

—— "Sainsbury's retreat in cola war", 11 May 1994

—— "Cola war hits Coke", 11 May 1994

—— "Roll up, roll up and sell the game", 22 May 1996

—— "Euro '96 coins enjoy royal approval", 22 May 1996

—— "Euro '96 is a big draw for small firms with the right sales pitch", 18 June 1996

—— "The £903 million story behind big names in daily cereal", 16 August 1996

University of Chicago Law Review, Comment, "The Anti-Competitive Aspects of Trade Name Protection and the Policy Against Consumer Deception" (1962) 29 *University of Chicago Law Review* 371

WADLOW, C., "Passing-off Enters the Supermarket Age" [1990] *European Intellectual Property Review* 104

WALL, D., "Taking Care of Business" (1997) 147 *New Law Journal* 540

WALSH, P., "Comparative Advertising and the UK Trade Marks Act 1994", May 1995, *Trade Mark World* 33

—— and WATTS, J., "Honest Practices in Comparative Advertising in the UK", March 1996, *Trade Mark World* 26

WALTON, A., "A Pervasive but not Explicitly Characterised Aspect of Passing-off" [1987] *European Intellectual Property Review* 159

WEINRIB, A. S., "Information and Property" (1988) 38 *University of Toronto Law Journal* 117

WEINRIB, E. J., "The Fiduciary Obligation" (1975) 25 *University of Toronto Law Journal* 1

WELKOWITZ, D. S., "Re-examining Trade Mark Dilution" (1991) 44 *Vanderbilt Law Review* 531

WILLIMSKY, S. M., "Comparative Advertising: An Overview" [1997] *European Intellectual Property Review* 649

WINNER, E. P., "Right of Identity: the Right of Publicity and Protection for a Trade Mark's Persona" (1981) 71 *Trademark Reporter* 193

REPORTS

Report of the Departmental Committee on the Law and Practice Relating to Trade Marks (Goschen Committee), Cmd. 4568 (London, 1934)

British Trade Mark Law and Practice (Mathys Committee), Cmnd. 5601 (London, 1974)

Report on Copyright and Designs Law (Whitford Committee), Cmnd. 6732 (London, 1977)

Reform of Trade Marks Law, Cm 1203 (London, 1990)

Fine Fragrances: A Report on the Supply in the UK for Retail Sale of Fine Fragrances, Cm 2380 (London, 1993)

Index